Stories of Fathers, Stories of the Nation

# Stories of Fathers, Stories of the Nation
*Fatherhood and Paternal Power
in South African Literature*

**Grant Andrews**

UNIVERSITY OF KwaZulu-Natal Press

Published in 2021 by University of KwaZulu-Natal Press
Private Bag X01
Scottsville, 3201
Pietermaritzburg
South Africa
Email: books@ukzn.ac.za
Website: www.ukznpress.co.za

© 2021 Grant Andrews

All rights reserved. No part of this publication may be reproduced or transmitted in any form or by electrical or mechanical means, including information storage and retrieval systems, without prior permission in writing from the publishers.

ISBN: 978 1 86914 478 4
e-ISBN: 978 1 86914 479 1

Project manager and editor: Sally Hines
Layout: Patricia Comrie
Proofreader: Alison Lockhart
Indexer: Christopher Merrett
Cover design: Marise Bauer, M Design
Cover art: 'Animus' by Maritha van Amerom

The financial assistance of the National Institute of Humanities and Social Sciences (NIHSS) towards this publication is hereby acknowledged. Opinions expressed and conclusions arrived at are those of the author and are not necessarily to be attributed to the NIHSS.

Printed and bound in South Africa by Creda Communications

# Contents

Preface                                                                                           vii

Chapter 1: Narrative Power and Paternal Narratives in
           South African Fiction                                                       1
Chapter 2: Paternal Narratives at the Dawn of Apartheid:
           *Cry, the Beloved Country*                                                 40
Chapter 3: The Stifled Narrative Power of Daughters:
           *In the Heart of the Country* and *Burger's Daughter*                      91
Chapter 4: Paternal Narratives in the Transition from
           Apartheid: *The Smell of Apples*, *Ways of Dying* and
           *The Quiet Violence of Dreams*                                            150
Chapter 5: Fatherhoods in Post-Transitional South African
           Novels: 'The Declining Patriarch'                                         218
Chapter 6: Conclusion                                                                             283

Select Bibiography                                                                                289
Index                                                                                             301

# Preface

In South African literature, the father reflects the nation. Of course, this is not a uniquely South African literary tradition. Fathers have been used in almost all storytelling patriarchal societies to reflect their cultural values and to prescribe the ways of living and being for their groups.

Father figures are often the centre of founding myths or narratives of independence in many nations, and they are given moral authority, agency and dominance in stories. In fact, the image of the righteous or dominant father figure is ubiquitous, from oral traditions in Africa to fairy tales from Europe and the Middle East. For example, the West African folklore character Anansi, who is both rebellious son and authoritative father, is conceived of as the god of knowledge and stories; the Middle Eastern collection *One Thousand and One Nights* uses the framing story of the character Shahryār, who is prevented from executing his bride Scheherazade through being distracted by a series of stories; and in European fairy tales such as 'Rumpelstiltskin' by the Brothers Grimm, the fate of a daughter is dictated by a story, told by her father, that she can spin straw into gold. These stories of fathers, across cultures, countries and historical periods, have many overlaps: the father's power is constituted through and negotiated around narratives, the stories he weaves or is enmeshed in, and often these stories would have major consequences for his sons or daughters. These stories seem to reflect the patriarchal values of the authority and centrality of older men as designers, creators and gatekeepers of knowledge and meaning. Many of these stories, too, came to define cultures, and they were told to children or members of cultural groups as ways of maintaining traditions and identity.

Stories of fathers were also foundational for how many cultures saw themselves or were seen in the world. These include myths of ancient

Greece, Egypt or Rome with father figures Zeus, Osiris and Jupiter, and their offspring in constant conflict with their dominance. For much of recorded history, the father in narrative is the embodiment of authority, justice, violence and control.

This book originated from my interest in understanding the role of the father figure in South African literature, and how the major political shifts in the country affected the image of the father. Could new states of the nation impact on how the father is represented? Could the father come to mean different things in literary texts based on political and social shifts, especially during the seismic movements from pre-apartheid to apartheid eras, then to states of emergency, mass protests and violent uprisings, and then to the transitional and post-apartheid eras?

I look at how stories of fathers reflect states of the nation, and how these narratives serve to grapple with social and political changes in relation to power dynamics in South Africa. Sons, predominantly, are used in the various texts to reflect the power of the fathers, and they are able to reproduce the paternal narratives in ways that show symbols of power. These transmissions of power through symbols are very similar to how political and social enculturation take place in the highly patriarchal South African society; sports, the military, guns, religion and other male-dominated domains symbolise how sons take up the mantle of patriarchal roles and values from fathers. These narratives, just like the historical myths and fables described above, show the passing on of power from father to son, with daughters and mothers often secondary, controlled and *narrated* characters.

This book looks critically at how fathers are reflected in English novels during different periods, starting with Alan Paton's *Cry, the Beloved Country*, where the central fathers are represented as morally unyielding leaders capable of healing a nation that is descending into apartheid divisions, and it ends with texts in the post-transitional period where fathers are represented very differently. In recent texts, fathers are spectral, dying and morally bankrupt. Sons and daughters are given centrality in these narratives, and they can distance themselves from the stifling influence of their fathers. What these texts show, through gradual changes influenced by (and perhaps influencing) massive social shifts, is the uncertainty surrounding paternal narratives; these narratives might be failing a nation that has never truly redefined itself or truly healed after the pain and trauma of apartheid.

I wanted to write this book as a longitudinal study of what fathers have meant in the popular imaginary, how fathers were able to act as the voice of different groups within South Africa, either representing racist and exploitative power or the power of resistance and revolt. I drew on theories of narrative and theories of gender to conceive of the *narrative power* of fathers. I, however, did not want to flatten interpretations of these texts by forcing them through a narrow lens, but instead wanted to see how they could speak to one another and offer insights into the anxieties, conflicts and disruptive moments that defined each era, and the tensions that still characterise representation in South Africa today. For example, how does a white author write a black character, and whose voice does this capture? How do African cultures and literary traditions allow for rethinking realism and magical realism? What was the influence of the global women's liberation movement on literature in South Africa? How do descendants of those who voted for and fought for apartheid see themselves in post-transition South Africa? How do black queer characters see themselves in a society where their identities are marginalised?

While these might seem disparate questions, unable to be woven together in any meaningful way through a project on paternal narratives, I answer that they can all be spoken to through how we imagine the father. The father is Paton, who writes his white liberalism into the characters of *Cry, the Beloved Country*. The father is Mark Behr's male relative, who recruited him as an apartheid spy, written obliquely through his paternal characters in *The Smell of Apples* and *Kings of the Water*. The father is K. Sello Duiker, who imagines himself as gentle and loving to the children of South Africa, and to himself, through the character of Tshepo in *The Quiet Violence of Dreams*; these children might be the queer South African students who picked up his book and saw themselves represented for the first time, as I did many years ago, and the black writers who pay tribute to his enduring influence.

The fathers in these texts fascinated me: how they speak to what South Africa was, is and what it might become. When the images were violent, dangerous or threatening, they could symbolise fears about moral ambiguities in the face of social changes, the prevalence of toxic masculinities, or the horrors of rape and domestic violence that South African women and children endure at the hands of men. When the images were gentle, introspective and seeking redemption, they could speak to new possibilities for men to redefine themselves, to disrupt restrictive gender norms that harm them, and to find loving ways to understand their diversity in sexuality, parenting styles, and racial and cultural identities, especially in post-apartheid South Africa.

I argue in this book that stories of fathers can be read as stories of confronting and defining the nation and national identity, and I read these stories here in ways that are cognisant of, but simultaneously seek to challenge, what paternal narratives have traditionally meant. Importantly, despite the traditional conception that the father's power is univocal, the South African imaginary shows multiple, diverse images of fatherhood. These multiple stories offer possibilities for productive new readings, rereadings and counter-readings that offer a reimagining of South Africa's story. Perhaps, too, fatherhoods in South African society might be seen through new lenses, which offer men and fathers the chance to forge new meanings and new stories of themselves.

CHAPTER 1

# Narrative Power and Paternal Narratives in South African Fiction

Literature and society interact in various ways, and for the purposes of this book the links between historical epochs, political shifts and the production of particular forms of narratives will be examined in the South African context. Analyses of particular texts highlight how societal shifts impact on literature as well as how literature can act as a tool in both reflecting and reimagining social realities.

I follow two traditions of narrative theory and literary criticism, New Historicism and gender studies, to explore not only patriarchal constructions within texts but also how these texts inform understandings of society. Harold Veeser explains that within New Historicism literature is treated as an important product of cultural production, which impacts on and is affected by other spheres, such as law and politics: 'New Historicism has given scholars new opportunities to cross the boundaries separating history, anthropology, art, politics, literature and economics. It has struck down the doctrine of non-interference that forbade humanists to intrude on questions of politics, power, indeed all matters that deeply affect people's practical lives' (1989: ix). New Historicists hold that the dynamics of particular cultural products can be indicative of broader realities, and they examine specific forms, such as works of literature, to expose the general ideologies underpinning them as well as overlaps with other cultural products. New Historicism aims to 'expose the manifold ways culture and society affect each other' (x).

Using this interpretive lens allows for an analysis of the dynamics of how paternal narratives in literature interact with societal power structures, and it enables a rich comparison of images of fathers from different historical epochs. Importantly, current New Historicism has been greatly influenced by post-structuralism and deconstruction. A key idea in post-structuralism is that the meaning of a text is always destabilised and contingent on context, and that texts can be read to have a multiplicity of meanings. Roland Barthes emphasises that the author, in post-structuralist thinking, is no longer the sole arbiter of the meaning of a text, but the reader also brings meaning to a text based on cultural, social and historical context. Barthes contends that 'literature is that neuter, that composite, that oblique into which every subject escapes, the trap where all identity is lost, beginning with the very identity of the body that writes' (2001: 2). Post-structuralism was a reaction to the rigidity of structuralist thinking, which theorised structures and hierarchies in language and social phenomena. Jacques Derrida contends that meaning is only constituted through oppositional concepts, which are hierarchically positioned, but the power relations between these concepts are inherently unstable. By exposing the assumptions inherent in these constructions of meaning, deconstruction allows for the meaning of texts to be critically engaged with in ways that are not laden with cultural assumptions (Derrida 1976). By deconstructing the assumed power relations and exposing them as inherently unstable, new meanings can arise.

Feminist theory is often seen as an important sphere of the post-structuralist reading strategy, examining social and cultural artefacts and moments through the lens of the oppression of women and the privileged position of men in patriarchal societies, thereby destabilising and denaturalising the assumptions of gender that underpin these constructions. Susan Bordo, a feminist philosopher, describes how women are historically associated with the body whereas men are linked to the intellect and spirit (2003) – an important distinction that will be demonstrated in many of the texts investigated in this book. Other feminist theorists have explored social institutions, such as religion and law, and exposed their patriarchal underpinnings to demonstrate how women are oppressed through them, such as Simone de Beauvoir, most famously in her seminal text *The Second Sex* (1974). Theorists, such as Patricia Hill Collins (1986), have also demonstrated the intersectionality of oppression, where race, class, gender and other social categories create various intersecting levels of oppression.

By employing a combination of New Historicism and poststructuralism, this book critiques the paternal narratives underpinning the novels under investigation, while also showing how these paternal narratives, and the power relations they are informed by and in turn support, are inherently unstable and can be reimagined. The role of the father as arbiter of knowledge is shown to be a cultural assumption, especially in many of the early novels, but even here the father's authority is constantly undermined and slippery. These dynamics become clear in chapters 2 to 5, which closely analyse a wide variety of novels to demonstrate how paternal narratives have been destabilised and reconfigured during different historical periods.

Paternal narratives are understood as those narratives associated with father figures, which serve to benefit or reinforce the father figure's patriarchal power. These paternal narratives are often found in works of literature that primarily serve to reflect political or historical realities, as power is frequently represented through the symbol of the father. Paternal narratives do not need to relate directly to a character who is a father himself, but can also be reproduced through reference to the authority of symbolic fathers, such as political leaders, lawmakers, police or the military, and religious symbols, especially God. Examples of these symbols of patriarchal power are common, and their function, within the framework of paternal narratives, is to reinforce the structures that allow for patriarchy to be maintained. The father's role is also frequently tied to creation; the father is framed as the creator of the child in the same way that he creates and has authority over the law, the nation, the military and religion. The paternal narrative allows for the complete authority of the father figure to be supported through ideology and myth, or stories that then become widely reproduced.

Narrative is always linked to power, and there are power structures discernible within any particular narrative moment. Fathers will be shown to have the greatest narrative power, which includes the power to narrate but also the ability for narratives to gain more power due to the authority associated with the father figures. The father is also able to be the hero within the narratives that are produced, constructing and perpetuating structures such as religion, history and law, and identity concepts such as race, gender, ethnicity and sexuality. Because masculinity is an important component of patriarchal power structures, the paternal narratives often make reference to symbols of traditional masculinity in order to reinforce and assert their power, such as money, sport, the voice, violence and weapons. The paternal narrative is decidedly and narrowly masculinist in its construction, and it relies on clear gender binaries for this reason. Threats to these gender binaries, such as queer characters, are often constructed as an affront to the father because they symbolically threaten his patriarchal power by unsettling the narrow view of masculinity that supports paternal narratives. This trend is variously evidenced in texts such as K. Sello Duiker's *The Quiet Violence of Dreams* (2001) and Mark Behr's *Kings of the Water* (2009), where gay protagonists have antagonistic relationships with their fathers. As Lynne Segal notes: 'Masculinity is structured through contradiction: the more it asserts itself, the more it calls itself into question . . . As it is represented in our culture, "masculinity" is a quality of being which is always incomplete' (1990: 123).

However, these paternal narratives are not simply reproduced in uncritical ways, either within a given work of fiction or within a society that reproduces its own narratives. There is always a precariousness to paternal narratives, and by their very nature they are contested and unstable. I show how the rebellion of the son against the narratives of his father is a way for him to gain his own narrative power, a necessary ingredient in the continuation of the patriarchal system. I demonstrate that changing social realities, such as the recent critical stance towards patriarchy, men and the father himself, all lead to shifting paternal narratives and to more multivocal stories about fathers, such as in Zukiswa Wanner's *Men of the South* (2010), discussed in Chapter 5. The father's voice is not given ultimate authority, especially within more recent works of South African fiction, as society and authors become more widely critical of power structures in an era of post-apartheid or post-liberation ideology.

South African literature offers an important site of investigation into the nature of paternal narratives as there were major power shifts within the country that were often tied to dominant patriarchal social myths and constructs, such as religion, race and ethnicity. Investigating how literature responded to these moments, and how paternal narratives are reflected in fiction at different times, offers a longitudinal view of how narratives can reflect social changes. Robert Mossman emphasises the uniqueness and importance of South African literature within global literary studies, explaining:

> The literature of South Africa provides a unique microcosm for examining issues of race, class, and gender. The lessons about how and why literature is created in South Africa have implications for the entire world as polarization on racial, economic, class, and political grounds intensifies. In South Africa, the so-called 'first' and 'third' worlds exist side by side in stark contrast (1990: 41).

Michael Chapman also explains why African literature is so culturally and politically relevant:

> There are good reasons, too, why the literary text should be regarded primarily as a social document. African literature, at least in the colonial language, is the direct result of a political act: that of colonisation. The literature is itself, in consequence, often a political act. It is expected that the African writer address the big sociopolitical issues of the day. The writer who does not may end up being considered irrelevant (2003: 1).

Novels discussed in this book were purposely selected to include those with prominent, central father figures, but should not be considered to give a comprehensive view of the historical period in any way. It must be acknowledged, however, that this focus led to many necessary omissions, particularly of black South African writers during the apartheid era, who did not generally publish novels of wide reach but often wrote more political shorter works of fiction, such as poetry and short stories. Annie Gagiano notes that 'in South Africa, colonial and apartheid-era writing tended to be dominated by white writers – for various reasons, both political and cultural (the latter term could be taken to include greater familiarity with the protocols of prize-winning writing)' (2004: 814).

## The centrality of narrative

The very definition of the term 'narrative' has been expanding to include a wide range of products and processes that act as carriers of meaning.[1] Narrative is seen as a way of making sense of one's environment, and of constructing meaning and significance out of events through interpretive frameworks. J. David Velleman explains: 'A story does more than recount events; it recounts events in a way that renders them intelligible, thus conveying not just information but also understanding. We might therefore be tempted to describe narrative as a genre of explanation' (2003: 1). Narrative thus creates links between events in order to make them significant to one another as well as meaningful to those constructing, reproducing or engaging with these stories. Hanna Meretoja characterises this by saying that 'narratives project a false order on the disorder of human existence' (2014: 90). One is never simply objectively relating events, but these events are always framed through perspective and social constructs, in line with Peter Berger and Thomas Luckmann's claim that our knowledge of reality is always socially defined and that 'definitions are always *embodied*, that is, concrete individuals and groups of individuals serve as definers of reality' (1991: 134). Jean-Paul Sartre succinctly captures how narrative frames experience: 'A man is always a teller of stories, he lives surrounded by his own stories and those of other people, he sees everything that happens to him *in terms of* these stories and he tries to live his life as if he were recounting it' (1964: 64). Sartre here highlights the fact that human agents are not simply producing or reading narratives, but are also always significantly affected by the

---

1. Brian Richardson explains the expanding boundaries of what constitutes narrative: 'Now, narrative is everywhere. The study of narrative continues to grow more nuanced, capacious, and extensive as it is applied to an ever greater range of fields and disciplines, appearing more prominently in areas from philosophy and law to studies of performance art and hypertexts. Nor is there any end in sight: the most important new movement in religious studies is narrative theology, and there is even a new kind of psychological treatment called "narrative therapy." Cognitive science offers experimental evidence for a claim that only recently was the hyperbolic boast of a practitioner of the nouveau roman: that narrative is the basic vehicle of human knowledge' (2000: 168).

narratives they encounter and produce. Narratives are social in nature and constitute understandings of the self, others and of the world.

Jerome Bruner expands on this point by showing that there is a fundamental link between narrative and the construction of culture. Using a constructivist approach, he explains: 'What creates a culture, surely, must be a "local" capacity for accruing stories of happenings of the past into some sort of diachronic structure that permits a continuity into the present – in short, to construct a history, a tradition, a legal system, instruments assuring historical continuity if not legitimacy' (Bruner 1991: 20-1). His emphasis here on legitimacy is important, as it shows that stories, or representations of events, real or imagined, are used to justify and legitimise cultural systems and ideologies. As Robert Anchor notes: 'Historical narratives, no less than fictional narratives, always serve in one way or another, to legitimize an actual or ideal social reality' (1987: 133-4). Literature, thus, is also given significance within the narrative paradigm as it constitutes narratives that inform understandings.

Storytelling is the important link between the past, present and future through the vehicle of culture, and reproducing certain stories from one generation to the next allows for the creation of cultural structures represented in the concepts of 'beliefs, traditions and history' (Ahn and Filipenko 2007: 279). These stories could refer to works of fiction or any other form of narrative within society. Bruner refers to this process as 'narrative accrual' (1991: 18), where the repetition of certain interpretations of events or the process of confirming events as part of a larger cohesive narrative over time create powerful cultural understandings in law, history, ideology, and even ideas of the self. All of these cultural forms rely on storytelling, and all of them are retrospective in nature, relying on making past events fit into the narrative coherence of current understandings. Fredric Jameson holds that even though history itself 'is *not* a text, not a narrative . . . it is inaccessible to us except in textual form, and . . . our approach to it and to the Real itself necessarily passes through its prior textualization, its narrativization in the political unconscious' (1981: 20). By refiguring new events into already constructed narratives, these interpretive frameworks gain legitimacy and thus more cultural reproductive power. Bruner refers to thinkers such as Hayden White,

Victor Turner and Paul Ricoeur, who assert that 'narrative is centrally concerned with cultural legitimacy', constructing a cogent and unified understanding of the world (Bruner 1991: 15).

Narrative thus creates interpretive paradigms, which link past events in ways that give them meaning and significance, and that also allow for the reproduction of cultural systems into the future. In addition, the narratives that frame cultures also frame ways of reading, and the individual will interpret new events or new perspectives through the familiar narratives that he or she is already entangled within. Jameson explains in his seminal book *The Political Unconscious: Narrative as a Socially Symbolic Act*:

> We never really confront a text immediately, in all its freshness as a thing-in-itself. Rather, texts come before us as the always-already-read; we apprehend them through sedimented layers of previous interpretations, or - if the text is brand-new - through the sedimented reading habits and categories developed by those inherited interpretive traditions (1981: ix-x).

By being immersed in culture, and the cultural structures that have already gained legitimacy through their narrative confirmation, the individual will read new narratives through these lenses, and thus understandings of the world are already situated within these frameworks.

Jameson continues by employing Marxist thought to demonstrate that all texts are interpreted through a political lens. He argues that 'there is nothing that is not social and historical - indeed . . . everything is "in the last analysis" political' (Jameson 1981: 5). He calls this interpretive framework 'the political unconscious', and highlights that all texts are read essentially through political dimensions, informing, reproducing or challenging the meaning of political and social systems.

This conception of reading is important in this book, which explores how narratives reflect or challenge political realities within apartheid and post-apartheid South Africa, but it also points to the important factor that interpretation is not univocal or uncontested.

There are always multiple ways of reading and of engaging with narratives, and cultural and political realities can inform many alternative readings of texts.

Jameson highlights this view when he gives the example of how religious texts have been read through many different lenses, and he offers the following: anagogical, moral, allegorical and literal. These, he says, are indicative of 'pluralism' in reading styles, even though he undercuts this by claiming that there are hierarchies of legitimacy in these various readings (Jameson 1981: 16). Thus, even though readings of texts are informed by past readings, there is always space for reinterpretation, although new interpretations might not always be given the same legitimacy.

In addition, narrative allows for the construction of a sense of self within these political and social frameworks. An important form of narrative in this process is the personal narrative, allowing individuals to understand themselves as constructed by a series of life events, and also as tied to grander social narratives of belief, tradition and law. Jiryung Ahn and Margot Filipenko propose:

> Narrative is not only a vehicle for informing and preserving cultural identity; it is also a vehicle for constituting reality and of conferring meaning on experience. Sharing narratives and reflecting on what such narratives mean, how they have affected and continue to affect an individual, opens the possibility for a much greater understanding of self (2007: 279).

But narrative can be expanded even further beyond this already broad definition, and, indeed, Walter Fisher's (1984) narrative paradigm offers an important framework for understanding how the individual constitutes narratives in every interaction – an important conception in understanding paternal narratives. Every new interaction or self-reflection is a part of constructing narrative. Alasdair MacIntyre calls this 'enacted dramatic narrative' where 'man is in his actions and practice, as well as in his fictions, essentially a story-telling animal' (1981: 200, 201). Fisher explains this approach in what he calls the narrative paradigm, where all understanding of reality is constructed through narration:

> When I use the term 'narration,' I do not mean a fictive composition whose propositions may be true or false and have no necessary relationship to the message of that composition. By 'narration,' I refer to a theory of symbolic actions – words and/or deeds – that have sequence and meaning for those who live, create, or interpret them. The narrative perspective, therefore, has relevance to real as well as fictive worlds, to stories of living and to stories of the imagination (1984: 2).

Every action, interaction and moment of communication is thus a narrative moment, either creating a personal narrative, communicating a narrative to the other, or linking to a larger political or cultural narrative, either through confirming or confronting it in some way.

What is significant in this approach is the fact that narrative's role in shaping the individual and culture demonstrates that fictional narratives as well as biographical, historical or cultural narratives can impact on cultural formation, and all act as tools for cultural reproduction or change. In his work *The Power of the Story: Fiction and Political Change*, Michael Hanne highlights how works of fiction have often been seen to intersect with, inform or catalyse political moments, such as the example of the religious debate and outcry around Salman Rushdie's *The Satanic Verses* (Hanne 1996: 2). He also explains:

> Storytelling . . . is always associated with the exercise, in one sense or another, of power, of control. This is true of even the most common and apparently most innocent form of storytelling in which we engage; that almost continuous internal narrative monologue which everyone maintains, sliding from memory, to imaginative reworking of past events, to fantasizing about the future, to daydreaming (Hanne 1996: 8).

Even in the most basic form of narrative, where events are related from one person to another, Hanne argues that 'it invokes, then, an interactional process, an assertion of power not only over the matter shaped into narrative but over the audience for the story' (1996: 9). Thus, reproduction of narrative can be seen as a form of exerting power over others and a way of claiming the legitimacy of a particular narrative.

Mark Freeman expands on this discussion of power in narrative by claiming that by creating a personal narrative, the subject reclaims a sense of power over their own identity. Freeman uses the example of Jill Conway's *The Road from Coorain* (1989) in which Conway discovers her own narrative power, not only in telling her story but also in breaking free from the confines of her surroundings and choosing her own path, or in other words, challenging the many dominant narratives of ideology that she is situated within and finding her own identity. Freeman explains: 'The environment, whatever force it could exert on those who inhabited it, could still be acted upon and changed' (2015: 189). He continues by exploring Michel Foucault's conception that power is not merely about the liberation of the self from dominant narratives, but is always the subjugation of the other, claiming 'every religious or moral or political sentiment we hold, Foucault tells us, every truth we speak, is nonetheless contingent upon the exercise of power'. Narrative allows for the self to gain a sense of power, in the same way that it allows for structures of power, or ideologies, to be reproduced when these narratives become dominant within a society.

This broad framework, which will be adopted in this book, places narrative as central to understanding the real and as something inherent in humanity; all meaning, all understanding, all power relations and even the self are dependent on narrative. Additionally, all narratives inform these understandings, be they social, structural or literary. Meretoja expounds the epistemological and ontological nature of narrative as theorised by prominent thinkers, offering a concise summary of the many discussions above:

> Theorists have been divided into those who conceive of narrative primarily as a cognitive instrument for imposing meaningful order onto human reality or experience (for example, Hayden White, Louis Mink, Daniel Dennett) and those who consider it to be primarily an ontological category that characterizes the human way of being in the world, that is, something constitutive of human existence (for example, Paul Ricoeur, Charles Taylor, Alasdair MacIntyre) (2014: 89).

Meretoja proposes a combination of these approaches, giving narrative epistemological and ontological centrality in human existence. These various theoretical approaches offer a useful framework for understanding the concept of narrative power and linking this to the systems of patriarchy. The theoretical background also allows for the significance of literary texts in refiguring as well as being influenced by social narratives.

**Narrative and power, and narrative power**
It has been argued that history, law, belief systems, political realities and class divisions, indeed, all cultural systems, are related to narrative, and the synthesis of these into cohesive ideologies or the formation of supporting systems based on ideologies can be seen as the result of the proliferation of dominant narratives that frame societies. Andrew Brown points out that social organisations and the identities of these institutions can be understood within the narrative paradigm. He sees these organisations 'as locales symptomised by relations of domination and resistance, hegemony and control. It is by focusing attention on identity narratives . . . that organizations can most easily be analysed as power effects' (Brown 2006: 732). Brown thus links narrative to the perpetuation, resistance and reclaiming of power within the individual and groups, and he claims individual narratives are tied to institutional or ideological narratives and the power relations that define them.

It is important to note that narrative is always framed within ideology. This ideology relates to the systems of power represented in a text or at play within an institution, as well as to the culture that informs and is influenced by the text or institution. Ideology thus allows for texts and institutions to interact with the individual in ways that construct the self within hierarchies of power. Luc Herman and Bart Varvaeck explain how ideology functions within narrative fiction:

> In the context of narrative fiction, ideology may be defined as the frame of values informing the narrative. This frame installs hierarchical relationships between pairs of oppositional terms such as real vs. false, good vs. bad, and beautiful vs. ugly. These preferences may be explicitly stated in the text or remain more or less implicit (2005: 1).

Thus, ideology deals with power relations constructed through narratives, either expressly fictional narratives in literature or storytelling, or societal narratives that organise human existence through institutions or ideology. Louis Althusser shows how ideology arises from a sort of imaginary or indeed a fictional relation between the self and the real world, in a stance that can be read as social constructionist and narrativist, as the individual is always situated unconsciously within ideology:

> In truth, ideology has very little to do with 'consciousness' . . . It is profoundly *unconscious*, even when it presents itself in a reflected form . . . Ideology is indeed a system of representations, but in the majority of cases these representations have nothing to do with 'consciousness': they are usually images and occasionally concepts, but it is above all as *structures* that they impose on the vast majority of men, not via their 'consciousness' (Althusser 2005: 233).

By framing ideology as a system of representations and symbols, Althusser locates it within the narrative paradigm, and, importantly, he shows how these structures are learned and inform the way people see themselves and understand their worlds. He continues: 'In ideology men do indeed express, not the relation between them and their conditions of existence, but *the way* they live the relation between them and their conditions of existence: this presupposes both a real relation and an "*imaginary*", "*lived*" relation' (Althusser 2005: 233). Ideologies can thus be seen as stories, or the meanings attached to stories, which link the individual to the real, but they do not accurately, objectively reflect the real. Narrative is the only way to understand the world, and power structures are inherent in narratives.

Althusser then makes a distinction regarding how ideology is approached by individuals, explaining that the individual is not powerless and does not lose all agency in engaging with ideological thought. Since ideology is a representation of socially constructed power relations, the way that the individual reacts to an ideological framework through narrative will necessarily either be reproducing these power structures or challenging them. He explains: 'In ideology the real relation is inevitably invested in the imaginary relation, a relation that *expresses a will* (conservative, conformist, reformist or revolutionary), a hope or a nostalgia, rather than describing a reality' (Althusser 2005: 234). Althusser offers a sense of narrative power to the individual, either adhering to and reinforcing established ideologies and power relations through conservative and conformist approaches, or challenging them through reformist or revolutionary approaches. Even though the individual is always situated within narratives, and the perpetuation of narrative relies on a sense of 'nostalgia', there is always the possibility for 'hope' in order to challenge or overcome narratives that might be stifling, which, in Althusser's Marxist interpretation, are made up of myths surrounding capitalism, which lead to the subjugation and exploitation of the working classes. Althusser directly shows how ideology, and the 'myth' or stories that support it, lead to the perpetuation of power relations, using the example of capitalism: 'The bourgeoisie *lives* in the ideology of *freedom*[,] the relation between it and its conditions of existence: that is, *its* real relation (the law of a liberal capitalist economy) *but invested in an imaginary relation* (all men are free, including free labourers)' (234). Ideology informs power structures, and it is maintained by myths and narratives that fictionalise relations and it is perpetuated by individuals who subscribe to, reiterate and thereby legitimise these narratives. Althusser explains that the individual is always already constructed within ideology through a process of 'interpellation' (22), which makes the individual a subject in relation to dominant ideologies. As Robert Paul Resch explains:

> For Althusser, the individual is 'always already subject' and, as such, always already enmeshed in the practices and rituals of ideological recognition. These rituals, inscribed in material institutions, assure that the majority of individuals will reproduce the existing relations of production. They are subjects in both senses of the word: (1) free subjects, with a free will, and (2) subjected beings stripped of all freedom (1992: 210).

Individuals are, according to Althusser, always interpellated by ideology, but they have the power to challenge ideology as well.

Herman and Varvaeck explain how narratives and ideology intersect through binary oppositions, which 'are present in the ideological, seemingly natural system pervading the narrative' (2005: 9). This is linked to Jeremy Tambling's conception of 'the everyday life beliefs that operate through a culture' (1990: 3). These beliefs are presented in a system of 'oppositions, which seem natural and seem to dictate their own terms [but] are cultural, part of a conventional way of thinking that is so automatic . . . that they are passed off as natural ways of thinking' (25). The focus again is on binaries and hierarchies, with some elements gaining more legitimacy and more power within ideological thought than others.

More clearly, ideologies are constructed by narratives that position the self as subject who is already prefigured by the established narratives in many respects, but still has power to challenge these narratives. Certain narratives have been afforded more legitimacy within societies than others due to their functioning as supportive of the power structures of those who have the power to narrate. Therefore, those with the greatest positions of power within a society will also be those afforded the greatest narrative power, and their narratives will carry the greatest legitimacy.

This is the process known as cultural hegemony, theorised by Antonio Gramsci. Hegemony was traditionally conceived to explain the reproduction of capitalist ideologies, but can also be used to demonstrate how all ideologies are reproduced within societies. As Gramsci explains, hegemony is 'the "spontaneous" consent given by the great masses of the population to the general direction imposed on social life by the dominant fundamental group; this consent is "historically" caused by the prestige (and consequent confidence) which the dominant group enjoys because of its position and function in the world of production' (2006: 89). Sally Ward Maggard expands on this conception of hegemony in a useful extended passage:

> The economic and political power associated with patterns of ownership and control is integrally related to another form of power – the power to set the terms of a community's self-understanding. People with that power fashion the tools we use to interpret everyday life. The ability on the one hand

> to influence values and self-perceptions and on the other hand to control access to information constitutes a form of cultural power . . . Those individuals in the most powerful positions in a society attempt to universalize their own beliefs so that a world view emerges which legitimates their positions . . . To generate a world view, powerful interests attempt to use and influence a whole range of social structures and institutions – such as schools, churches, unions, the family, and the media (1983: 67).

This reproduction of power through ideologies and institutions allows the powerful members of society to maintain their power. What Maggard refers to as the 'cultural power' (1983: 67) that underlies hegemony and maintains dominant ideology can be reconceptualised, within the narrative paradigm, as narrative power: the power to construct meaning about the world in ways that demonstrate or maintain power, broadly through the employment of narratives. Maggard's view of controlling access to information can be seen as linked to the censorship, canonisation, proliferation or legitimacy of particular texts or narrative forms within a society, and those with the power to dictate these terms can be seen as possessing a form of narrative power.

Gayatri Spivak expands on the discussion of hegemony by locating narrative power and the power of representation, particularly in the West, and further with Western men, using Gramsci's conception of the subaltern as the represented Other: 'If, in the context of colonial production, the subaltern has no history and cannot speak, the subaltern as female is even more deeply in shadow' (Spivak 1994: 82–3). By asking the question 'Can the Subaltern Speak?' in the title of her article, Spivak demonstrates the link between power and the narrative or historicising voice, which she demonstrates as constructed in terms of masculine traits, particularly those found in Western men. These agents, in light of the above argument, can be seen to possess the greatest narrative power.

Spivak's conception is supported by theorists such as bell hooks (1992) and Patricia Hill Collins (1986), who look at the multiple layers of how patriarchy intersects with race, class, gender and other factors, or the intersectionality of oppression. They argue that 'it is incorrect to build research and feminist theory on a binary opposition of women and men when race and social class produce many categories of women and men that form hierarchical stratification systems in societies' (Lorber 1994: 5). This results in the 'domination by upper-class white men *and* women and subordination of lower-class women *and* men of color' (5). These multiple layers of oppression show that patriarchy is not a simplistic social structure, but is highly complex and multidimensional, producing vastly different narrative power across these social divisions.

The term 'narrative power' has been used in many senses within academic discourse. In Stewart Clegg's work 'Narrative, Power and Social Theory', he refers to the 'narrative power of revelation' (1993: 16) in the social theory of functionalism, where applying social theories in a narrativist approach could serve to reveal certain underlying realities in historical events. The narrative thus has potentiality in reconstructing understanding. Alice Nelson, in her discussion of the concept of narrative power in *Political Bodies: Gender, History, and the Struggle for Narrative Power in Recent Chilean Literature*, explains the concept as referring to 'a notion of history as a material and symbolic struggle for the ability to tell one's story and the story of one's community, and to enter into social dialogue' (2002: 22). She explains that within the Chilean context, 'a single official story had been imposed to replace a multiplicity of voices – "order" was to replace "chaos"'.[2] Reclaiming narrative power is thus being able to tell 'alternative stories', and she clarifies that 'by "stories," I mean communicative forms like performances and demonstrations, as well as texts with words' (22-3). Narrative power is thus the power to engage in narratives, either official, dominant narratives, or resistant, alternative, multivocal counter-narratives.

---

2. This analysis can easily be applied to the South African context where the dominant narrative was heavily controlled by means of censorship, selective historicising and the suppression of human agency by denying the majority of the population from engaging in democratic processes and the enactment of oppressive laws. This resulted in the 'silencing' of not only literary narratives but also social narratives of oppressed people in South Africa, be they female, queer, black or those who were critical of the apartheid system.

Melissa Schaub uses diverse conceptions of the term 'narrative power' in her article 'Queen of the Air or Constitutional Monarch? Idealism, Irony, and Narrative Power in *Miss Majoribanks*', referring to the 'subversion of . . . gender myths' (2000: 197) as demonstrating power over narrative or the narrative's power to resist hegemony, where a character can 'manipulat[e] . . . textual roles provided by society [and gain] mastery of narrative' (204). Narrative power is also demonstrated when a character can gain or maintain power within a narrative, as well as through the construction of events or people within narratives, as characterised by the character Lucilla. Schaub explains: 'The ability to assess a situation for its conventional dramatic potential is the source of Lucilla's power, because other people will always fall in with her planned narrative if she can establish it convincingly and conventionally enough' (205). Lucilla thus uses established narrative devices in order to gain power.

Various conceptions of the term 'narrative power' are useful within the framework of how narratives create meaning and self-definition, provide agency, shape ideology and reinforce hegemony. Narrative power thus operates at four interconnected levels. Firstly, the figure who is represented within a narrative as possessing the greatest power through the structural conditions created within the text is said to have narrative power. Secondly, having the power to construct narratives, or, in other words, having the resources, abilities and social capital in order to construct narratives either within a text or within a society that produces texts is a function of narrative power, and this is associated with agency and self-determination or the spreading of a narrative to others. This means that the author of a given literary text has a certain level of narrative power, and when these texts gain cultural significance and proliferation, it can be seen as having greater narrative power than obscure or oppressed texts have. Thirdly, reproducing hegemonic narratives that reiterate or strengthen ideologies or institutions with which the self identifies, and thereby reinforcing the power of the self through identification with these institutions, is also a form of narrative power. Finally, certain narratives are viewed as more significant, are more respected, or are more pervasive within a society, giving these narratives greater cultural power.

The four levels of narrative power are not necessarily complementary. For example, in Nadine Gordimer's *Burger's Daughter* (2000), Lionel Burger can be seen as having narrative power as he gains many followers and is able to challenge the apartheid government, but his communist and non-racial ideology runs counter to the dominant ideology of apartheid, an ideology that has much greater narrative, symbolic and systemic power. These clashing forms of narrative power eventually lead to Burger being imprisoned and dying, effectively robbing him of at least some of his narrative power.

By understanding how narrative and power intersect through the concept 'narrative power', the ways in which ideology is reinforced and contested through works of fiction can be analysed. Power relations present in works of fiction can either reflect and thereby reinforce those relations functioning in a given society, or unsettle and challenge them. Within the narrative paradigm, the narrative power of characters within a text or the narrative power of the author and the text itself can constitute rich sites of analysis to demonstrate how patriarchal structures are engaged with in works of literature. Due to the fact that many of the texts within this book are regarded as canonical, they can be seen as having great narrative power, and their role in engaging with paternal narratives is important in the South African literary and social context.

## The paternal narrative and the father as narrator

If narrative informs an understanding of the world and the self and involves power relations, it is important to investigate which members of society are given narrative power to reproduce narratives and give certain narratives legitimacy, which characters are commonly given the greatest narrative power within texts, as well as which texts gain the greatest narrative power within societies, particularly, in this book, South African canonical texts. Of course, in the narrative paradigm, every subject has certain forms of narrative power, since narrative happens constantly, whether consciously chosen or unconsciously reproduced. However, as Jameson highlights, there are hierarchies of legitimacy and certain narratives are more pervasive than others (1981).

Laura Donaldson sheds some light on which members of society are afforded the greatest narrative power. She begins by criticising

Althusser's implied conception that all narrators have access to similar narrative power, claiming 'interpellation ignores the fissures that the violent and subterranean pressures of patriarchal society open between men and women [which constitute] a false conflation of masculine and feminine subject positions' (Donaldson 1988: 71). Within patriarchal structures, men and women are differently interpellated, have different narrative power and are able to reproduce power structures differently. Nancy Chodorow elaborates on the gender dynamics of subjectivity by explaining that 'women experience a sense of self-in-relation that is in contrast to men's creation of a self that wishes to deny relation and connection' (2012: viii). Chodorow elaborates on the male's need for 'independence' within this ideological context, and she highlights the way that men are socially constructed to be driven to create a sense of self, a factor strongly interconnected with narrative power. De Beauvoir characterises the symbolic subjugation of female subjects clearly when she explains the assumed gender dynamics of subjectivity: 'Humanity is male and man defines woman not in herself but as relative to him; she is not regarded as an autonomous being . . . she is simply what man decrees . . . He is the Subject, he is the Absolute – she is the Other' (1974: 13). This important location of subjectivity with masculinity exposes how men are afforded greater narrative power, even over women, who are relegated to objects rather than subjects. Katherine Nelson-Born explains:

> The existence of women and other minorities too often remains defined by the dominant culture in power and remains relegated to the periphery of such a power structure, subsumed by . . . a monological narrative that dominates and marginalizes the voices of those who would dissent against those who remain in power (1996: 1).

Thus, within a patriarchal system, men remain the primary subjects within the production of narratives, which serve to legitimise their positions of power.

The important concept of patriarchy must be employed in order to understand ideologies of control, especially in gender and generational binaries. Max Weber categorised patriarchy as 'a system of government in which men ruled societies through their positions as heads of households. In this usage the domination of younger men who were not household heads was as important, if not more important than the element of men's domination over women *via* the household' (in Walby 1990: 214). In this understanding of patriarchy, not only are men given the greatest power in societies, but older men are necessarily constructed as ideologically dominant over younger men, especially their sons in the family setting. Even though Sylvia Walby argues against the inclusion of the generational aspect of patriarchy as it undercuts the domination of women, it is still a factor widely cited in social and even narrative theories, where the father is given the highest degree of narrative power.

The father is able to shape the reality of those who follow his narrative. Jacques Lacan famously conceptualised the 'symbolic father' who bestows 'symbolic regulation' within the family setting, as 'it is in the name of the father that we must recognise the support of the symbolic function which, from the dawn of history, has identified his person with the figure of the law' (Lacan 1977: 67). Elizabeth Grosz explains that the father

> can represent law, order, and authority for the child. It is not, however, the *real* or generic father, but the *imaginary father* who acts as an incarnation or delegate of the *Symbolic Father*. In the case of his absence or failure to take up the Symbolic function, other authority figures – the teacher, headmaster, policeman, or ultimately, God, – may take his place in instilling in the child the sense of lawfulness and willing submission to social customs (2002: 68).

The father's role, or the symbolic paternal role of social institutions, is to perpetuate patriarchy through reproducing dominant social myths and narratives, such as law, tradition or religion and practising power over women and the son in order to maintain the current social structure. Within this patriarchal structure, the father is the symbolic subject, who gives meaning to the system, whether actively practising his power in the family unit or merely being represented in narrative or institutions. Graham Lindegger, using Jung's conception of archetypes, explains: 'The father archetype may show itself in many forms, often including the elder, lawmaker, king, and father-in-heaven. The father is the embodiment of the logos principle, that is, the principle of thought and wisdom [and shows a] preoccupation with power and control' (2006: 122). Anthony Stevens explains that the father's 'attributes are activity and penetration, differentiation and judgement, fecundity and destruction' (2004: 105). The father is afforded the dominant narrative power, and patriarchy, which has 'reproduction as its sole basis' (Walby 1990: 218), is able to continue through these narratives.

Paternal narratives, thus, are those narratives produced by fathers in order to legitimise their privileged positions within patriarchal systems. By reproducing narratives that give subjectivity, authority and dominance primarily to the father, as most dominant narratives in the patriarchal system do, the position of the father is embedded and his narrative power is reinforced. This is clearly articulated by Lahoucine Ouzgane and Robert Morrell when they see masculinity as a 'fictional construct' (2005: 10), linking the power of men to narratives, and when they question how societies reproduce the power of men:

> How are myths of masculinity reinforced or challenged in literature and the popular media? Do the new practices reinscribe or modify conventional understandings of men and masculinities by offering different images, different roles, and different options for men? What modified forms of sexualities and genders are produced and maintained in the hybrid societies of postcolonial places? (2005: 10-11)

Importantly, the generational struggle for authority between fathers and sons within patriarchal conceptions often casts these figures as oppositional in narratives that inform or support ideology, such as religious, historical, traditional or national myths and narratives. Women are often only reflected on the periphery of these narratives, as objects to be controlled, protected, owned or dominated. Thus, in narratives involving mother or daughter figures, they are frequently not given the same narrative power as fathers or even sons. The sons, as inheritors of the paternal narratives and assumed future fathers themselves, are able to subjectively engage with these narratives, but, in trying to claim a subjectivity for themselves, they often resist their position as objects in the narratives of fathers, resulting in father-son narratives being fraught with conflict. In the construction of traditional masculinity that the father engenders, conflict and aggression are necessary ingredients, as Michelle Toomey explains: 'To be a man is to be in charge. To be gentle is to be a wimp, a weak excuse for a man, an object of derision, and ridicule' (1992: 44).

The father is the possessor of power, tied to his masculinity, and he demonstrates this power through traditional masculine symbols of dominance, through links to patriarchal systems and institutions that support his power, such as money and material possessions, religion, tradition, nationalism and ethnic separatism, politics, education, and through symbols related to the phallus as representative of male dominance, such as guns and monuments. The father is also linked to violence, aggression and sexual dominance, and this essential connection of men with forms of violence and control is theorised by Suzanne Hatty when she explains: 'Violence, as a modern strategy, guarantees both individual and social control, while maintaining and perpetuating hierarchy and inequality' (2000: 10). Paternal narratives or narratives about the father need to reflect and reinforce his connection with these forms of dominance in order to serve their patriarchal function.

Many myths and religious tales that deal with father-son relationships show the inherent distance and violence found in these relationships within representations, as well as the role of material possessions and the required obedience of sons to their fathers, which many sons disobey with severe consequences. In Western psychoanalysis's founding story, Oedipus is left to die by his own father and eventually kills him and takes his crown as king of Thebes without any knowledge that the man he has succeeded is his biological father. Liongo Fumo, great Swahili poet and seemingly undefeatable warrior, is deceived and killed by his son Mani Liongo (Werner 1926). In Greek mythology, Zeus, not being the creator of either mortals or gods, still takes on the role of protector and disciplinarian atop Mount Olympus with thunderbolt in hand, a symbol of his dominance through the threat of violence.

The first son in Judeo-Christian belief, Adam, is shown to disobey God, his father, and suffers God's wrath through exile from the perfect Garden of Eden. God's law is sacred in this narrative, and the disobedience of his symbolic children casts them out of his benevolent protection. The Bible is full of references to obedient or rebellious sons, all of which show the inherent power of the father and required submission of the son so that order can be maintained, such as in the parable of the prodigal son or when God tasks Abraham with killing his own son, Isaac, to test his obedience. The ultimate obedient son, Jesus, is shown to be a perfect reflection of the father himself; indeed, they are seen as parts of the same entity. This is why, when he is on the cross, Jesus does not understand the seeming absence of his father, who, here, would be expected to fall into the protector role of his perfect son, and he is left wondering: 'My God, my God, why have you forsaken me?'

Ask, Adam's Nordic counterpart, is shown to have many father figures in the form of Nordic gods, and he was apparently not conceived with any womanly influence. In this myth, the role of the fathers is hyperbolised as the only essential creative force, negating the role of mother. In Egyptian mythology, Horus undertakes to avenge the death of his father Osiris, bringer of law, agriculture and religion, and god of the underworld. Horus eventually reinforces the link with his father by replacing him as king of Egypt, inheriting his title and dominion, and also cementing his bond with Osiris by obeying his order to avenge his death.

Even national or political narratives emphasise the role of the father, and a large number of nations have a political father figure, most often one who led a political revolution in colonised countries. The leaders of the American Revolution who founded the United States of America are known as the Founding Fathers, indicating their narrative power in defining a new nation, with the first president, George Washington, known as the father of the nation. In South Africa, the end of apartheid and the birth of a democratic country was ushered in by a symbolic father in Nelson Mandela, who is often referred to as Tata, the isiXhosa word for father.

Social theories and philosophies about fatherhood latch on to the same themes of power struggles, narrative, control of possessions, and how 'patriarchy is often confused with paternity, and manhood with fatherhood' (Muponde 2007: 19). Desmond Lesejane provides five criteria for what he calls 'manly and fatherly conduct', namely, the man/father must be 'a custodian of moral authority; a leader with responsibility; a primary provider of material needs; a protector of family; and a role model' (2006: 176). Tamara Shefer and Keith Ruiters also hold that masculinity is 'predominantly associated with a man's capacity to exercise power and control' (1998: 39), and suggest that this is sustained through heterosexuality. In this model, fathers exercise their power and demonstrate their masculinity by controlling their wives and children. Paul Ricoeur argues that father-son relationships entail 'a battle of wills struggling for recognition' (in Oliver 1997: 45), and Lacan and Sigmund Freud associate 'the Father with the Law or the Name' (in Oliver 1997: 46).

Even narratives of science rely on a multitude of father figures and very few mother figures, such as Democritus and Thales being cast as the fathers of science, Galileo Galilei as the father of modern physics, Pythagoras as the father of number theory, and Freud as the father of psychoanalysis. The position as knowledge builder and the title of father serve as patriarchal formations and demonstrate the narrative power of men in these societies.

Many links can be drawn between stories of father-son relationships from various cultures and disciplines. These stories often show how the father is given agency and can weave an uncontested narrative through rules, role modelling, or allowing and disallowing access to money, possessions and power, which the father has supreme power over. At times, the son is given the chance to retaliate and claim power for himself, as in the case of Oedipus, but as a matter of course the father is endowed with the power to narrate and control the son's life and the relationship between himself and his son, and the son's disobedience of the father is constructed as leading to disorder and many negative consequences.

This essentialised view of fatherhood as heterogeneous, hegemonic and as conflated with masculinity is problematised by the notion that 'there are multiple versions of how to be a man in any particular society, and the relations between them are a crucial part of the makeup of gender relations in general' (Crous 2007: 19-20). Ane Kirkegaard also explains that 'men are not just men among men. They are differently positioned in relation to each other, depending on a number of hierarchical structures, including sexual orientation, age, class and racial differences' (2007: 122). A view of masculinities and fatherhoods as homogeneous serves to subvert and deconstruct the aforementioned views of the sole authorship of father figures. It also highlights that not all fathers will have equal access to narrative power, and, in a country like South Africa, with a racially divided past, extreme wealth inequality, and widespread homophobic violence and prejudice, power will usually still rest with wealthy, white, heterosexual fathers who demonstrate their links to traditionalist institutions that support patriarchy. These fathers will usually be represented as most powerful within paternal narratives, and they will be able to engage in the construction and perpetuation of narratives most effectively.

It is important, however, to note that not only fathers, and not even only men, are able to reproduce paternal narratives within society or within literature. These narratives, even though they are in the service of the authority of men and father figures by underpinning patriarchal structures, are also widely and uncritically disseminated by women who subscribe to them, especially women afforded some measure of relative power themselves. This can be seen in the figure of Mrs Lithebe in Alan Paton's *Cry, the Beloved Country* (2003), who can prescribe more 'feminine' behaviour for Gertrude in the novel due to her age and the respect she demands, or even by Marion's mother Helen in Zoë Wicomb's *Playing in the Light* (2008), who is able to gain power by 'playing white' and thus seeks to maintain racial boundaries. However, it is predominantly the father who is concerned with reproducing paternal narratives in many of the texts under investigation.

## Masculinity and fatherhood in the South African setting

Fatherhood is understood to serve as a rite of passage into manhood for many men (Morrell 2007: 89), and becoming a patriarch or father is an important factor in the performance of traditional conceptions of masculinity (Clowes, Ratele and Shefer 2013). Morrell explains that hegemonic masculinity is associated with 'private and public power' (2005: 84), and fatherhood enables the enactment of this power within the family setting as well as garnering status and respect within communities. Morrell argues: 'Fatherhood [is] associated with manhood. Manhood is a station that requires responsibility and obliges respect' (2007: 89). Furthermore, in the South African context of widespread unemployment, 'fatherhood is synonymous with manhood and fatherhood is the primary signifier of masculinity because other signifiers (for example, work) are not immediately available'. In addition to how fatherhood reinforces the masculinity of the father, it is also argued that fatherhood is a site where the requirements of successfully performing masculinity can be modelled and transmitted to sons. Natasha Cabrera et al. hold that fatherhood is linked to successful 'sex-role and gender-identity development' in boys (2000: 128). Through the influence of the father, the son learns how to be a man.

Judith Butler's concept of performativity in constituting self-definition and gender identity can be linked to the narrativist approach. Butler argues that gender is constructed through corporeal performances that mostly reiterate gender expectations, and deviation from gender norms is punished in societies in order to maintain clear gender binaries. These performances and the ideologies that they reproduce become so commonplace that they seem natural, and most people will not realise that they are merely performances and not defined through essentialist notions of gender or sex. Thus, gender performativity is not an everyday choice, but rather an ingrained code of expectations and reiterations that order social structure. She explains:

> The tacit collective agreement to perform, produce, and sustain discrete and polar genders as cultural fictions is obscured by the credibility of its own production. The authors of gender become entranced by their own fictions whereby the construction compels one's belief in its necessity and naturalness. The historical possibilities materialized through various corporeal styles are nothing other than those punitively regulated cultural fictions that are alternatively embodied and disguised under duress (Butler 1988: 522).

Judith Lorber elaborates on how gender is not simply linked to biological sex but is informed by a multiplicity of social codes and values. She explains that gender can be seen as 'an institution that establishes patterns of expectations for individuals, orders the social processes of everyday life, is built into the major social organizations of society, such as the economy, ideology, the family, and politics, and is also an entity in and of itself' (Lorber 1994: 3). Lorber goes on to describe how different feminist theories have located the construction of gender in the sexual oppression of women, the division of labour, the law and family relationships, with psychoanalytic feminists particularly locating patriarchy in 'the symbolic rule of the father through gendered sexuality and the unconscious' (4).

Cabrera et al. suggest that the father is the main exemplar of these performative codes for the son (2000). This relationship of performing masculinity necessitates a power difference between fathers and their children, especially sons: the father is shown to prescribe and direct the way in which the son expresses his gendered identity, essentially becoming the narrator of the son's performance of the power that is linked to maleness. However, paradoxically, this paternal narration is also seen as a limit to the masculine power and agency of the son, who seeks to narrate his own existence independent of the influence of his father. Robert Muponde explains that 'the son as an aspiring author of his own destiny is weighed down by the imponderable and castrating fact of his being already situated, figured and narrated [by his father]' (2007: 28). In this way, the research shows that the father simultaneously serves to direct or model the masculinity of the son, as well as acting as a limit to this masculinity through his overpowering narrative influence.

One such narrative can be found in the concept of legacy, the story of the father's life and how he practises his 'public power' (Morrell 2005: 84), and the influence of the family name, which also creates expectations and limits for the life of the son or daughter. Other forms of paternal narratives include the sharing of myths, values and traditions, which sometimes might contradict the views of the sons and daughters.

This conception of conflicting narrative agencies becomes significant in understanding the tensions inherent in many conceptions of fatherhood, in which the fathers and their sons struggle to maintain narrative control of their own lives, as well as seeking to control and influence the narrative of the other party in order to assert their own masculinist power. Kizito Muchemwa proposes that 'psychic struggles mark the relations between fathers . . . and their children, especially sons . . . The space that separates children from their fathers engenders emotions of endearment strangely mixed with violence' (2007: 1). It is important that Muchemwa maintains the focus on narrative as symbolic of the paternal role, and closely links narrative to masculinity. Narrative can be seen as a binding link between a father and his children, since the biological link is not as corporeally defined as it is in the case of mothers, due to pregnancy and breastfeeding. Narratives of fatherhood need to bridge not only this corporeal distance between fathers and children, but also the obstacle of patriarchal masculinity, which resists fatherly affection as this is linked to the 'feminine' traits of emotion, nurturing and affection. Narrative is also conceptualised as a masculine endeavour as it involves creativity, the assertion of subjectivity, and often a claim to historical authority – realms that have traditionally been viewed as masculine and which allow for the production of power (Nochlin 1978: 146). The son, through his own struggle for masculine power, aims to create his own life's narrative, resisting the emasculation of already being narrated by the legacy and control of the father. The father and son are thus shown to be competing in their masculinity, each threatened by the authorship of the other. This book explores representations of this tension between fathers and their sons, and the struggle for masculinity and power, which is linked to this tension.

The father's threatened masculinity is also examined through the lens of relationships with daughters who challenge the father's authority as narrator: Eva in *Skinner's Drift*, Marion in *Playing in the Light*, Rosa in *Burger's Daughter* and Magda in *In the Heart of the Country*.[3] In the context of feminist theory and the women's liberation movement, narrative power has increasingly been claimed by women, and the daughter's quest for narrative power is also explored as conflicting with the masculinist dominance of the father. The focus is on how literature allows for these types of narratives to be represented, reproduced and renegotiated. This shows how literature offers a space

---

3. An example not explored at length in this book is J.M. Coetzee's most famous novel *Disgrace*, in which Lucy challenges her father's authority in many ways.

for the narrative power of sons and daughters to be expressed, and how representations within literature speak to the societal shifts in conceptions of fatherhood.

Culturally, fatherhood has become a major focus in gender studies and social activism in South Africa, through the establishment of the Fatherhood Foundation of South Africa in 2008 by prominent actor and activist Zane Maes with major corporate partners, as well as projects such as the Sonke Gender Justice's Fatherhood Project. These initiatives are linked to a global trend of focusing on fatherhood as a point of intervention in tackling social issues. Programmes such as these are often aimed to address the so-called 'crisis of fatherhood' (Richter and Morrell 2006: 6) – a fairly recent conception that proposes that the influence of the father is vital in providing stability within the family, and that many fathers are no longer successful in fulfilling this role. While many academics are critical of the conception that fatherhood is necessary for family and social stability (Samuels 2003), and while many researchers show that there are many forms of successful, loving fatherhood in South Africa (Prinsloo 2006; Richter and Smith 2006), the prevalence of social programmes aimed at the crisis of fatherhood shows that this conception still has wide currency.

A major factor in these conceptions of unsuccessful fatherhood is the issue of absentee fathers. Stephen Baskerville points to the fact that 'virtually every major social pathology has been linked to fatherlessness: violent crime, drug and alcohol abuse, truancy, teen pregnancy, suicide – all correlate more strongly to fatherlessness than to any other single factor' (2002: 695). While absentee fathers seem to have negative effects on sons and daughters, absenteeism might be understood within the conception of masculinity as defined through sexual freedom, non-domestic roles and emotional distance, and it thus constitutes an active denial of the emasculating role of fathers who are present. Jeanne Prinsloo claims:

> The private [domestic] domain is identified with the feminine and women are therefore allocated the caring parental role . . . Locating men and masculinity within the privileged public sphere effectively excludes the private sphere from

significance. Within this discourse, the primary role of the father is constrained to bringing home the bacon (but not cooking it) (2006: 134).

While fatherhood is a prerequisite for performing successful masculinity, it simultaneously presents a struggle to maintain this masculinity, as the father is at once expected to protect and provide for his sons and daughters as well as to maintain emotional distance from them in order to avoid the feminine realm of warmth and care. Lindegger also notes that 'there is a pervasive fear that warm fathers will be effeminate and stir the development of homosexuality in their sons' (2006: 123), highlighting the heteronormative restrictions of masculinity that do not allow for 'homosocial' relationships with sons.

In addition, in order to maintain masculine status, many men, especially young men, seek to maintain sexual freedom and power even once they have become fathers. Christine Varga, in studying a group of young men from KwaZulu-Natal, explains that for these men 'having multiple sex partners [is] a particular status symbol, the yardstick by which masculinity, intelligence and success [are] measured among one's male friends . . . [Having] many partners [is seen] as a reflection of male intelligence, cunning, and wit' (1997: 55). Thus, committed relationships and the nuclear family structure might actually threaten the masculinity of these men, and many of them have children with multiple partners who they do not actively care for.

The father, in many contexts, seems to be expected to be largely absent from the lives of his children in order to maintain his masculinist power. This necessary distance helps to dispel some of the conflict that threatens the masculinity of the father, as he no longer faces the aforementioned antagonistic narrative power of his sons and daughters. However, he also risks losing his own narrative power over the lives of his sons and daughters through this distance. He is no longer able to be a gender model or have influence over the lives of his sons and daughters, as Francis Wilson shows that fatherlessness might lead girls to distrust men, and that for boys 'the consequences can be even more destructive as they seek to navigate the turbulence of growing up without the guidance of someone whom they love and trust' (2006: 33).

Various factors are thus shown to influence the social phenomenon of fatherlessness, and these factors are linked to the performance of masculinity as well as to the difficulties encountered when men are unable to fulfil the expectations of masculinity. Mamphela Ramphele and Linda Richter highlight that unsuccessful fatherhood might be deeply shameful for fathers, and that failing to fulfil the masculine role of provider might also lead to further distancing:

> Desertion by fathers is often prompted by their inability to bear the burden of being primary providers. The burden of failure becomes intolerable for those who lack the capacity to generate enough income as uneducated and unskilled labourers. Desertion is not always physical, it can also be emotional. Many men 'die' as parents and husbands by indulging in alcohol, drugs, or becoming unresponsive in their families (2006: 79).

The research shows that fatherhood and masculinity interact in complex and often paradoxical ways. Fatherhood is influenced not only by pervasive patriarchal conceptions of masculinity, but it is also contingent on cultural, economic, social and political factors. The ideas of fatherlessness and the crisis of fatherhood, while prevalent, do not seem to encompass the realities of the many loving, caring fathers who negotiate the role of father positively and who demonstrate that fatherhood is important to them (Richter 2006).

Mark Hussey highlights the importance of critically analysing societal conceptions of fatherhood as well as paternal narratives, seeing the construction of father figures as parodic in their reliance on hegemonic and tenuous masculinity. He latches on to the cultural significance of 'threatened' masculinity that needs to be 'defended', and the so-called 'decline of males' and absent fathers. He argues that 'this father is in many ways rooted in caricature', and that 'the parodic figure of the domestic autocrat has dominated our cultural narratives, and, indeed, it can often seem that the entire western literary tradition is the endlessly repeated story of the struggle between fathers and sons' (Hussey 2003: 163). He calls for shifts in these simplistic constructions of fathers linked to hegemonic masculinity, shifts that this book shows have become evident in recent South African novels, arguing that 'the work of making gender visible, then, must include new stories about men as fathers, as husbands, as sons – stories that illuminate how these social categories produce masculinities, stories told from many different points of view' (Hussey 2003: 163).

While there has been much research on the state and significance of fatherhood in the South African context, as highlighted in this discussion, there has not been a comprehensive and unifying focus on how these aspects of fatherhood have translated into representations through fiction. Fatherhood is pervasive in this medium, and the depictions are varied, including representations of absent fathers, oppressive paternal narratives, disconnected and conflicting relationships between fathers and their sons and daughters, and also, rarely, representations of loving and nurturing father figures.

The father is constructed as the univocal narrator and is expected to display this power at all times, and yet he is at odds with the narration of his sons and daughters who try to refigure him within narratives that threaten his power. South Africa offers unique challenges to fatherhood as a country undergoing transformation, where the tensions between generations are affected due to drastically different societal values and national narratives between fathers and their sons and daughters. National identity can be seen as reflected through the way fathers are represented in literary fiction, and representations of fatherhood seem to signify anxieties around national identities. Not only do the fictional works discussed in this book reflect social issues relating to fatherhood, but they also offer possibilities for how fatherhood can be reimagined. This involves the representations of attentive father figures who are not necessarily the biological father, such as in Duiker's *The Quiet Violence of Dreams*, as well as complex and tumultuous relationships with father figures who are unable to reconcile their paternal roles, as demonstrated in Achmat Dangor's *Bitter Fruit*.

Morrell stresses that a new model of masculinity is emerging socially, especially in the developed world, which 'stresse[s] tolerance, peace, democracy, domestic responsibility, sensitivity and introspection' (2005: 84), but that these models have not been shown to be effective within the poorly resourced African context. This book explores whether these models are finding expression in representations in South Africa. It shows that these conceptions are often linked to more successful depictions of fatherhood in South African fiction, in which the father is able to abandon heteronormative, sexually dominant, traditionalist versions of fatherhood in favour of a more loving and nurturing role, as seen in Zukiswa Wanner's *Men of the South*.

Additionally, this book looks at the types of representations and narratives that are available to or associated with mothers and women generally. These maternal narratives, in a context where the woman is viewed as Other, have very different structures and functions to paternal narratives. Instead of serving control or dominance and reinforcing patriarchy as paternal narratives do, maternal narratives offer alternative possibilities for expression and understanding, without limiting or denying any of these possibilities. Whereas paternal narratives are often shown to be stoical, dominant or oppressive, maternal narratives are seen to be emotional, caring and allow for the reclaiming of lost power. The mothers in these novels are usually linked to vulnerable narratives, ones that are uncertain and frequently play into the mother's role as subjugated. They are narratives of unbridled creativity and difference, seeking understanding of divergent ideas. Importantly, not all mothers engage in maternal narratives, and similarly not all fathers engage in traditional paternal narratives. Many women perpetuate patriarchy, simply reproducing and not questioning the paternal narratives that frame them, and many men challenge patriarchal ideals and structures by resisting the symbols, institutions and myths that inform them. However, the association of these narrative types with gender is implied in the patriarchal system: when the mother can narrate in a way that challenges paternal narratives, she is transgressing not only her position as Other, subaltern and object to the father, but she is also beginning to challenge the assumed legitimacy of restrictive paternal narratives and creating new, fluid narratives. The mother, as an othered, often voiceless and nurturing figure, can represent resistance to rigid paternal narratives. The stories associated with mothers offer a range of possibilities for self-expression in characters in these works of literature, allowing them to move outside of the stifling narratives of the father.

## Paternal narratives in South African fiction

Many iconic South African texts written before 1994 use the idea of disconnected fatherhood to represent the failings and conflicts of national structures of power, such as Gordimer's *Burger's Daughter* and Paton's *Cry, the Beloved Country*. These pre-1994 texts are used as background to demonstrate the shifts in representations that have been produced after 1994. I argue that the fathers in each of these novels act as symbols of political subversion. They are given paternal power through creating national narratives and through providing legacy, but in these cases the narratives run counter to the established relations of power in the racially divided South Africa. As Rosa's father, Lionel Burger, realises in Gordimer's text, 'white people worship the God of Justice and practise discrimination on grounds of the colour of skin; profess the compassion of the Son of Man and deny the humanity of the black people they live among' (Gordimer 2000: 25). The paternal narratives are shown to be deeply entrenched, but contradictory and incompatible with nature. Each of these novels also signifies a shift, where narrative power is granted to sons and daughters. I show that this narrative shift is a tool to highlight the necessity of refiguring established national narratives of racial division. The fathers and their sons and daughters reach greater understanding through gaining more equal narrative power. Even though the sons and daughters live under the influence of their fathers, in these cases fathers are represented as honourable, at least in the view of liberation politics.

This representation obviously runs counter to apartheid-era texts such as Athol Fugard's *'Master Harold'... and the Boys* (2009), where the protagonist, Hally, is shown to have an overwhelmingly negative relationship with his biological father, a physically absent and yet ideologically ever-present figure who is shown to hold racist ideas. The father is demonised in order to represent his social views as detestable, and his influence over his son can be seen in the way that Hally eventually repeats a racist joke and seeks to assert his dominance over two black workers, who also act as father figures to him.

In J.M. Coetzee's *In the Heart of the Country* (2004), the paternal narrative and generational conflict is hyperbolised into a tale of murder and sexual dominance. The text offers another example of a daughter's narrative power, but, in this case, the white protagonist,

Magda, through her disapproval of her father's affair with a black woman and her own relationship with a black farm worker, shows a complex unravelling of racial and sexual relations. Magda's rebellion might be explained in many ways: as a consequence of her own mental illness, as symbolic of her subjugated position in society, as reflective of her feelings of betrayal by her father taking a new lover, or as symbolic of her initial abhorrence of his interracial affair and her later realisation that she might desire such an affair as well.

Some of these apartheid-era texts represent fatherhood and father figures in an idealised form, encompassing what Morrell views as the most privileged version of fatherhood within the African context, which stresses 'responsibility, protection, provision, wisdom and communal loyalty' (2005: 84). This idealised father figure was used to create subversive narratives by opposing apartheid structures, and the deviant, reluctant or challenging sons and daughters are required to submit to the wisdom of the father. When the father is fulfilling his masculine paternal role, his political message is more resonant and effective. On the other hand, in the cases where the father figure is demonised, his complicity with racial divisions can be highlighted.

During the transition period from the release of Nelson Mandela to the end of the Truth and Reconciliation Commission, taken as the closing of the Amnesty Commission in May 2001, many texts represented the sense of powerlessness and emasculation of the apartheid system through the imagery of failed or threatened fatherhood. Njabulo Ndebele's *Death of a Son*, Zakes Mda's *Ways of Dying* and Rayda Jacobs's *My Father's Orchid* offer some examples of this disrupted fatherhood, and demonstrate attempts to repair paternal relationships or negotiate fatherly roles as reflective of a country in healing. Following the end of apartheid, fatherhood is often represented as linked to violence, oppression and absenteeism. Fathers are no longer represented in idealised political terms, but in many cases even became antagonistic to their sons and daughters and, by extension, to political change. Fathers are unable to negotiate the realities of a changing social and political climate, and they are shown to feel threatened by how these changes constitute an affront to their power. The narrative devices of rape and sexual dominance are considered in this context. Many of the texts under investigation involve at least one instance of rape, demonstrating how this act of violence and dominance becomes conflated with post-apartheid ideas of fatherhood. In *The Quiet Violence of Dreams*, *The Smell of Apples*, *Bitter Fruit* and *Disgrace*, rape and sexual dominance establish the fathers as masculine and powerful within the texts where their power is unsettled. Each of the fathers seems to promote traditional views of masculinity and power relations, which are at odds with the changing social climate. The loss of the father's idealised role in post-apartheid representation can be linked to the fact that the father is no longer necessary as a symbolic leader towards liberation. It could also be linked to disillusionment with leadership, both in the form of leaders who perpetuated narratives that maintained apartheid structures, as well as leaders who are not adequately addressing current problems in South Africa. The reality of unstable fatherhood in the light of widespread unemployment and the linking of fatherhood with violence are reflected in these novels. The subjectivities of fathers become unstable and anxious; whereas once fathers were represented as uncritically dominant or oppressive, now these roles become uncertain. The sons and daughters, who are now shown to be critical of the influence of their fathers, are also portrayed as uncertain of their own identities when confronted with unstable father figures.

In Dangor's novel, the protagonist Silas Ali has anxiety about his failure to protect his wife from rape by a white policeman, an act that resulted in her pregnancy with their only son Michael. Even though he is initially presented as an idealised father, his marriage eventually falls apart and he loses touch with his son, who goes on to murder his biological father. In *Disgrace*, David Lurie loses many of the markers of his masculine power, and he is unable to understand the motivations and choices of his daughter, Lucy. Again, in this novel, David is unable to protect Lucy from rape. In Behr's *The Smell of Apples* and Duiker's *The Quiet Violence of Dreams*, the sons need to negotiate their own identities in the light of their violent, oppressive fathers, who are both perpetrators of sexual violence. Tshepo in Duiker's novel is able to break free from the paternal narration that had defined his life, but Marnus in Behr's novel is never able to do this.

Literature published more recently demonstrates how understandings of South African fatherhood are shifting within the context of a country living in the legacy of apartheid and a country trying to renegotiate the role of fathers. Many images of dying fathers are employed in post-transitional texts to show the receding of the past, and many of these fathers are still seen to act as remnants of South Africa's racially divided history. In Wicomb's *Playing in the Light*, originally published in 2006 yet set in the mid-1990s, the protagonist Marion learns that her parents had been reclassified as white after being originally classified Coloured, and she is forced to deal with her own identity as a part of the democratic South Africa where race is still largely tied to class. Marion has a strained relationship with her father, and in light of this revelation she begins to grapple with his decision to 'play white'. In this novel, the father is out of place in the new social context, and Marion needs to negotiate an identity independent of the history that he represents.

In Lisa Fugard's *Skinner's Drift*, the protagonist, Eva, returns from abroad to her family farm and her dying father. She is conflicted about his accidental killing of a black child and struggles to identify with the image of a violent South Africa that he represents. In Behr's *Kings of the Water*, published in 2009, the protagonist, Michiel, is again an expatriate who returns to attend his mother's funeral. Michiel cares for his father once he returns, and their relationship is characterised by conflict as well as moments of tenderness, demonstrating the way in which the relationship with the father echoes feelings about national identity. Michiel's homosexuality becomes a point of disapproval for his father, showing how heteronormative masculinity is associated with the rigid values of the father. Similarly, in *Men of the South* by Zukiswa Wanner, published in 2010, the character Mzilikazi sees his homosexuality as a barrier between himself and his father. Images of young, urban, complex fatherhoods are highlighted in this novel, showing how the concept of fatherhood has become interrogated in contemporary South Africa.

The next chapter closely examines the fathers in Paton's *Cry, the Beloved Country*, demonstrating how this pre-apartheid text constructed the father as an authoritative moral compass for sons, and for the nation, which was fast solidifying racial exploitation and oppression into law. Various symbols of paternal power in the novel are discussed to demonstrate how the idealised father figures are able to gain narrative power and thereby criticise the apartheid structures. Paton's novel is a useful bookend for the many representations of fatherhood discussed throughout this book, and, indeed, many later texts can be seen as speaking back to the iconic paternal figures of Stephen Kumalo, James Jarvis and James's deceased son, Arthur, who was similarly a caring, attentive father and community leader. These idealised fathers served to reflect the voices of liberal writers and activists like Paton, and to offer powerful narratives of hope, resistance and pious certitude at a tumultuous moment in South Africa's history.

CHAPTER 2

# Paternal Narratives at the Dawn of Apartheid
## Cry, the Beloved Country

South African literature in English is often understood to have been spearheaded by two famous pre-apartheid novels, Olive Schreiner's *The Story of an African Farm*, published in 1883, and Peter Abrahams's *Mine Boy*, published in 1946.[1] These early novels already represented the strict paternalistic racial, religious, gendered and economic structures that would lead to the development of apartheid policies with the election of D.F. Malan's National Party in 1948. The two novels offer an interesting point of departure for this investigation; not only are they written by those who would have been denied narrative power during colonial and apartheid times in the context of a deeply patriarchal country, namely, a woman and a person of colour, but they also offer highly subversive reflections on South African society. These novels also introduce two of the prominent settings that would preoccupy many future texts – the rural farm setting and the mine, the latter closely linked to the city as a corrupting, exploitative and inhospitable space. Both of these sites are important in understanding the role of fatherhood and paternal narratives in South Africa, as they are spaces that are often associated with the authority of men and their power to narrate the lives of others.

Schreiner's novel was originally published under the pseudonym Ralph Iron, indicating the patriarchal nature of literature production at the time as she could only publish under a male name. As pointed out by several critics (for example, Driver 1988), it can be read as an

---

1. Other notable pre-apartheid novels in English are *King Solomon's Mines* (1885) by H. Rider Haggard, *A Burgher Quixote* (1903) by Douglas Blackburn, *Mhudi* (1930) by Sol Plaatje and *An African Tragedy* (1928) by R.R.R. Dhlomo.

early feminist novel, and it offers a powerful affront to patriarchy by providing nuanced representations of gender non-conforming behaviour, powerful free-thinking female characters and criticisms of religion, tradition and dogmatic thinking.

The farm becomes centrally important in many of the texts investigated in later chapters of this book, with this site indicating a sense of a contentious home to many characters who might distance themselves from the history of oppression, which the farm is often linked to. This is evident in texts ranging from Nadine Gordimer's *July's People* and *Burger's Daughter*, where farm settings are used to indicate a sense of legacy for white South Africans, which is jealously guarded. In J.M. Coetzee's *In the Heart of the Country*, the farm is used as a central site of struggle between father and daughter, and also importantly a site of enacting the power associated with whiteness over black workers. In Mark Behr's *The Smell of Apples*, the farm and the tradition of farming, including the protagonist's uncle who farms the titular apples, are a link to authentic Afrikaner identity. In Behr's *Kings of the Water* and Lisa Fugard's *Skinner's Drift*, the farm is the site where the expatriate son and daughter confront their dying fathers. The farm comes to represent South Africa for the two protagonists in these novels as well, a place that both of them had wanted to escape from for different reasons. From these examples, it is clear that Schreiner's early representation of this setting prefigures a central dynamic that would become important throughout the history of South African literature, namely, that the farm is a site of paternal power, which also acts as a site of conflicting identity politics in terms of race, gender, history and culture. Coetzee characterises the farm in South African literature by explaining: 'Somewhere intermediate between the infinitesimal and the infinite, the farm asserts its own measures of time and space, and on these axes carries out its own self-absorbed existence' (1986: 2). Nicole Devarenne sees this site as encompassing 'a deterministic relationship between genre and ideology . . . justifying the disenfranchisement of blacks and the disempowerment of women' (2009: 627). Devarenne also notes that the *plaasroman* traditionally 'lent credibility to a story about Afrikaners' rural origins that provided an illusion of continuity in South African history and a description of an unchanging Afrikaner identity'. These dynamics construct the farm as a place of isolated power, particularly for the Afrikaner characters associated with the positions of power within it, as well as sites for the enactment of apartheid ideology and patriarchy.

Abrahams's novel focuses on the experience of a black migrant worker who leaves his rural home to work in the mines of Johannesburg, a narrative structure commonly referred to in South African fiction as the Jim Comes to Jo'burg trope, where the struggles of city life are contrasted with the purity and goodness of rural life (Samuelson 2008).

The migrant labour system created many dysfunctional dynamics within rural black South African families. Many short stories during the apartheid era refer to this phenomenon as devastating for men, such as shown in the short story collection by Mtutuzeli Matshoba, *Call Me Not a Man*, published in 1979. The stories in the text refer to how the dynamics of the migrant labour system, as well as apartheid systems more generally, impact on masculinity and particularly on fatherhood.

While these two novels by Schreiner and Abrahams offer a fertile starting point for investigating South African novels, the work that is most widely cited as having the greatest impact on early English literature in South Africa is Alan Paton's novel, *Cry, The Beloved Country*. Jack Cope noted that 'with this book, South African fiction really came into its own' (1970: 13). Andrew Foley shows how the novel still has relevance in South Africa today, explaining:

> Problems such as unemployment, poverty, insufficient housing, inadequate educational opportunities, as well as, most evidently, the unacceptably high crime rate, remain crucially pertinent. In fact, reading the novel today inspires the uncanny feeling that, in terms of its portrayal of social ills, it might have been written in 1998 rather than 1948 (1998: 89).

The novel also engages with the rural farm setting as well as the migrant labour system and mining in many interesting ways. The farm setting in Paton's novel, as well as the rural village of Ndotsheni, are linked much more naively with an authentic masculinity and with paternal narratives than later and current literature would allow for.

James Jarvis had wished for his murdered son Arthur to take over his farm, High Place, creating a sense that the farm was a symbol of bonding and inherited ownership between father and son. The farm is also the site where reconciliation takes place at the end of the novel, as James is able to offer produce and assist the agricultural efforts of the local community in order to revitalise the village of Ndotsheni. The rural village is a site of yearning for fathers and young men, who are shown to have left for the city as 'the soil [of the village] cannot keep them any more' (Paton 2003: 4), and this loss of men leaves the village desolate and seemingly hopeless. These constructions of the rural setting indicate the importance of men in the maintenance of stability, prosperity and power relations, a particularly patriarchal construction explored in this chapter.

The mining industry is demonstrated as oppressive towards black workers in the novel, exploiting the labour of black people for the benefit of white people. The exploitation in the mines is also criticised in an idealistic reflection that mines should be 'for men, not for money' (Paton 2003: 171), empowering men to use the money gained from mining to provide for their families. The novel also appeals to the sense that white men in these settings, those who hold power, should somehow use their power to rebuild families and communities for black men and women.

The novel has a precarious relationship with the history of South Africa. Indeed, Paton himself, in the introduction to the novel, considers whether it can be seen as 'true', noting: 'In these respects therefore the story is not true, but considered as a social record it is the plain and simple truth' (Paton 2003: vii). Paton also highlights how his story can be seen as transgressive of paternal narratives of tradition and patriarchal values often associated with white South Africans, and he offers a multivocal perspective even at this early stage when apartheid was about to be entrenched in society. In his introduction, he explains that the novel 'stands by itself; it creates rather than follows a tradition . . . It is a story; it is a prophecy; it is a psalm. It is passionately African, as no book before it has been; it is universal. It has in it elements of autobiography; it is selfless' (xi). Fred H. Marcus's analysis of the novel might be useful in understanding its relation to social and historical realities, as he explains: 'The novel, then, emerges out of the racial problems in South Africa. We must assess it – not for its sociological content, nor outside its sociological content – as a work of art attempting to re-create experience in a world ordered by the writer' (1962: 609–10).

Stephen Watson is critical of these historicising claims, suggesting that 'whilst the fictional portions of the book seem to trivialize the historical, the historical merely serves to empty out the imaginative substance of the fictional – with the result that the novel fails both as fiction and as social document' (1982: 43). Watson argues that by oversimplifying the extremely complex racial, economic and political issues in South Africa and offering solutions that rely on white benevolence and religious symbolism, Paton misrepresents the historical situation.

The novel has been interrogated from various perspectives in the decades since its publication, and indeed the autobiographical elements become very significant in the wake of Peter Alexander's biography of Paton. John F. Cronin notes that 'it helps towards an understanding of [Paton's] career to know that he grew up at a time when South Africa's racial issues were not yet as violent and clear-cut as they [were during apartheid] . . . it was only from 1948 on that *apartheid* began to be applied at all points as a deliberate governmental policy' (1967: 74). Cronin thus argues that Paton might have had an idealistic and naive view of how to overcome racial conflict in South Africa, perhaps not seeing the need for 'extreme solutions' (75). Watson claims that Paton might be viewed in this context as espousing the idea that 'liberalism still seemed to provide an answer to South Africa's problems' (1982: 29). Paton's novel has also been read as favouring a paternalistic view where white people could be the solution to the problems faced by the black majority. Watson quotes an anonymous reviewer in *The Times Literary Supplement* in 1957 as saying that Paton's novel 'presents a picture of optimism, together with an assumed confidence in the European's ability to lead and guide Africans to a better condition. Today it is regarded by many who would have praised it then as an old-fashioned paternalist book, which portrays Africans in a sentimental and unrealistic light' (30). Foley, in his article '"Considered as a Social Record": A Reassessment of *Cry, the Beloved Country*', says that the novel has 'been condemned by a diversity of critics as paternalistic, naïve, simplistic and irrelevant, and its author labelled misguided, conservative and anachronistic' (1998: 64). Contrary to Watson's characterisation of the novel as misrepresenting the South African situation, Foley argues that it does offer a 'depiction and analysis of South African social and political conditions on the eve of the advent of apartheid' and 'provides a keen insight into the problems facing South African society at the time, an informed and subtle understanding of contemporaneous socio-political debates, and a sensitive appraisal of the possibilities for the country's restoration on a number of different levels'.

Watson characterises Paton's primary concern as being 'to expose a certain state of affairs in South Africa; namely, the social consequences of the destruction of the tribal system by the whites and the general disintegration, both moral and otherwise, which characterises South African society as a whole' (1982: 30). Watson sees the novel's intention as speaking to political shifts in the country: 'Through the personal sagas of the Reverend Stephen Kumalo, James Jarvis, and their respective sons, [Paton] wishes to reveal some of the tragic consequences of this social disintegration.' Watson also links this to the particular religious bent in the novel: the suffering of the son brings about redemption, which he sees as 'a Christian message of comfort and hope despite the prevailing desolation', which allows for the novel to 'appeal to the liberal consciences of . . . readers'.

It is useful to look at Paton's own life and his ideological affiliations in order to contextualise the concerns of the novel. Paton was born in Pietermaritzburg in the then British colony of Natal in 1903. Alexander, in his biography of Paton, explains:

> Almost wholly dominating [Paton and his siblings'] world as they grew up was their father, a small, intense man with a walrus moustache and a tormented personality. Young Alan in particular was deeply influenced by him . . . and everything he wrote about his father is deeply inhibited by his desire to do justice to a man for whom he had felt passionate dislike (1994: 4).

Alexander explains that Alan's father 'James Paton was in fact a domineering man who enforced his will on his wife and his children'

(1994: 9). In *Towards the Mountain*, Paton elaborates on his father's 'authoritarianism maintained by the use of physical force' (1980: 14). He expands on this by explaining: '[James's] use of physical force never achieved anything but a useless obedience. But it had two important consequences. One was that my feelings towards him were almost those of hate. The other was that I grew up with an abhorrence of authoritarianism.'

Paton's upbringing was extremely conservative and Christian, under the rule of his devoutly Christian father. He also explains in *Towards the Mountain* that he was 'brought up to respect . . . almost revere, the law' (1980: 310). Foley claims that Paton was raised in a racially conservative family, and that his commitment to liberalism, in Paton's own recounting, came about while working as the principal at Diepkloof Reformatory for African Boys (1998: 65). Foley characterises Paton's central concern by explaining that for him 'it is the human individual who constitutes the primary unit of social and political value. This view represents the core principle of liberalism as a political philosophy, which may be seen to underpin the fundamental meaning of the novel [*Cry, the Beloved Country*] as a whole' (64). This focus led to Paton's strong commitment to liberalism and spirituality. As Michael Black explains: 'Challenging the law, challenging authority, after 1948 was something [Paton] could only do by manufacturing a higher moral authority of his own' (1992: 53).

Paton wrote extensively about crime and race in South Africa in the years preceding the publication of *Cry, the Beloved County*. In fact, Paton seems to suggest that the character of Arthur Jarvis might represent his own attempts at theorising and promoting liberalism by referring to the title of one of his own articles as one of the speeches given by Arthur in the novel, namely 'Who Is Really to Blame for the Crime Wave in South Africa?' (Paton 2003: 72). Paton argued in many of his critical works that the 'disintegration of traditional African society under pressure of the impact of Western social and economic forces' (Foley 1998: 67) was the driving force behind crime in South Africa. He saw this as a moral and spiritual decay, and argued that it 'can be stopped only by moral and spiritual means' (Paton 1945: 8). Paton claimed that his liberalism was an extension of his Christian faith: 'Because I am a Christian I am a passionate believer in human freedom, and therefore, in human rights' (Paton 1974: 278). He also argued that white societies deny the rights of black people due to fear (Foley 1998: 67). Foley argues that this demonstrates how Paton's novel serves as a social record of his own extensive experience in racial politics (68).

Paton wrote three novels and several short stories in his career, with all of his fiction reflecting on racial issues and the restrictive laws and practices in South Africa. *Too Late the Phalarope*, published in 1953, deals with an Afrikaner policeman, Lieutenant Pieter van Vlaanderen, who is charged under the Immorality Act for having sex with a black woman. He is eventually ostracised from his family and his community, with his father rejecting him completely as he has broken not only his allegiance to the law and to Christian morality, but also to the Afrikaner 'nation'. However, his mother and his sister still show love and understanding for him and question the laws that led to the charges brought against him, indicating how women are more easily afforded the maternal narratives to reimagine and to connect with sons and daughters in Paton's fiction. His third novel, *Ah, but Your Land Is Beautiful*, was published in 1981, and contains six sections, with many characters who are also confronted with strict apartheid laws. The novel seeks to give a multivocal depiction of how the laws negatively affected diverse people. These novels demonstrate Paton's central concern with opposing racist ideology and the restrictive laws that supported apartheid, while humanising and creating sympathy in readers for many different segments of the South African population. Paton, furthermore, wrote a series of autobiographies, which served to cement and contextualise these central concerns, including *Towards the Mountain* (1980), *Save the Beloved Country* (1987) and *Journey Continued* (1988).

Paton's seminal novel *Cry, the Beloved Country* was published in 1948, the year in which the National Party was first elected into power and the system of apartheid became entrenched into South African society. It was written in 1946, a time when, as Foley explains, 'South Africa seemed to be on the verge of political liberalisation' (1998: 88). However, 'D.F. Malan's National Party won a shock election victory in May 1948, just a few months after the publication of *Cry, the Beloved Country*, and plunged the country into more than forty years of apartheid rule.'

The novel has been read in multiple ways: as a narrative of racial injustice, as a story of reconciliation, as a religious morality tale, or as a study of white liberal paternalism. My reading of the novel will highlight the important theme of fatherhood and the role of the fathers in the novel, showing that it is an early example of how the national identity becomes articulated through paternal narratives. The familiar tropes of the absent, tyrannical, wise, misunderstanding, domineering, but always authoritative father are central to Paton's novel, and the fission and tension between fathers and their sons can be likened to a divide between the stifling national narratives and the thwarted freedoms of the South African populace. Indeed, this familial tension highlights the greater divisions in society, and the struggle of sons to find their own narrative voice is symbolic of the many barriers to freedom within the apartheid system. The father becomes the nation, or, in many ways, is a symbol of God the father, and his narrative power is his way of asserting his control over those he is meant to shepherd. This is evident when Paton, in his autobiography *Towards the Mountain*, links a symbolic benevolent father figure in the form of the pre-apartheid deputy prime minister, Jan Hendrik Hofmeyr, with the state itself, personifying the state as once kind but transformed after apartheid: 'After all the State had been good to [me]. In a way Mr Hofmeyr had been the State, but now Mr Hofmeyr had been replaced by a new breed of Afrikaners' (Paton 1980: 310). In this conception, the new father figure in the form of D.F. Malan and the apartheid state is the tyrannical and cold father, whose paternal narratives of racial exploitation and apartheid must be resisted by the son. An appeal to other paternal narratives, in this case religion and the rule of law, becomes the new framing dogma for Paton, represented through his characters. The conflation of father, law, religion and the nation state form a useful background for understanding how paternal narratives operate in the novel.

### The paternal narrative power of Kumalo and Jarvis
The novel tells the story of Stephen Kumalo, a black pastor from the rural village of Ndotsheni, who travels to Johannesburg to visit his sister and search for his son Absolom. He discovers that Absolom has

shot and killed a white man named Arthur Jarvis, who is a prominent political writer. Stephen learns that Arthur was the son of a farmer who lives near Ndotsheni, a man named James Jarvis. He feels great shame and confusion about what could have led his son to commit this crime, and seems to suggest that the corruption within the city of Johannesburg and Absolom's distance from his so-called tribal homeland led him astray.

This family story is linked throughout with changes in the national setting. Foley characterises the first movement of the novel as presenting 'the parallel experiences of Stephen Kumalo and James Jarvis as they are forced to recognise and to understand the nature and the full extent of their society's problems for the first time in their lives' (Foley 1998: 68). The mining industry was expanding rapidly at the time, with a growing number of black men leaving their rural homes to work in the mines and live in the surrounding compounds. This system created great family division, which the novel extensively criticises. This is highlighted by John Kumalo, Stephen's brother, during a political rally, in which he proclaims:

> They say that higher wages will cause the mines to close down. Then what is it worth, this mining industry? And why should it be kept alive, if it is only our poverty that keeps it alive? They say it makes the country rich, but what do we see of these riches? Is it that we must be kept poor so that others may stay rich? (Paton 2003: 184)

The fathers in the novel are presented as conflicted figures. Stephen and James are shown to be endowed with power, leadership and virtue, but these factors are undermined in many ways in the novel: the black fathers are largely unable to adequately provide for or protect their families or communities due to economic exploitation, and they are dehumanised and infantilised by apartheid. Absolom, as a father-to-be, is the perpetrator of crime, which robs him of his moral authority and his role as protector of his family. Additionally, the fathers are always shown to be at a distance from their offspring, and demonstrate a failure to understand the choices and the subjectivity of their children. Stephen does not understand what could have led his son to become a killer, and James does not connect with the liberal politics of his son. Foley characterises Stephen's journey as 'try[ing] to find three missing members of his family and re-unite the family structure', but this quest 'ends in failure' (1998: 68). Stephen is enacting his paternal role of attempting to protect his family and maintain the family structure, but he is thwarted by the realities of crime, violence and economic exploitation that he encounters on his journey.

Watson offers a critical view on how the novel frequently mystifies and obscures the harsh realities of society at the dawn of apartheid, even when it seems to be representing many different voices in the South African setting in compassionate ways. The novel often relies on simplistic paternal narratives to offer solutions to problems faced by all the protagonists. Watson highlights how the novel emphasises the certainty and importance of religion, the law and the value of 'tribal' culture (1982: 30). He argues that these strategies, of first mystifying then oversimplifying the harsh realities of racial oppression, offer no real solutions to the underlying issues. Watson notes that 'just as many aspects of human existence are surrounded by a nimbus of mystery, so the law is deified, is put into a position where it cannot be questioned; it is treated as a divine institution which requires unquestioning awe and respect as an utterly objective arbiter over the subjective follies and anarchies of men' (32). Paton himself, in his autobiography *Save the Beloved Country*, espouses the importance of the law, stating emphatically: 'The Rule of Law is the greatest political achievement of humankind. The Rule of Law is a miracle; it is nothing less than man protecting himself against his own cruelty and selfishness' (1989: 283). The law is again linked to a spiritual framework, highlighting the confluence of these ideologies for Paton. This construction of the law is clearly a reflection of a paternal narrative, highlighting the underlying paternalism of Paton's novel, similar to how religion is constructed in the text when Watson argues:

> The series of misfortunes which his novel relates are definitely not the result of the obscure workings of gods (or of God) whose ways and whims cannot be discovered by man. Like the law which has been formulated as an expression and defence of the interests of white South Africa alone, these misfortunes are

quite explicable in terms of the man-made reality and historical conditions of South Africa in the first half of the century (1982: 33).

Paton, Watson suggests, uses these paternal narratives in a way that obscures the true causes of racial oppression rather than offering meaningful explanations and realistic solutions for them.

The murder of Arthur Jarvis is frequently constructed within the framework that is symptomatic of a country that has been broken because of the systems of racial oppression, resulting in fear of black crime on the part of white people and the loss of a traditional culture by black people. As a result, the country has lost both the rule of law and the spiritual integrity to function optimally. This can be seen in Watson's discussion of how Paton often appeals to the generosity and leadership of white people as the ideal solution to the problems in South Africa. Watson refers to this as Paton's preoccupation with representing the '*good* white man', such as 'the advocate who takes on Absolom Kumalo's case *pro deo*, Father Vincent, and those helping blacks at the school for the blind' (1982: 39). Arthur is constructed, in Watson's view, as 'the *good* white – the liberal hero . . . who is destroyed by the harsh South African reality – as a representative figure who atones through his death for the collective guilt of the whites' (39–40). The religious overtones here are clear, but racially Arthur's death is important as it signifies that the white benefactor, who in Paton's construction is crucial for change in South Africa, becomes a victim to the horrors of South African society. In fact, Watson argues that 'the *good* black man' is merely included as 'conciliation', which can 'allay the suspicions and the hostility of whites towards blacks' in a position with implicit and explicit paternalism (40). Indeed, the novel can be seen to be enmeshed in a paternal(ist) narrative about the power of white people over the lives of black people, casting them as saviours of the black people whom they have disenfranchised. Through the murder of a white character who was working towards a liberal agenda, it signals the death of a figure who would have served the paternal narrative role, someone with enough narrative power to perhaps have aided the black characters in the novel. These concerns give added weight to the crime that Absolom commits, and construct him, as much as Arthur, as a victim of a brutal social system.

This murder is a matter worthy of national mourning as it signals a sense of hopelessness since Arthur was working towards reuniting the father with his family, and criticised the compound system as well as the hypocrisy of apartheid. At Arthur's funeral, as focalised through his father James, this idea is highlighted:

> And the Bishop too had said that men did not understand this riddle, why a young man so full of promise was cut off in his youth, why a woman was widowed and children were orphaned, why a country was bereft of one who might have served it greatly. And the Bishop's voice rose when he spoke of South Africa, and he spoke in a language of beauty, and [James] Jarvis listened for a while without pain, under the spell of the words. And the Bishop said that here had been a life devoted to South Africa, of intelligence and courage, of love that cast out fear, so that the pride welled up in the heart, pride in the stranger who had been his son (Paton 2003: 148).

The funeral is shown to be a moment of connection between father and son, as James Jarvis is able to feel a sense of pride for his son. However, Arthur is still constructed as a 'stranger' to him, indicating that the ideologies of father and son were vastly different.

Arthur's funeral is attended by people of all races, and all mourn the loss of this great man. This funeral closely resembles what Paton called one of the transformative moments in his life in terms of his awareness of racial relations in South Africa, namely, the funeral of Edith Rheinallt Jones (Paton 1961: 24). Rheinallt Jones had worked at the South African Institute of Race Relations and the Wayfarers. At her funeral in 1944, Paton witnessed many diverse people, 'their hates and their fears, their prides and their prejudices, all for the moment forgotten'. Paton continues by valorising the plight of Rheinallt Jones:

> In that church one was able to see, beyond any possibility of doubt, that what this woman had striven for was the highest and best kind of thing to strive for in a country like South

Africa. I knew then I would never again be able to think in terms of race and nationality. I was no longer a white person but a member of the human race (1961: 24).

The experience seemed to create a sense of awareness in Paton of the impact that one person can have, as well as allowing him to see commonalities in diverse people towards the goals of reconciliation. Indeed, Arthur Jarvis might be seen as representing the entire South African liberal movement and many of the figures involved, such as Rheinallt Jones and Paton, in his quest to be a voice for the black South African plight.

By locating this important symbolic figure in the character of Arthur Jarvis, Paton masculinises his message, distancing it from the female Rheinallt Jones, in order to link it to a lost father as well as a lost son, both roles filled by Arthur, who is also a father of two as well as the son of James Jarvis. These symbols, just like the fathers who leave rural villages to work in the mines, indicate a crucial loss that plagues the country within the context of the novel. Without the white man to work towards reconciliation, in this case Arthur Jarvis, Paton's entire construction of liberalism is in danger. Jarvis's message is one of respect and benevolence from white people to black people, similar to the liberal politics that Paton espoused in his life. With Arthur's death, the future of the nation can be seen as symbolically jeopardised, and only through the reconciliatory efforts of the two other father figures in the novel, especially Arthur's own father James in providing assistance to Stephen Kumalo, is the novel able to end on a note of rebuilding and reconciliation.

In this way, the role of the father is often linked to national concerns, and specifically to the leadership and restoration of the nation. The loss of the father signals a sense of hopelessness for the nation. An extract from one of the reflective sections of the novel demonstrates the link between the loss of the father and the brokenness of the nation, again reinforcing the patriarchal vision of South Africa as lost without the paternal narratives and authority, which men, especially fathers, can provide: 'Cry for the broken tribe, for the law and the custom that is gone. Aye, and cry aloud for the man who is dead, for the woman and children bereaved. Cry, the beloved country, these things are not yet at an end' (Paton 2003: 66). The father's death, immediately linked to ideas of custom, tribe and law, indicates the fundamental aspects that Paton believes underlie the problems in South Africa. The father's role is one of maintaining order, and his death or absence leads to disorder.

Absolom is put to death when he is convicted of murder, and Stephen discovers that Absolom was to become a father as well, creating another absent father in the novel. Interestingly, Arthur and Absolom take on the dual roles of fathers and sons in the novel, and their deaths are shown to be both the loss of a father to his family and to the nation, as well as a loss to their fathers.

Stephen reflects of Arthur: 'There was a white man, a good man, devoted to his wife and children. And worst of all – devoted to our people. And this wife, these children, they are bereaved because of my son' (Paton 2003: 109). Stephen here not only seems to display a sense of culpability that his son had destroyed the life of a good father, but also points to the irony that Absolom had taken the life of someone devoted to remedying the injustices of South Africa, the very injustices that the novel portrays as leading to black crime.

Through these aspects of the novel, it becomes clear that fathers, successful fatherhood and cohesive family structures are victims of the national system of racial oppression and exploitation and this leads to social ills. In addition, it robs fathers of their sons and of an active role in the lives of their children, or at least of a tangible connection to the new narratives that their sons forge for themselves. This is demonstrated when the judge in Absolom's case summarises his defence by saying that it amounts to 'the disastrous effect of a great and wicked city on the character of a simple tribal boy. [Absolom's lawyer] had dealt profoundly with the disaster that has overwhelmed our native tribal society, and has argued cogently the case of our own complicity in this disaster' (Paton 2003: 199). The killing of Arthur Jarvis becomes South Africa's crime.

The father's position as narrator is highlighted throughout the novel, and fathers are given the power to shape their own realities and the realities of those whom they encounter, at least as far as the oppressive political system will allow them. By contrast, women are shown to rely on the power of men, especially those in the role of father, in order to shape their lives. Stephen's sister Gertrude and Absolom's young bride rely on Stephen to give them direction when they have little hope in Johannesburg. The narrative role of the father is to propagate and protect traditional culture and religion, to give direction and leadership, and to provide protection and sustenance to his family and by extension to the nation. In addition, the father is often shown to desire that his son maintain and mirror his ideologies, and is unsettled and disappointed when his son chooses his own path, demonstrated by both Kumalo and Jarvis.

The narrator role is shown symbolically and functionally at many points. At the first introduction of Reverend Stephen Kumalo, he is writing, highlighting his position as writer and arbiter of ideals and tradition. James Jarvis also demonstrates the desire to have his legacy maintained, showing the construction of paternal narratives as carried on through the mirroring of sons. He points to the fact that he had inherited his farm from his father, and that 'it had been his wish that his son, the only child that had been born to them, would have taken it after him. But the young man had entertained other ideas' (Paton 2003: 131). However, this desire seems tempered when the son can become a father himself, and he can enter the form of masculine power that fatherhood affords:

> He had married a fine girl, and had presented his parents with a pair of fine grandchildren. It had been a heavy blow when he decided against [working on the farm] High Place, but his life was his own, and no other man had a right to put his hands on it (Paton 2003: 132).

There is obvious irony in this reflection by James, since Arthur had been killed, and another man had 'put his hands' on his life. The paternal narrative was threatened, and, as the novel suggests, this was a result of the political tensions in the country. It is clear here that even though James would like his own paternal narrative of farming at High Place to be continued in Arthur, he gains a sense of acceptance for the narrative power of his own son to make a different choice.

Arthur Jarvis, as father, is also a writer, and he expresses the desire to have his children maintain his legacy as well. However, paradoxically,

Arthur fears that his legacy might compromise his other fatherly requirements, such as his role as protector and provider, as he might be seen to be jeopardising the continued superiority of whites in South Africa. About his political convictions, he is happy that his wife shares his thinking, but he explains:

> My children are too young to understand. It would be grievous if they grew up to hate me or fear me, or to think of me as a betrayer of those things that I call our possessions. It would be a source of unending joy if they grew up to think as we do. It would be exciting, exhilarating, a matter for thanksgiving. But it cannot be bargained for. It must be given or withheld, and whether the one or the other, it must not alter the course that is right (Paton 2003: 175).

Arthur holds that justice, and his obligation to the nation, exists outside of the success of paternal narratives, and outside of children mimicking their fathers. While he presents the familiar desire for the continuation of his paternal narrative, he holds that the advancement of the country would be worth sacrificing this role. Whether his children subscribe to his thinking, it does not alter the justice that he speaks of. He hints that he might be seen as 'betraying' his paternal role, and allowing himself not to be the securer of possessions. This signals Arthur as a different type of father in the novel, who seeks for a different form of narrative that exists outside of the traditional paternal narrative. Instead, these narratives seek to lead to a greater sense of community and understanding, and, as will be shown, these link more closely to maternal narratives.

James has access to Arthur only through his writing after his son is killed, giving written narrative a heightened power in the novel as it can even transcend death. In this novel, there is a reversal where the father seeks to understand the son and to gain access to the son's narrative. The son's narrative also has power here over the father, as Foley explains: 'Jarvis undergoes his own spiritual and political enlightenment and comes to question and eventually reject his previously held conventional and conservative views. Jarvis finds his own attitudes challenged and changed to a large extent by reading his son's articles and essays' (1998: 72).

Importantly, Arthur functions as both father and son in the novel, being given narrative power to reproduce paternal narratives, but also producing transgressive counter-narratives that resist dominant ideology. His connection with both roles of father and son can be shown through an analysis of his study in his home, which his father visits after his death. Foley explains that the study has 'pictures of Christ and Abraham Lincoln and [a] great variety of books [which] gives an initial impression of the quality of the son's character – broad-minded, tolerant, enlightened, compassionate and deeply concerned about his fellow man' (1998: 72). His association with the idyllic son figure Christ, who sacrificed himself for the will of his father, and the idyllic father figure Lincoln, the American president who oversaw the dissolution of slavery in the United States, emphasises this dual role. Patrick Colm Hogan also points out that both Christ and Lincoln were also 'murdered liberators' (1992: 209), lending Arthur both religious and political significance. His link to books and his political writings indicate that he will use these roles to work towards combatting racial injustices in South Africa.

Stephen, similarly to James Jarvis, cannot understand his son and why he made the choices he made. When he visits Absolom in prison, he reflects on how his son has lost his way and is no longer the boy that he had known:

> He is a stranger . . . I cannot touch him, I cannot reach him. I see no shame in him, no pity for those he has hurt. Tears come out of his eyes, but it seems that he weeps only for himself, not for his wickedness, but for his danger (Paton 2003: 109).

The construction of both Absolom and Arthur as 'stranger[s]' to their fathers is significant here, indicating again the power struggles between the narratives of fathers and sons. Stephen relies on the narrative of how Absolom was raised, as his only avenue for understanding is memory, and indeed many of his reflections of Absolom are through the lens of memories of when he was an innocent child. What is most distressing for Stephen seems to be that his son has strayed from his parental influence, and he no longer holds the morals that Stephen has tried to instil in him: 'Can a person lose all sense of evil? A boy, brought up as he was brought up? I see only his pity for himself, he who has made two children fatherless' (Paton 2003: 109). Stephen does not yet realise that a third child, Absolom's own unborn child, will also be rendered fatherless by his actions. The two great violations that Absolom has committed here are disobeying the paternal narrative of Stephen, and destroying the chance of these children having the presence of a father in their lives.

Importantly, even though the novel might place the ultimate culpability for these crimes on the system of inequality and the exploitation of black people in South African society, Absolom still needs to be held accountable for his actions because of Paton's preoccupation with the rule of law and religion. By violating these two central narratives that Stephen and, by extension, Paton espouse, Absolom's death penalty becomes justified in the text as the only logical, righteous conclusion.

Despite Absolom's violation of Stephen's paternal narratives, Absolom is still clearly shown to be a son captured within the narrative of the father. When Stephen visits him and asks why he has committed the crime, Absolom again relinquishes all power to his father, and becomes childlike. Stephen reflects:

> If I say to him, do you repent, he will say, it is as my father says. If I say to him, was this not evil, he will say, it is evil. But if I speak otherwise, putting no words in his mouth, if I say, what will you do now, he will say, I do not know, or he will say, it is as my father says (Paton 2003: 109).

Absolom is shown to have no narrative power of his own, and to simply be situated within the narrative that his father constructs of his own crime, one of religious certainty through the symbols of evil and repentance.

Later, when it is said that Absolom is to be sent to his execution in Pretoria, he is again infantalised in the presence of his father:

> At those dread words the boy fell on the floor . . . and he began to sob, with great tearing sounds that convulsed him. For a boy is afraid of death. The old man, moved to it by that deep compassion which was there within him, knelt by his son, and ran his hand over his head (Paton 2003: 207).

The fear and uncertainty of being sent to death reduces Absolom again to a child who needs the protection of his father, and, indeed, he relies on the paternal narratives: '[Stephen] stood up, but the boy caught his father by the knees, and cried out to him, you must not leave me, you must not leave me. He broke out again into the terrible sobbing, and cried, No, no, you must not leave me' (Paton 2003: 208).

Stephen still tries to practise his narrative power over the life of his son in these moments, appealing to a sense of religious propriety by insisting that Absolom marry the mother of his child. Importantly, this allows Absolom some form of narrative power over the life of his own child, as he is fulfilling the religious traditions that form part of the narrative of his own father. Despite this, he will be an absent father as well, and at the wedding Father Vincent emphasises this religious narrative when he says to Absolom and his bride that they should 'bring up what children there might be in the fear of God' (Paton 2003: 205), but there will be no more children as Absolom is to be put to death, and he will have no role in caring for or instructing the child they are already expecting. Interestingly, Absolom has only chosen a name for a future son: 'If the child is a son I should like his name to be Peter . . . if it is a daughter, I have not thought of any name' (206), showing the importance of father-son relationships in maintaining and perpetuating masculine power. He is able to fulfil one role of the father by providing money for his child as he leaves money in a post office book. Absolom is a father with no access to his son, but he tries to maintain his paternal narrative power through these acts of tradition.

James engages in a different form of narrative, this time not relying on written narrative or memory to gain access to his son, but rather engaging in fantasy. He mentally recreates the circumstances of his son's killing, and thinks about what could have been if Arthur had been told to stay out of danger. He imagines that if Arthur had been warned, he could have avoided death. This creative reimagining falls within the maternal narrative structure and signals a shift in James. Unlike Stephen, who merely judges his son and tries to lead him to Christian redemption through paternal narratives, James tries to gain a greater sense of understanding of his son through these various strategies.

There are hints that James is already moving away from his distant, restrictive paternal narrative. He begins to question his own understanding of his nation as well, and he starts to truly engage with the narrative of his son and even adopts his perspective. But this shift is unnerving for him. As James gains slightly more understanding of his son and his son's path, differing from the paternal legacy, he seems to also lose his link to the nation and his simplistic understanding of the country. Whereas at the start of the novel James was able to look upon his farm at Ndotsheni lovingly and feel a close connection to it, once he begins to engage with Arthur's ideas, 'these skies of a strange country told him nothing' (Paton 2003: 176). There is the implication that losing his son and having to abandon his simplistic paternal narratives and engage with the ideas of his son have rendered James unsettled and vulnerable.

Stephen expresses a similar disorientation when he experiences the fear for his son when he first leaves for Johannesburg: 'Deep down the fear for his son. Deep down the fear of a man who lives in a world not made for him, whose own world is slipping away, dying, being destroyed, beyond any recall' (Paton 2003: 14). Stephen is also unable to comprehend the world around him, when once he had simplistically viewed the world from his religious perspective. In these instances, the father is shown to be dislodged from his position of power when he engages with the diverging narrative of his son. He is unable to reconcile the realities that his son engages in with his own understandings.

## Disrupted urban fatherhoods

While Stephen and James are presented as positive symbols of fatherhood, who seek to fulfil their paternal roles, the novel is also fraught with depictions of absent and disempowered fathers. Johannesburg seems to exist as a city that steals fathers from families, and it also causes fathers to be corrupted. Stephen's sister, Gertrude, loses her husband to the city:

> She came to look for her husband who was recruited for the mines. But when his time was up, he did not return, nor did he write at all. She did not know if he were dead perhaps. So she took her small child and went to look for him (Paton 2003: 23).

As discussed above, Absolom is also to become a father, just as he is about to be sent to prison for murder, and before this he has already abandoned the mother of his unborn child without any explanation, indicating another disrupted fatherhood.

The loss of fatherhood is linked to a sense of brokenness in masculinity as well. When discussing opinions of politics in South Africa, the novel explores the idea that '[some] cry away with the compound system, that brings men to the towns without their wives and children, and breaks up the tribe and the house and the man' (Paton 2003: 78). In this instance, the familial and so-called tribe bonds are broken, and indeed these structures seem to be unsustainable without the influence of the father. In addition, it is stated that it breaks up the very essence of the man as well, as he is taken from his role as father. He is no longer a complete man if he cannot fulfil this paternal role, and the loss of his manhood is a severe loss not only to himself, but to all those who he is meant to support through his paternal and masculine influence.

The role of men and of their children are constructed as pivotal to the continuation of 'tribal culture',[2] and the loss of these men and young people to the city is also shown to cause irreparable damage to the tribe. Importantly, the tribe is constructed as a succession of paternal voices, and the tribal identity offers these men a nurturing influence, as Stephen notes: 'The tribe that had nurtured him, and

---

2. The concept of 'tribal culture' as employed in the novel has been extensively criticised as Eurocentric and limiting (Mafeje 1971). Archie Mafeje wonders: 'Might not African history, written, not by Europeans, but by Africans themselves, have employed different concepts and told a different story?' (1971: 253). He continues by explaining: 'In South Africa the indigenous population has no word for "tribe"; only for "nation", "clan", and "lineage" and, traditionally, people were identified by territory – "Whose [which Chief's] land do you come from?"' (254). Despite these contentions, the concept is uncritically employed in the novel and is argued to be a part of the construction of paternal narratives. Thus, it will be used at many points in this chapter in order to frame the conceptions of ethnicity and ethnic separatism within the unique South African setting, where ethnic identity is an important part of the national discourse, and where racial segregation and apartheid laws further solidified the ideas of 'tribal culture' by segregating people to their allotted 'homelands'.

his father and his father's father, was broken. For the men were away, and the young men and the girls were away' (Paton 2003: 88). Through the loss of fathers and children to the city, the tribe and the paternal narratives and lineage that it represents will be destroyed. Arthur Jarvis, in his letters found by his father after his death, also denounces the practice of removing fathers from families through the compound system, saying: 'It is not permissible for us to go on destroying family life when we know that we are destroying it' (145).

Not only is the father lost to the city, but children are lost to it as well. While the loss of the father is linked to the broader, metaphysical realm of nationhood and culture, the loss of these children is symbolised through the destruction of the earth and the soil, as the children represent the possibility for newness and growth, and they are also linked to the more visceral, grounded narratives of the mother. Through the loss of children, the soil and the earth become destroyed, and this loss is likened to that which is felt in the soil. The narrator reflects that the valleys of Ndotsheni are 'valleys of old men and women, of mothers and children. The men are away, the young men and the girls are away. The soil cannot keep them any more' (Paton 2003: 4). Later, Stephen's wife says to him, when he dreams of sending his son to St Chad's for his education: 'Absolom will never go to St. Chad's . . . He is in Johannesburg, she said wearily. When people go to Johannesburg, they do not come back' (8). At this, Stephen already begins to speak of his son in the past tense, as though the city had devoured him and stolen Stephen's chance at maintaining his paternal role:

> We had a son, he said harshly. Zulus have many children, but we had only one son. He went to Johannesburg, and as you said – when people go to Johannesburg, they do not come back. They do not even write any more. They do not go to St. Chad's to learn that knowledge without which no black man can live. They go to Johannesburg, and there they are lost, and no one hears of them at all (Paton 2003: 9).

This loss again signals a sense of hopelessness for Stephen, as he does not seem optimistic at the thought of finding his son, and he is also downcast about the state of his village, using similar language when describing Ndotsheni and the disappearance of Absolom. This is shown when he is travelling to Johannesburg, and he shares stories of Ndotsheni with other travellers:

> He told them too of the sickness of the land, and how the grass had disappeared, and of the dongas that ran from hill to valley, and valley to hill; how it was a land of old men and women, and mothers and children; how the maize grew barely to the height of a man; how the tribe was broken, and the house broken, and the man broken; how when they went away, many never came back, many never wrote any more (Paton 2003: 22).

By using the same language in these descriptions, Stephen links the two forms of loss and the absent fathers to the destruction of the land. With the loss of men and sons, there is little hope for the land to be restored in the context of the novel.

The city is further shown to destroy morals and traditional values for many characters, again weakening the paternal narrative in the form of religious and cultural values that Stephen represents. This is shown in the way that Gertrude becomes a sex worker and makes bootleg liquor in Johannesburg, where she had gone to search for her husband. Msimangu, a minister in Johannesburg and Stephen's companion once he arrives there, says of Gertrude: 'I do not know if she ever found her husband, but she has no husband now. [Msimangu] looked at Kumalo. It would be truer to say, he said, that she has many husbands' (Paton 2003: 23). Stephen later universalises the corrupting influence of the city when he reflects: 'His son had gone astray to the great city, where so many others had gone astray before him, and where many others would go astray after him' (87). Additionally, there seems to be a loss of humanity itself, and a loss of manhood, in the city, as Stephen wonders of Absolom: 'What broke in a man when he could bring himself to kill another?'

While the exploitative city and the system of racial oppression are shown to destroy the role of the father, the father himself is still a powerful force in rectifying this. The father is afforded the power to criticise the systems of power, he is given the ability to bring together the family again, he is given moral authority, and he is shown to be able to shape his surroundings in positive ways. Stephen reflects, soon after coming to Johannesburg and offering Gertrude the chance to return to Ndotsheni, 'One day in Johannesburg, and already the tribe was being rebuilt, the house and the soul restored' (Paton 2003: 32). He is eventually able to take the young girl who is carrying Absolom's child with him to Ndotsheni, and he is able to negotiate for the betterment of the community with the chief and the headmaster of the local school. Similarly, at the end of the novel, James begins to help to transform Ndotsheni through improving the farming capabilities of the land and feeding the children there with milk. The father is able to exercise his power in many ways that women and children are not.

Various symbols of traditional masculinity are linked to the father in order to demonstrate his power, and these afford him the tools to not only demonstrate his authority, but also to weave and propagate his narratives among his community. These symbols include religion, ethnic culture, money and business acumen, weapons, and the power of words or the voice. These symbols are presented in complex ways, and are shown to be powerful tools for promoting a moral society while simultaneously being criticised. In this way, paternal narratives and the symbols that are employed in their promotion and reproduction are seen as both stifling and potentially liberating. The novel suggests that only through engaging with these symbols in a way that simultaneously is conscious of their limiting nature will they be able to lead to true change in society. Also, only by engaging with maternal narratives, and adopting aspects of these, will the country and the characters themselves be able to overcome the oppressive nature that paternal narratives can often manifest. Essentially, the paternal narratives seek to contain meaning and to limit divergent or alternative thinking, whereas maternal narratives seek a stronger sense of communal meaning-making, understanding and acceptance of diverse narratives and the power of love.

## Religion as paternal narrative

The symbol of masculinity most clearly linked with Stephen Kumalo is religion. Coetzee explains that 'Paton's fable bears the invariant content of religious tragedy: that the dispensation under which man suffers is unshakeable, but that our pity for the hero-victim and our terror at his fate can be purged by the ritual of re-enactment' (1992: 17). Through representation, the religious tragedy offers meaning to the suffering of the religious yet fallen subject or to the unbearably complex issues facing a society. Coetzee continues: 'The tragic hero is the scapegoat who takes our punishment. By his suffering we undergo a ritual of expiation, and as we watch in sympathy our emotions are purged.'

Watson, similarly, criticises the simplicity that religious explanations and symbolism offer in the novel:

> Paton's characteristic simplicity of tone and language reads as intolerably *faux-naïf*; his 'Biblical' style and its pieties (particularly evident whenever he touches on law and order, and family life) are simply not equipped to deal with the complex conflicts of the fifties . . . Clearly one cannot develop much in the way of an historical debate if one is bound by the language of the Sunday school (1982: 42).

Stephen relies on the certainty of the Bible, his paternal narrative of choice, taking comfort from the predictability that it offers him in the face of an inscrutable world: 'The humble man reached in his pocket for his sacred book, and began to read. It was this world alone that was certain' (Paton 2003: 14). In his moments of comfort in the face of harsh realities, he gives thanks to God, such as when he spends time with Gertrude's son: 'Now God be thanked that here is a beloved one who can lift up the heart in suffering, that one can play with a child in the face of such misery' (62).

However, when he discovers Absolom's crime, he feels abandoned by God as a father figure: 'There are times, no doubt, when God seems no more to be about the world' (Paton 2003: 74). But, for the most part, religious answers seem to be comforting, unwavering narratives that give simple answers to highly complex questions, and Stephen seems aware of this when he becomes frustrated with Absolom for saying that what made him kill 'was the devil' (100).

Religion is also shown to be an inadequate form of meaning-making when Jarvis reflects on Arthur being seen as a missionary. James reflects on religion and how it is passed on similarly to paternal, stifling narratives, but does not really offer any material change in the lives of people and might not have been relevant to the lived realities of many who follow it: 'There was a mission near him, at Ndotsheni. But it was a sad place as he remembered it . . . A dirty old school where he had heard them reciting, parrot-fashion, on the one or two occasions that he had ridden past there, reciting things that could mean little to them' (Paton 2003: 141).

Religion is also criticised when it is used for propaganda, since God the Father becomes manipulated to reflect racialist ideology. Arthur points to the hypocrisy of religious people practising exploitation and dehumanisation, and says:

> We are . . . compelled, in order to preserve our belief that we are Christian, to ascribe to Almighty God, Creator of Heaven and Earth, our own human intentions, and to say that because He created white and black, He gives the Divine Approval to any human action that is designed to keep black men from advancement. We go so far as to credit Almighty God with having created black men to hew wood and draw water for white men. We go so far as to assume that He blesses any action that is designed to prevent black men from the full employment of the gifts He gave them (Paton 2003: 154).

The religious narratives are used to justify oppression and exploitation in this way, and Stephen's own reliance on these narratives is called into question. Through his uncritical adoption of the paternal narrative that supports his own oppression, Stephen personifies an obedient son figure to God the Father, but shows how this role stifles his own freedom. Only once he is able to question the validity of this narrative through his anger with Absolom's answer is he able to gain a sense of freedom from it as well, and focus on more practical ways to effect change in Ndotsheni.

John Kumalo, Stephen's brother, who lives in the city, most clearly voices the criticism of religion as a stifling paternal narrative that limits the freedom and empowerment of those who blindly follow it. He also shows how religion is ineffective as a solution to social injustices, which are at the crux of the novel. He says to Stephen and other companions:

> I do not wish to offend you gentlemen, but the Church too is like the chief. You must do so and so and so. You are not free to have an experience. A man must be faithful and meek and obedient, and he must obey the laws, whatever the laws may be. It is true that the Church speaks with a fine voice, and that the Bishops speak against the laws. But this they have been doing for fifty years, and things get worse, not better (Paton 2003: 36).

John criticises religion in relation to chiefs and 'tribal' culture, and sees both as symbols of white power and oppression. Watson shows that the ideological conflict between John and Stephen is important since it highlights Stephen's convictions and his strategy towards overcoming societal ills: 'Stephen is an advocate of "Change from Within", of spiritual purification, and is in favour of passivity, submission, meekness and guidance; John is a proponent of "Change from Without" and of the activism, domination and calculation which this programme for social change demands' (Watson 1982: 37). Watson highlights that Stephen's convictions can clearly be seen as those favoured by the novel, highlighting passivity and a 'revolution of hearts . . . rather than . . . a revolution in social or economic structure'. Watson shows further that Stephen, for the most part, does not recognise the failings in his ideology and his simplistic reliance on religious answers to social questions: '[Stephen] himself does not seem to realize (though John Kumalo makes this clear) that although Christianity might offer profound spiritual strength to people . . . it also imparts a political weakness which dictates, however necessarily and realistically, an acceptance of the hegemony of the oppressor' (37–8).

Importantly, Stephen Kumalo is never able to reflect fully on the precariousness of his reliance on religious narratives, but the tensions in this novel clearly demonstrate that paternal narratives such as these were inadequate in transcending societal ills and the novel's focus of unsuccessful fatherhoods. Towards the end of the novel, Stephen adopts a more nuanced view of his devotion to religion, understanding that it does not supplant practical concerns: 'Kumalo began to pray regularly in his church for the restoration of Ndotsheni. But he knew that was not enough. Somewhere down here upon the earth men must come together, think something, do something' (Paton 2003: 195). So, in the end, the novel does seem to steer away from a simplistic religious focus as the answer to social ills.

## The paradoxes of rural 'tribal' culture and urban capitalism as patriarchal structures

The issue of traditional 'tribal' culture and the ethnic separatist system of apartheid is important in highlighting the difference between John and Stephen Kumalo. Naively, Stephen seems to demonstrate a belief that the tribe can be rebuilt and that the rural tribal system is still the answer for South Africa. Foley notes that 'what Kumalo comes fundamentally to understand is that the root cause of [societal] degradation and corruption lies in the disintegration of traditional African society' (1998: 69). The degradation is so severe that even Stephen, as an authoritative father figure, is unable to restore his family. Foley expains: 'Kumalo's failure to re-unite his family and restore the traditional kinship structure suggests, metonymically, the impossibility of restoring the former tribal system generally.' This tribal system, symbolised through the disintegration of the family, does not offer a simplistic solution to South Africa's social and economic problems. Despite this, Stephen seems to lament its loss and sees it as idyllic. John, in contrast, is disillusioned with the tribal system. He sees the tribal chief as the 'white man's dog . . . a trick to hold together something that the white man desires to hold together' (Paton 2003: 35). It is thus in John's estimation a structure that seeks to maintain power for white South Africans and to exploit and oppress other groups.

The chief is constructed as a paternal figure in the tribal setting. He has power and is a leader, but this power is subverted in the novel and shown to be merely symbolic. The chief is disrespected in many ways, especially by white people. When Kumalo expresses concerns about the community, and tries to find ways to make sure that young people do not leave, he reflects on the position of the chief:

> For who would be chief over this desolation? It was a thing the white man had done, knocked these chiefs down, and put them up again, to hold the pieces together. But the white men had taken most of the pieces away. And some chiefs sat with arrogant and blood-shot eyes, rulers of pitiful kingdoms that had no meaning at all (Paton 2003: 230).

The power of the chief is compromised and only propped up by the paternalistic system that still sees him as a puppet of white power. When Stephen sees the chief with the group of white men, planting sticks in the ground in order to delineate the limits of a new dam in the area, which James commissioned, he reflects:

> Now the chief was not to be outdone by the white men, so he too got down from his horse and took some of the sticks, but Kumalo could see that he did not fully understand what was being done . . . The chief, embarrassed and knowing still less what was to be done, got back on his horse and sat there, leaving the white men to plant the sticks (Paton 2003: 242).

The chief, for all the ceremony and pomp of his position, is rendered powerless. His paternal narrative is not truly reflecting his own power, but rather the power of an oppressive system. The chief, as a male figure of power and authority, is constructed in the tribal narrative as one who is meant to offer leadership and to be respected by the tribe, but his role is subverted and the so-called tribal system is shown to be a measure of control and a stifling paternal narrative that relies on ideologies of difference and division.

Interestingly, John, who is one of the main critics of these systems of oppression, espouses an answer in the form of capitalism. He ironically does not acknowledge that exploitative capitalism is the major driver behind many of the systems that he criticises, including the mining industry. The novel presents a version of capitalist South Africa that relies on widespread oppression for its continuation, and indeed capitalism itself is a paternal narrative. Even though they are poor and exploited, black people keep the capitalist system operating through their cheap labour, as John explains:

> It is they who dig the gold. For three shillings a day . . . We live in the compounds, we must leave our wives and families behind. And when the new gold is found, it is not we who will get more for our labour. It is the white man's share that will rise . . . They do not think, here is a chance to pay more for our labour. They think only, here is a chance to build a bigger house and buy a bigger car (Paton 2003: 36).

Arthur Jarvis, in his letters, calls out this exploitation as well: 'It is not permissible to add to one's possessions if these things can only be done at the cost of other men. Such development has only one true name, and that is exploitation' (Paton 2003: 145). He points to the many negative consequences of exploitation, stating that it results 'in the disintegration of native community life, in the deterioration of native family life, in poverty, slums and crime'.

Importantly, economic disparity also creates a crisis of fatherhood. The inability of the father to provide for his family is linked to many social problems, and the racial structure of this exploitation results in a sense of moral degeneration among black people. According to Arthur:

> The old tribal system was, for all its violence and savagery, for all its superstition and witchcraft, a moral system. Our natives today produce criminals and prostitutes and drunkards, not because it is their nature to do so, but because their simple system of order and tradition and convention has been destroyed. It was destroyed by the impact of our civilization. Our civilization has therefore an inescapable duty to set up another system of order and tradition and convention (Paton 2003: 146).

Arthur constructs a sense of moral, intellectual and economic superiority of white people, and this places a paternalistic burden on them to care for black people. The parallels here are clear: the white race is the father figure to black groups, and has to construct paternal narratives that not only maintain their own power and are self-perpetuating, but that also aim to understand the emerging narratives of the child figure, which is seen as representative of black people in

South Africa.[3] Importantly and ironically, Arthur does not allow for the voices of black people or their own narrative power in constructing these narratives, but sees it as solely the responsibility of white people. They need to create a new paternal narrative, but this time one that shares power.

Watson also highlights how this paternalistic construction is ignorant of many important considerations and extremely simplistic. He argues that the novel's central problem is 'social disintegration' (Watson 1982: 35), which he identifies as 'the detribalization of blacks by whites and the lawlessness and moral corruption which this enforced social disintegration has caused' (34). Watson explains how paternal narratives are used to understand these shifts by white characters, particularly Arthur Jarvis, and father figures like Stephen Kumalo:

> A certain ideology, which is an amalgam of liberalism and Christianity, is brought to bear upon this problem . . . It is through this . . . that the major mystification of *Cry, the Beloved Country* is perpetrated. Through the mouthpiece of Kumalo and Msimangu, Paton attempts to solve what is clearly and statedly a material, sociological problem by means of metaphysics; against the multiple problems caused by detribalization and urbanization he advances the solution of love (1982: 35).

---

3. J. Grenfell Williams, in his review of the novel published in 1949, demonstrates this inherent paternalism as it is practised by the author as well, as Paton is given the power to narrate the lives of black people in South Africa and to analyse their situation in ways they seem unable to do. He explains: 'In some books about Africa the attempt to reproduce in English the rhythm and the idiom of an African language achieves only self-consciousness or an awful kind of whimsical sentimentality. But not here. Mr. Paton knows his Africans. He knows that they are neither whimsical nor sentimental though their phrases have a beauty of their own. His Africans talk in short, hard, almost brittle sentences; the only softness is that which comes, naturally enough, at the end of Zulu conversations "Go well", "Stay well". They shy away from the complex thought that has to be put into words and when Mr. Paton speaks these thoughts for them he speaks like an Old Testament prophet' (Williams 1949: 79).

This idea of love is purposely vague in the novel, and has been criticised by Watson, but the full implications of Msimangu's message will be explored in context later in this chapter.

Capitalism is again ironically espoused as the answer to social ills in one of the novel's reflective sections, where many segments of the South African population are focalised. Money is shown as a symbol of masculine power, contradicting the corrupting force of money and capitalism that is often highlighted in the novel. In a section that sympathises with the voice of white, wealthy city men, it is explained:

> It is wrong to say . . . that Johannesburg thinks only of money. We have as many good husbands and fathers, I think, as any town or city, and some of our big men make great collections of works of art, which means work for artists, and saves art from dying out; and some have great ranches in the North, where they shoot game and feel at one with nature (Paton 2003: 170).

Again, nature and the rural landscape are contrasted with the city, and shown to be linked to purity. The section, however, comes across as an ironic representation of the goodness of these men, and it deconstructs itself in the presentation. The 'good husbands and fathers' seem to inherently contradict the idea of the city, as was already demonstrated in the rest of the novel, which here is undone with the important hesitation in the form of 'I think'. The more feminine symbols of nature and art are also shown to be valued by these men, but interestingly these are always mediated through masculine symbols of power in the form of money and guns. These men are not shown to be truly linked to nature or art, which are representative of more maternal, imaginative narratives, but instead they seem to merely have control over them, 'sav[ing]' artists or 'hav[ing] great ranches . . . where they shoot game'. There is still the sense of control and domination linked with father figures, especially white fathers.

After this reflection on the role of wealthy white men, it is suggested that money should be in service of the family and strengthening the role of the father as provider, and not jeopardise the family or undermine its functioning. Money is shown to be dangerous when it is an end in itself, as in the exploitative capitalist system demonstrated in the novel's representation of Johannesburg, and instead the functions of money and how it can strengthen the family are valued. The reflection proceeds:

> For mines are for men, not for money. And money is not something to go mad about, and throw your hat into the air for. Money is for food and clothes and comfort, and a visit to the pictures. Money is to make happy the lives of children. Money is for security, and for dreams, and for hopes, and for purposes. Money is for buying the fruits of the earth, of the land where you were born (Paton 2003: 171-2).

John Kumalo represents the pursuit of money that is criticised in these sections, and sees capitalism as his route to 'freedom' (Paton 2003: 35). Even though he does seem to recognise it as a stifling system, similar to religion and tribal culture, he claims that it gives him a measure of freedom. He explains that money gives him a sense of personhood and of masculine power and influence, and it allows him to weave a paternal narrative of control that he could not experience in his tribal homeland. He explains to Stephen:

> Down in Ndotsheni I am nobody, even as you are nobody, my brother. I am subject to the chief, who is an ignorant man. I must salute him and bow to him, but he is an uneducated man. Here in Johannesburg I am a man of some importance, of some influence. I have my own business, and when it is good, I can make ten, twelve, pounds a week . . . I do not say we are free here. I do not say we are free as men should be. But at least I am free of the chief (Paton 2003: 35).

Ultimately, however, the power that money affords is claimed to lead to corruption and deterioration. John recognises this, even when he praises money as his own route to a sense of freedom. The exploitative capitalist system, represented by the mining industry and Johannesburg as a whole, is shown to lead again to corruption, and this solution to regaining a sense of masculine power is also inadequate. Stephen's companion Msimangu shares this observation when reflecting on John's comments about power:

> Because the white man has power, we too want power, he said. But when a black man gets power, when he gets money, he is a great man if he is not corrupted. I have seen it often. He seeks power and money to put right what is wrong, and when he gets them, why, he enjoys the power and the money. Now he can gratify his lusts, now he can arrange ways to get white man's liquor, he can speak to thousands and hear them clap their hands. Some of us think when we have power, we shall revenge ourselves on the white man who has had power, and because our desire is corrupt, we are corrupted, and the power has no heart in it. But most white men do not know this truth about power, and they are afraid lest we get it (Paton 2003: 39).

### Violence and crime as routes to power

When all of these avenues to gaining power are rendered futile, another symbol of masculine power is exposed: violence.[4] In the novel, crime and violence are often blamed on these systems of inequality, and on the destruction of a sense of personhood and especially masculinity in oppressed groups. When men are systematically disempowered and their ability to determine their own lives is taken away, they are shown to enact violence and crime. In the novel, this disempowerment happens at two levels: the paternalistic and racist system of exploitation and migrant labour, and the oppressive paternal narratives that stifle self-determination. For the black son, he operates under both of these pressures, and Absolom, as a disempowered black man whose reality is ill at ease with the religious and tribe-based

---

4. Importantly, Paton was a staunch pacifist, denouncing political violence as a solution to racial inequality. This might explain his valorising of black characters in the novel who espouse spiritual solutions to social ills, and how these characters never consider the possibility of militant resistance. Paton notes: 'By temperament and principle I am opposed to the use of violence. By intellectual conviction I am opposed to its use in South Africa, believing that it will not achieve its declared purpose of making this country happier and better' (1965: 2).

narratives of his father, is symbolic of how the novel constructs the origins of crime.

When Stephen first arrives in Johannesburg, he discusses the city with Msimangu and others, and when he sees how race is linked to crime, he reflects:

> They talked of young criminal children, and older and more dangerous criminals, of how white Johannesburg was afraid of black crime. One of them went and got him a newspaper, the *Johannesburg Mail*, and showed him in bold black letters, OLD COUPLE ROBBED AND BEATEN IN LONELY HOUSE. FOUR NATIVES ARRESTED (Paton 2003: 22).

This is then explicitly linked to the broken family and to the broken tribe, as well as to 'the man that falls apart when the house is broken' (Paton 2003: 25). Masculinity and fatherhood are threatened by oppression, and crime is the response to that threat. Msimangu explains:

> The tragedy is not that things are broken. The tragedy is that they are not mended again. The white man has broken the tribe. And it is my belief – and again I ask your pardon – that it cannot be mended again. But the house that is broken, and the man that falls apart when the house is broken, these are the tragic things. That is why children break the law, and old white people are robbed and beaten (Paton 2003: 25-6).

Children are shown to break the law because they have lost the influence of their 'broken' fathers and live in 'broken' homes. Through a loss of masculine power in the exploitative capitalist system, the man has to find ways to reassert his control and power, and often these are shown to be violence and crime. Again, through asserting control, claiming possessions, and altering their own narratives, the perpetrators of crime experience a semblance of regaining their masculine power. They are often shown to employ one of the traditional masculine symbols, namely, guns or other weapons, which highlight their masculinity. Ultimately, weapons give Absolom and his cousin Johannes the ability to harm others: Johannes uses the bar that he carries to strike Arthur's domestic worker, and Absolom uses the gun to 'frighten' (Paton 2003: 163), affording him a form of strength.

Arthur, as a victim of crime, is presented as a victim of this system of disempowerment, and importantly his loss is represented prominently as a loss to his father James. This is demonstrated when Stephen shows great shame in his admission to James that he is Absolom's father: 'This thing that is the heaviest thing of all my years, is the heaviest thing of all your years also . . . It was my son that killed your son' (Paton 2003: 181). Arthur's death symbolically highlights the dangers of racial exploitation, as well as the loss of children to violence, which leads to the destruction of the family. When James is confronted with the violence of his son's death, seeing the blood stain on the floor where Arthur was shot, he remembers his son as an innocent child again, but interestingly also couples this with a symbol of masculinity in the form of a gun: 'He took off his hat and looked down at the dark stain on the floor. Unasked, unwanted, the picture of the small boy came into his mind, the small boy at High Place, the small boy with the wooden guns' (147). The gun here might serve to foreshadow the means of Arthur's death, but it is also representative of an image of innocence. Both sons are shown with guns, Arthur using a toy gun as a plaything and Absolom using it to frighten and to kill. This symbol is used in a way that represents life and vitality, and the power to control or dominate others. The use of this masculine symbol emphasises the ability of the sons to enact power over their worlds.

Hogan, however, explains that this association between black oppression and crime might not capture what the novel constructs as the cause of crime. He links it more powerfully to the role of paternalistic notions of white moral and intellectual superiority in the novel and to the novel's preoccupation with intact family structures with strong father figures: 'And what is the cause of these problems? Again, it is not political oppression and economic exploitation. Rather it is the lack of an adequate familial structure in which a strong moral tradition can be handed down, and specifically the failure of Europeans to provide such a system, their failure to accept parental responsibilities' (Hogan 1992: 209). The crime represented in the novel is ultimately, and again paternalistically, the responsibility of white people to find solutions for.

### The father's power represented through his voice

The final symbol of masculine power, closely linked to the theme of narrative, is the use of the voice. The voice articulates control and dominance, and allows the sharing and relaying of narrative and ideology to others. Stephen demonstrates the power of the voice when he tells stories to Gertrude and to her son. He turns to his nephew for companionship, and telling these stories allows him to construct a sense of the idyllic homeland to which they can return. He practises his paternal role in order to re-establish power over the wayward Gertrude and to remind her of where she belongs, and also as a way to bond with her son. By constructing Ndotsheni as a beautiful, idyllic place, he practises the paternal narrative role of maintaining a sense of commitment to the traditional homeland.

However, when he realises he has lost his own son Absolom to the city, the stories are unsettled, and finally his narrative power wanes when Gertrude's son becomes restless, no longer allowing him to practise his paternal narratives. He begins to realise that the appeal to the values of the homeland are out of place in the city, which he sees as corrupting, and it signals a sense that he is critical of the validity of these narratives.

John Kumalo expresses a paternal narrative through the use of his voice as well, this time not through storytelling but through his speeches at political rallies, such as his speech to mine workers; his voice is animalistic, referred to as a 'bull voice' (Paton 2003: 183), and linked to images of power: 'A lion growls in it, and thunder echoes in it over black mountains.' Es'kia Mphahlele explains that 'John Kumalo is a political speech-maker; he always seems to be addressing a crowd even when he speaks to one person' (1962: 37). John is aware of the power of his voice. His voice allows him to have influence over others, as he manages to capture thousands of listeners at political rallies, but this time his narrative captures the entire continent: 'It is as though Africa itself were in it' (Paton 2003: 183). John uses his voice to communicate the inequality of the current exploitative system of racial division and the mining industry, referring to a link between the people and the land, similar to the call back to the rural landscape that Stephen Kumalo proposes. But this time he shows a link between the gold found in the mines and the people as well, saying: 'It is the gold of the whole people, the white, and the black, and the coloured, and the Indian. But who will get the most of the gold?' (184). His voice is dangerous to the institution of racial exploitation, and at the rally the police become nervous about the power he wields to unsettle the national narrative. He is practising a form of rebellion against the dominant narratives of capitalism and racism, even though he ironically benefits from the capitalist system. He represents a son disobeying the father, using his own voice to weave an alternative narrative that threatens the power of the nation. His voice and ideas have been used to challenge all the dominant paternal narratives in the novel, from religion to tribal chiefdom to capitalism, and he realises the threat he poses.

The police wonder what would happen if his voice 'should madden [the crowd] with thoughts of rebellion and dominion, with thoughts of power and possession? Should paint for them pictures of Africa awakening from sleep, of Africa resurgent, of Africa dark and savage?' (Paton 2003: 184). Africa is linked to the oppressed here, something that has been drawn to slumber under the rule of the paternal narratives of colonialism and racial exploitation. By imagining Africa as once again powerful, John is a threat to the paternal power of the state, weaving new narratives that threaten entrenched ideologies.

John Kumalo links this rebellion to the inability of the system to foster effective fatherhood. He explains that without the ability to adequately provide for their families, the role of the father is destroyed: 'It is only our share that we ask, enough to keep our wives and our families from starvation. For we do not get enough' (Paton 2003: 184). Money is not merely a way to heighten the paternal and paternalistic influence, as was the case with the wealthy white men who can control their environments, but money is also necessary for the basic functioning of fatherhood and the paternal role. The provider and protector role depends on money, and without it the father's power, and by extension his masculinity, necessarily fail. John continues: 'We only ask for those things that labouring men fight for in every country in the world, the right to sell our labour for what it is worth, the right to bring up our families as decent men should.'

However, despite his realisation of his own narrative power through his voice and his ability to weave a new narrative, John stops his speech due to fear. His spell on the crowd is broken: 'But the man is afraid, and the deep thundering growl dies down, and the people shiver and come to themselves' (Paton 2003: 184). Msimangu and Stephen, having witnessed the rally, then comment on why John is ineffective in creating a new narrative or in pursuing his own narrative power. A reflection on John clarifies that he seeks only the power and recognition of the words:

> There are some men who long for martyrdom, there are those who know that to go to prison would bring greatness to them, these are those who would go to prison not caring if it brought greatness or not. But John Kumalo is not one of them. There is no applause in prison (Paton 2003: 186).

Msimangu says to Stephen after hearing John's speech: 'Perhaps we should thank God he is corrupt . . . For if he were not corrupt, he could plunge this country into bloodshed. He is corrupted by his possessions, and he fears their loss, and the loss of the power he already has' (Paton 2003: 187). Msimangu shows that John is a slave to the very paternal narratives that he tries to challenge, failing to truly challenge the inequality and exploitation since he fears the loss of his own relative wealth and power. However, the ease with which Msimangu is able to dismiss John is glaring, judging him only by his moral character rather than by the content of the speeches he is giving and the political realities he points to. Watson notes that this is a convenient way for the novel to ignore political conflicts with its decidedly liberal and Christian ideology: 'John Kumalo's *moral* corruption is emphasized to the extent that his actual political worth, the substantial accuracy of his many brief analyses, are ultimately ignored and glossed over . . . In short, because John Kumalo is not a good man, his politics are not good' (Watson 1982: 39). In light of Paton's commitment to pacifism, it is important to note how John, as a potential revolutionary and political dissident who might be seen as inciting violence, is portrayed as a negative, corrupt character in the novel. Foley explains: 'John Kumalo . . . does nothing in the service of others and can offer the people little more than his "golden voice," which is disparagingly contrasted with Msimangu's "golden words"'

(1998: 83). Msimangu is given moral authority through his 'golden words', whereas John's message seems to be delegitimised due to what is seen as his corrupt character. In Foley's summary, John's 'depiction as a selfish coward and corrupt hypocrite detracts from the several valid points which he makes in conversation and speeches' (83-4).

## The possibility for maternal narratives and destabilising power structures

The voice becomes a symbol of masculine power, which offers the possibility of escaping stifling paternal narratives, but this is still shown to be impossible for the characters due to the structural and systemic inequality and powerlessness created by the paternal narratives of religion, tribal culture, tradition, capitalism and race. While the fathers are always immersed in these narratives and use them to perpetuate and cement their own authority and power, these narratives also limit them in many ways by disabling their ability to understand realities outside of these simplistic frameworks and to challenge or reimagine ways of understanding the world. The symbols of masculine power discussed above offer men, and especially fathers, the ability to reclaim their power, but they do not ultimately lead to the reconciliation and societal shifts that are shown to be lacking in the novel. The reliance on paternal narratives limits the fathers from understanding or connecting with their own sons, and limits the agency of these sons. In this light, it becomes necessary to engage in maternal narratives, which are linked to mutual understanding, nurturing, emotion and reimagining. Edward Callan notes that the novel includes a 'multitude of voices', which '[talk] incessantly about problems - problems of race, problems of language, and problems of living space' (1982: 35). By integrating the paternal and maternal forms and engaging in discourse critical of the stifling paternal narratives, as Arthur began to do before his death and as John showed the potential to do as well, the novel shows the possibility of redemption and reconciliation across racial and economic boundaries.

While these maternal narratives are depicted as complex and are not offered as unproblematic solutions to the challenges raised in the novel, they do offer the most powerful means of criticising patriarchal power structures as well as allowing for true reconciliation. Mothers are shown to have a closer link to the new narratives woven by the son, but fathers experience distance from these narratives since they contradict their own realities or the established systems of power. Black, in his review of Paton's relationship with the rule of law, explains that women were often given the role in Paton's novels of contesting restrictive laws. He focuses on the nationalism of Afrikanerdom, saying that it is 'the most patriarchal of societies. Paton clearly explores an idea time and again that there is a silent disquiet about apartheid and its "fierce laws" amongst its women' (Black 1992: 69). Black's observation that it is a 'silent disquiet' is pertinent here, as it demonstrates how women are not associated with the power to narrate their own lives, nor with the image of the voice as fathers are, but in order to express their dissent they often engage in the imaginative maternal narratives that allow them to transcend the restrictions of the patriarchal nationalism of South African society at the time. Black explains that 'it is through the women that the true unhappiness of the Afrikaner male apartheid supporters and lawmakers is always revealed'. In *Save the Beloved Country*, Paton describes the men who construct the restrictive apartheid laws as those who hold the 'disastrous belief that peace can be maintained by force, that law is the equivalent of justice, and that order is to be preferred above freedom' (Paton 1989: 232). This can be clearly linked to paternal narratives, which seek to restrict and maintain power relations, and contrasted with maternal narratives, which resist and reimagine these relations.

The mother in *Cry, the Beloved Country* is often linked to the body, to the visceral, to the life and death of the child, and to innocence. James reflects on his son's activism and political ideologies: 'For this boy of his had gone journeying in strange waters, further than his parents had known. Or perhaps his mother knew. It would not surprise him if his mother knew. But he himself had never done such journeying, and there was nothing he could say' (Paton 2003: 140). James is shown to be located firmly within the certain and narrow domain of his known experience and of traditional narratives, while Margaret, Arthur's mother, seems to be able to connect with the new narrative that Arthur forms a part of, a narrative that contradicts traditional paternal values. The image of 'journeying in strange waters', which Margaret is able to do along with Arthur, demonstrates how women can deviate from the strict paternal narratives that fathers are variously linked to. James says to Margaret: 'You were always nearer to him than I was,' and she responds: 'It's easier for a mother, James' (142). The mother is shown to be more intimately connected with the child, and James says to Margaret: 'Although his life was different . . . you understood it . . . I'm sorry I didn't understand it . . . I didn't know it would ever be so important to understand it.' Even grief is gendered in the novel, as Harrison, Arthur's brother-in-law, says to James: 'It's always worse for the mother, Jarvis' (138). James, feeling this implies that he is distant from his son, actually counters Harrison's assertion: 'He pondered over it, and said then, I was very fond of my son, he said. I was never ashamed of having him.' This sense of shame that James refers to is interesting, as it can only refer to the ways in which Arthur deviated from the paternal narrative through not taking over High Place and through his progressive politics. By asserting that he was never ashamed, James signals his own grief as well, and contradicts the supposed closer link of the mother. It can be read as a sign that he is reconnecting with his son.

The mother also fulfils the nurturing role, especially physically caring for the child, as Stephen reflects of Absolom: 'The hand that had murdered had once pressed the mother's breast into the thirsting mouth, had stolen into the father's hand when they went out into the dark' (Paton 2003: 215). The father here again represents safety in the dark for the child, the protective and guiding role, while the mother is the nurturer. When the letter arrives at the end of the novel saying Absolom will receive no mercy and will be executed, this visceral and physical link with his mother is again emphasised, as Stephen hands the letter to his wife: 'With shaking hands he gave it to her, and she read it also, and sat looking before her, with lost and terrible eyes, for this was the child of her womb, of her breasts' (239).

This intimate link is again shown in another reflective section of the novel, in which a poor family living in an informal settlement with a sick child are represented. When the child dies, the mother reflects:

Oh child of my womb and fruit of my desire, it was pleasure to hold the small cheeks in my hands, it was pleasure to feel the tiny clutching of the fingers, it was pleasure to feel the little mouth tugging at the breast. Such is the nature of woman. Such is the lot of woman, to carry, to bear, to watch, and to lose (Paton 2003: 59).

While the mother is shown to understand and to be closely connected with the child, she is also shown to be ineffective in protecting or guarding the child from the dangers of the world, or of practising much agency at all. Watson offers an interesting interpretation of how the extreme emotiveness of this section could create a sense of helplessness, which defies the agency of black subjects, explaining in an extended passage:

The description of the misfortune is invariably converted into a drawn out characterization of the almost insuperable sorrow and mourning which it arouses. And although Paton could be said to follow this strategy in order to convey the very real helplessness and justifiable bewilderment of the simple-hearted, largely uneducated black in the face of a cruel and alien white world whose domination is ubiquitous and so unfathomable that . . . it takes on all the mysteriousness and arbitrariness of an unknown god, the function of his emphasis on blind, grief-stricken reactions is both to obscure the real reasons (and hence possible solutions) for the tragic incidents and to elicit from the reader a purely emotional identification with the suffering hero so that, again, the real reasons for a predicament are smothered under the flow of sympathy which the reader feels (Watson 1982: 33).

Thus, while this section might be shown to be representative of a potentially insightful maternal narrative, it could also serve to obscure the structural reasons for why these problems exist and thus disempower the focalised mother. In effect, Watson accuses Paton of further silencing these multivocal narratives, indeed the maternal narrative, through connecting these stories to heightened emotions and the helplessness of these subjects in the face of grander forces, such as religion, the law and ultimately racial exploitation.

While mothers are able to have access to the narratives that the sons weave, they are not able to influence the world around them in the way that men can. Only John is able to ensure the freedom of his son when he is accused, only Stephen is able to search for Absolom, and only James is able to rebuild the village of Ndotsheni at the end of the novel. Thus, while women are shown to have access to different narratives and levels of understanding than men have access to, they are not shown to have agency to construct their own narratives in the novel or to practise any political action.

Only Gertrude, interestingly, is able to offer an alternative maternal narrative. She eventually leaves her child because she fails at approximating ideal femininity in the novel, as she has sexual desire and is 'careless' with her laughter, which are qualities she is reprimanded for by Mrs Lithebe, the matriarch of the novel who Gertrude and Stephen live with while in Johannesburg. Gertrude thus leaves, ostensibly to become a nun, forging her own narrative that is separate from her maternity, but importantly still trying to fit into the traditional narrative of femininity that is imposed on her. Ultimately, the women are absent characters in the novel, who do not seem to offer real resistance or agency. Even though they have access to the new narratives of the children due to their closer bonds, they are not able to truly create their own narratives. The role of maternal, transformative narratives thus become the work of men as well, and many of the men, such as John, Stephen, Arthur and James, demonstrate the ability to have imaginative, alternative narratives. It becomes their task to change the material reality of their children and, by extension, of their communities. The community becomes symbolised as a child, which the leaders and fathers need to care for.

At the end of the novel, this message is emphasised in Stephen's conversation with the headmaster of Ndotsheni's school, and his paternal role of protector is expanded to include the entire community: 'The headmaster explained that the school was trying to relate the life of the child to the life of the community . . . everything in the valley was dead too; even children were dying' (Paton 2003: 233). The death of the children is a failure of the fathers, and it is their role to protect them, and as the children are symbolic of the community as a whole, the father's role is expanded to caring for the community.

One of the ways the fathers in the novel are able to do this is by establishing a closer link to the children and their narratives, and by refiguring the stifling paternal narratives, essentially practising the maternal narrative form. Only by engaging with the writing of his son does James gain the impetus to restore Ndotsheni, and, importantly, James provides milk to the children of Ndotsheni, a father-given sustenance that mirrors the mother's breast milk, which is often referred to in the novel to indicate the link with children. This shows his new inhabitation of maternal, community-based and reimagined narratives. Only after understanding and forgiving his son, after recognising the injustices of the colonial system, which destroys families and communities, and by critically confronting and working around the holders of power like the chief of Ndotsheni, does Stephen begin to rebuild his community. Their traditional, paternal power is refigured with more nurturing maternal narratives in order to reach for healing after the traumas to themselves, to their families, to the communities and to the country.

The maternal narratives, concerned with sharing and diversifying rather than stifling and concentrating power, are also linked to the power of love, which the novel values as the most effective mode of overcoming the fractures in society. Msimangu is one of the most vocal proponents of the power of love, and stands as a paragon of religious authority and grace in the novel. He explains:

> But there is only one thing that has power completely, and that is love. Because when a man loves, he seeks no power, and therefore he has power. I see only one hope for our country, and that is when white men and black men, desiring neither power nor money, but desiring only the good of the country, come together to work for it (Paton 2003: 39–40).

Msimangu shares these thoughts while reflecting on the corruption of John, and how, even though he challenges the systems of inequality, he will be unable to bring about change due to his own reliance on money and power. When Stephen later leaves after Absolom is sent to prison, he seems to have adopted these words and goes to see John, but in anger he mentions how Absolom was betrayed by John's son Johannes. John kicks him out, and Stephen reflects:

> Out there in the street, he was humiliated and ashamed. Humiliated because the people passing looked in astonishment, ashamed because he did not come for this purpose at all. He had come to tell his brother that power corrupts, that a man who fights for justice must himself be cleansed and purified, that love is greater than force. And none of these things had he done . . . He turned to the door, but it was locked and bolted. Brother had shut out brother, from the same womb had they come (Paton 2003: 212).

Once again the sense of connection is shown through the physical link to the mother, and Stephen was unable to resist his desire to hurt his brother with his words and to share the message of love that he had come to share. Msimangu's message of love as the remedy for injustice is lost in this angry moment, but the message remains with Stephen. He remembers more of Msimangu's words towards the end of the novel: 'It was Msimangu who had said, Msimangu who had no hate for any man, I have one great fear in my heart, that one day when they turn to loving they will find we are turned to hating' (Paton 2003: 276).

Watson is highly critical of using love as a solution, noting: 'Of course this is useless, the problem has not been caused by a lack of love in South Africa, and therefore to prescribe an antidote of love for it is simply naïve and beside the point' (1982: 35). Watson points out that the sociological problems highlighted in the novel cannot be solved through these ideological and metaphysical solutions that rely on religious underpinnings. He highlights the fact that even though the individuals in the novel might have gained resolution and James Jarvis undergoes a 'liberal change of heart', this does nothing to change the underlying problems of crime, poverty and racial exploitation that lie at the heart of the novel.

However, Foley expands on the concept of love, arguing that it is used in the novel in a particularly political sense:

> By 'love' as it is used here, Paton – via Msimangu – does not mean simply some vague notion of interpersonal goodwill. More properly, the term, 'love,' may be glossed here as the

desire to create and live in a just society, and so the act of loving may be thought of as right political conduct which will help bring about a more equitable socio-political order (Foley 1998: 81).

Love, Foley suggests, is the sharing of power and, by extension, the disruption of strict power hierarchies.

The father's role, the novel suggests, is to find narratives that support this vision and to instil them in children and communities. When Stephen returns to Ndotsheni at the end of the novel, he knows that this is his role now. It is a moment akin to a father returning to his family, and everyone in the community is reverent and happy. He reignites a sense of beauty and wonder in the village, as well as revitalising the spirit of Africa, which John's speeches alluded to earlier:

> There is calling here, and in the dusk one voice calls to another in some far distant place. If you are Zulu you can hear what they say, but if you are not, even if you know the language, you would find it hard to know what is being called. Some white men call it magic, but it is no magic, only an art perfected. It is Africa, the beloved country . . . They call that you are returned (Paton 2003: 222).

Watson notes:

> The social failure which is signified by the murder of Arthur Jarvis and the execution of Absolom Kumalo is transformed, by the twist of tragedy, into the moral victory of James Jarvis and the religious exultation of Stephen Kumalo who is restored to an intimation of ultimate order and meaning through his final sense of the nearness of God (1982: 36).

Watson comments, again, that the larger issues plaguing the country are obscured by this individual tale of ideological superiority. The paternal narratives allowed reconciliation for James and Stephen, but they did nothing to change the society, a fact that is glossed over in the reconstruction of Ndotsheni.

Later, however, there is the mournful reflection of a country broken, and the realisation that the sons born into it will be corrupted by it. There is a sense of innocence in the rural setting, but soon the youth will be corrupted by the stifling paternal narratives that they are growing into:

> Yes, God save Africa, the beloved country . . . Call, oh small boy, with the long tremulous cry that echoes over the hills. Dance oh small boy, with the first slow steps of the dance that is for yourself. Call and dance, Innocence, call and dance while you may. For this is a prelude, it is only a beginning. Strange things will be woven into it, by men you have never heard of, in places you have never seen. It is life you are going into, you are not afraid because you do not know (Paton 2003: 225).

The dance that will have 'strange things . . . woven into it' is symbolic of how the freedom of these boys to express themselves through their own narrative power, 'the dance that is for yourself', will be tainted by paternal narratives from 'men you have never heard of'. These boys will not be able to dance in 'Innocence' for long. Stephen's ability to recognise this by the end of the novel gives him the imperative to weave new narratives that allow for regeneration and change – maternal narratives that defy tradition.

The new narratives of the sons are represented by Arthur, in his writing, as well as Arthur's young son, who comes to Stephen to learn Zulu and to share a bond with him when he visits his grandfather James's farm. Marcus characterises this as 'symboli[sing] a hope for better future relationships between black and white in South Africa' (1962: 612). These narratives are also demonstrated by Napoleon Letsisi, a man hired by James to teach farming techniques to the community at Ndotsheni. Letsisi advocates that the community gives up on old tribal ways, such as the practice of lobola, if they are to successfully use the land at Ndotsheni. Letsisi's ability to engage in creative reimaginings is what situates him within maternal narratives, and the language used to describe his plans shows this: 'They all sat round the table, their faces excited and eager, for this young man could paint a picture before your eyes' (Paton 2003: 253). The promise of prosperity ignites the will to change in the people, especially Stephen. There is a sense of duty to the community in the new narratives, as well as a duty to nurturing children, and no longer duty to tribe, money or master, as Letsisi says:

> I could not work so for any master . . . we do not work for men . . . we work for the land and the people. We do not even work for money . . . We work for Africa, he said, not for this man or that man. Not for a white man or a black man, but for Africa (Paton 2003: 269).

They begin to rebuild the community, in collaboration with James and even with the chief. The symbols of masculine power, such as money, race and tribal culture, earlier shown to be inadequate and stifling, are resisted and transcended.

Watson notes that this conclusion to the novel does not serve as an ending, indicating a limit to the power of the paternal narratives to account for the future of the country. He argues:

> The evidence that this is not a genuine restoration . . . but only an instance of two men who have each, as it were, made a separate peace, is to be found in the fact that Paton quite literally cannot finish his novel. Although, in the final scene, the sun rises in the east and Stephen Kumalo rises in thanksgiving from his mountain vigil, the essential question remains unanswered – the 'mystery' of freedom and injustice remains to be solved (Watson 1982: 36).

Mphahlele similarly criticises the end of the novel and its ideological bent:

> Because the message keeps imposing itself on us in *Cry, the Beloved Country*, we cannot but feel how thickly laid on the writer's liberalism is: let the boys be kept busy by means of club activities and they will be less inclined to delinquency; work for a change in the heart of the white ruling class (Jarvis's final philanthropic gesture and his son's practical interest in club

activities together with his plea to South Africa indicate this) (1962: 39).

However, Foley argues that viewing the ending as paternalistic might be oversimplifying it, criticising Mphahlele and Watson's views as misreadings. He argues:

> Jarvis does not perform [his acts of generosity] in a patronising manner, or out of a desire to establish himself in a position of control over the people, or out of some misplaced sense of guilt. On the contrary, he acts from a wish to lend real practical assistance where it is manifestly needed (Foley 1998: 77).

Foley sees this as 'real moral progress' as James can finally recognise and address the needs of Ndotsheni. He notes that 'the novel suggests that through [Kumalo] and Jarvis's combined actions – a white man and a black man coming together and thinking and acting in concert – the land may at least partly be restored' (Foley 1998: 78). Despite Foley's reading of the character's motivation, it must be noted that symbolically it is a strikingly paternalistic moment, and, in the context of a novel that places white men's benefaction as the solution to the problems faced by black people, its simplistic, naive underpinnings cannot be ignored.

There is an ironic sense of hope at the end of the novel when it is viewed retrospectively, given that it was published at the beginning of the widespread implementation of apartheid laws and that there would be no transformative collaboration in the country for many decades to come. As his son is being put to death, Stephen is on a mountain watching the sun rise: 'Yes, it is the dawn that has come . . . But when that dawn will come, of our emancipation, from fear of bondage and the bondage of fear, why, that is a secret' (Paton 2003: 277). The father has lost his son but is reconnected with him, and he begins to recognise his role in rebuilding his community, but the widespread structural inequality was just beginning to take root in South Africa and would serve to disempower fathers for generations afterwards.

CHAPTER 3

# The Stifled Narrative Power of Daughters
## *In the Heart of the Country* and *Burger's Daughter*

During the apartheid era, the South African literary landscape was consumed with addressing racial oppression. There were many portraits of state cruelty and injustice, including André Brink's *A Dry White Season* (1979), Sipho Sepamla's *A Ride on the Whirlwind* (1981), Mongane Wally Serote's *To Every Birth Its Blood* (1981) and Richard Rive's *'Buckingham Palace', District Six* (1986). Prison narratives were also prominent, such as Alex La Guma's *The Stone Country* (1967) and Breyten Breytenbach's *The True Confession of an Albino Terrorist* (1985). Many texts explored racial tensions and subverted white positions of power, often through reflections on the rural farm setting, for example, Nadine Gordimer's *July's People* (1981), J.M. Coetzee's *Life & Times of Michael K* (1983) and Brink's *Rumours of Rain* (1978).

While many of these texts offer valuable insights into paternal narratives in literature during apartheid, and while they could provide the basis for a wealth of future research on this subject, Coetzee's *In the Heart of the Country* and Gordimer's *Burger's Daughter* were ultimately selected for analysis due to their central, powerful father figures and the interesting dynamic of daughters struggling for narrative control. Both novels were published in the 1970s, after the Soweto uprising, a symbolic moment of rebellion against paternalistic control that informs my reading of the texts; indeed, Gordimer's novel makes direct reference to these protests. Both authors also won the Nobel Prize in Literature later in their careers, reflecting the national and international impact they had; their contributions to the South African canon influenced many writers during the transition and post-transition eras, as will be demonstrated in chapters 4 and 5.

While *Burger's Daughter* and *In the Heart of the Country* each respond to racial and gender issues in South Africa, the former is in line with the dominant realist tradition in South African apartheid literature, while the latter challenges these conventions. The novels thus offer rich possibilities for comparison.

The period between 1948 and 1960 saw apartheid becoming entrenched in South African society, with widespread forced removals and the expansion of the legal framework that underpinned the system, from the Prohibition of Mixed Marriages Act in 1949, the Group Areas Act in 1950, the Immorality Act in 1957 to the Unlawful Organisations Act of 1960. The first state of emergency in South Africa followed the Sharpeville massacre in 1960 and saw the banning of the Pan-Africanist Congress (PAC) and the African National Congress (ANC), which led to the launch of their militant wings. The intermediary period, from the 1960s to the 1980s, saw violent clashes between resistance movements and state bodies, most prominently the June 16, 1976 student protest, and the 1985–1986 state of emergency, which saw many thousands being detained.

As detailed in Peter McDonald's *The Literature Police: Apartheid Censorship and Its Cultural Consequences* (2009), many books published before and during this period were banned in South Africa in an attempt to maintain racial policies and to silence dissent. Charles R. Larson, writing in 1973, explains: 'No book that attempts to depict life in South Africa accurately can be published there today. More books are censored in South Africa than in any other non-communist nation in the world' (1973: 54).

This trend shows how literature was often used as a political tool by those who challenged the apartheid government, and how censorship was used to counter this in an attempt to maintain a rigid, stifling ideology. *Burger's Daughter* was banned for only a few months after it was published, from July to October 1979, and Gordimer's next novel, *July's People*, which depicts a fictional future where apartheid is overthrown through civil war, was banned outright. In addition, many anti-apartheid writers at this time faced government restrictions and potential legal consequences, such as Athol Fugard, who was placed under police surveillance. Susan Gardner explains that many white writers and their books were 'selectively unbanned while most banned books by black writers (and many of these writers themselves) remained so' (1982: 61), explaining the dearth of novels from black South Africans at the time as their attention moved to drama and poetry. Gardner implies that censorship is another obstacle for the writer in the creative process, undermining and stifling his or her creative voice in the attempt to maintain hegemonic control of dominant ideologies.

The threat of banning and potential legal repercussions for writing politically dissident texts creates an interesting dynamic relevant to the theme of paternal narratives: the national narrative of apartheid, upheld through laws, force and a censorship board, is challenged by the narrative divergence of those who do not support the national narrative. By practising their own narrative power, imaginatively refiguring or questioning the narratives of their forefathers or paternalistic authority figures, many anti-apartheid writers during this period faced strong pressures from the stifling social and governmental forces that sought to maintain apartheid, but they were spurred by the impetus to use their writing as a tool for social change.

These political pressures on writers created what Gordimer herself referred to as the interregnum, which 'has the artist caught in trepidation between insecure structures and values' (Dimitriu 2000: 14). Iliana Dimitriu explains that 'while Gordimer gives us the emotional contours of people living amid large historical events, she is also "written" by the history of which she is a part. Despite her considerable novelistic imagination, she is overdetermined and limited in her writerly freedom' (12–13). These dual concerns, of being restricted by history in the artistic endeavour and facing censorship within hostile political climates, place limits on the narrative power of writers themselves. This has led some critics to question whether novels written during this time are artistically or culturally relevant for modern readers, as they were so strongly determined by the political objectives of their authors, as in Gordimer's work. Gareth Cornwell suggests:

> As time passes, [Gordimer's] novels will continue to be useful sources of historical data – South African society chronologically cross-sectioned, as it were – but are unlikely ever again to be as compelling to read as they were during the

dark years of apartheid. One would like to be able to say that the 'insider's' perspective that they afford is an intimate one charged with the textures of real life; or that the characters and situations represented are so fresh and free from cliché that they acquire an (as it were) independent life in the reader's imagination. But unfortunately, as the vast majority of her South African readers have attested, neither postulate is true (in Cornwell, Klopper and MacKenzie 2010: 12).

Dimitriu explains that there were 'contextual constraints' as well as 'critical methods that were appropriate to a time in which history, as J.M. Coetzee puts it, threatened to obliterate the allegorical act of fiction' (2000: 15). Gordimer's work, as with many texts written during apartheid, might have suffered under their own drive of creating narratives that describe national, political concerns and thereby sacrificed artistry or the representation of more personal concerns. However, Gordimer places her own pursuit of creative expression as paramount, saying that writing is more important to her than 'being answerable to some political or social problem' (Gordimer and Sontag 1985: 16), and she continues: 'I believe that you must do the thing you do best, and if you're a writer it's a mistake then to become a politician' (16). This conflict between creativity and politics, and the many dynamics of writing within repressed societies, might be reflected in the way in which the protagonist of her novel *Burger's Daughter*, Rosa Burger, struggles to narrate herself.

Tracing the literary landscape of South Africa from the dawn of apartheid until the Soweto revolt in the 1970s demonstrates how political concerns influenced the literature that was produced and published in South Africa. The 1950s saw the rise of the *Drum* writers, which Stephen Clingman characterises as 'part of the general ethos of multi-racialism that dominated the social and political opposition to apartheid at the time' (1986: 6). This era saw the representation of vibrant black townships and subjectivities through literature published in the popular *Drum* magazine. These narratives exposed the injustices of apartheid in an effort to bring about a more equal society. The emergence of dissident black voices through journalism and fiction demonstrated the power of the written word as a tool for resistance.

Prominent writers, such as Can Themba, Lewis Nkosi, Bessie Head and Richard Rive, worked for or published in *Drum* magazine during this era.

After the Sharpeville massacre, the treason trial of the late 1950s, the banning of the ANC and PAC, and the arrest of prominent resistance leaders during the 1960s, Clingman explains that the dominant ideology in the 1970s, 'in both literary and political terms, was that of Black Consciousness; this movement infused the renaissance of black poetry in this time as well as a much larger political revival' (1986: 7). The 1970s saw the publication of two prominent novels, which focus on the theme of fatherhood in very different ways: Gordimer's *Burger's Daughter*, in which she 'responds most deeply to the challenge of Black Consciousness – and the Soweto Revolt of 1976 to which it led' and Coetzee's *In the Heart of the Country*.

Each of these texts demonstrates the link between national narratives and paternal narratives, and importantly each of them uses narrative voice as a symbol of power. The ability to engage in self-definition and self-narration is linked to gender, generational differences and race. The figure of the white father is, in Coetzee and Gordimer's novels, shown to be the figure of narrative authority, and the narratives of the two daughters in these novels are always conflicted, diffused and uncertain. In both cases, the daughters claim to lose their narrative voice. The father is given the power to maintain or to resist power structures, and the daughters struggle to find their own narrative voices in the presence of overwhelming paternal narratives.

## J.M. Coetzee's *In the Heart of the Country*
### Critical perspectives
The second novel by Coetzee, *In the Heart of the Country*, was published in 1977 by United Kingdom publishing house Secker & Warburg. Hermann Wittenberg notes that the publication of this novel established him as 'a transnational author', or 'a writer whose literature is alert to the local but whose meaning is independent of it' (2008: 134). Indeed, the concerns of the novel can be seen to represent both the local, as it is set on a South African farm and deals with South

African racial themes, as well as broader concerns of gender, agency, colonialism and familial relationships. Brian Macaskill uses the novel to highlight how Coetzee's own writing can be seen as representing a 'middle voice':

> Coetzee's writing situates itself between: on the one hand, the less novelistic and often 'nonfictional' literary tradition long associated with black writing – poetry, autobiography, journalism, theatre, and 'protest' forms of short fiction – and, on the other hand, the narrative legacy of liberal realism in white writing inherited from Olive Schreiner and passed down through Alan Paton, Phyllis Altman, Harry Bloom, Dan Jacobson, early Nadine Gordimer, and a number of more recent novelists working in English or in Afrikaans (1994: 441).

This is done, according to Macaskill, in a way that allows Coetzee to at once inhabit as well as critically confront the tradition of liberal realism, which constitutes a large part of South African fiction. Macaskill suggests that Coetzee was 'surrounded by works with historical affiliations to distinct ideologies of South African literary production – from the Black Consciousness of Mtutuzeli Matshoba or Mongane Serote to the historical materialism of Nadine Gordimer's more recent work' (1994: 442). He highlights that in this position, 'Coetzee takes up a narrative position in a time and place replete with the awareness that history may "overtake" literary productions and thus affect the way those productions take place, causing them self-consciously to position or reposition themselves.'

Coetzee has been widely criticised for seemingly distancing his novels from historical materialism or even liberal realism, forms that were deemed to be politically necessary in a country as conflicted as apartheid South Africa. However, David Attwell counters this by asserting that Coetzee's writing can be seen 'as a form of situational metafiction, with a particular relation to the cultural and political discourses of South Africa in the 1970s and 1980s' (1993: 3).

In his second novel, the setting is a farm in rural South Africa, inhabited by the central character Magda, who presents herself as suffering under the oppressive control of her nameless father.

Magda is an unreliable narrator, frequently questioning her own understanding of events and her ability to narrate, and retelling parts of her tale with different outcomes. The novel is organised into short sections, which are numbered; as Coetzee himself explains in an interview with Joanna Scott:

> The enabling device in *In the Heart of the Country* turned out to be the numbering of the sections, because that enabled me to drop all pretense of continuity. After a few hundred words of prose, there comes a break – a three-digit number . . . They enable a certain sharpness of transition, or lack of smooth transition (Scott 1997: 89–90).

Within the tale the dominance of the father is violently challenged, as Magda kills her father in two of the longer narrative branches, but each time she is rendered confused, powerless or desperate without the presence of her father. Magda's violence is constructed as the only way she can overcome her state of being invisible to her father. Michela Canepari-Labib argues:

> It is therefore the need to be loved and included in her father's discourse, together with her rage at what she perceives as her father's attempt to exclude her from his world . . . that, if we are to believe Magda and take one of her versions of her father's killing as real, lead her to an extreme and desperate attempt to gain the man's love and recognition (2000: 116).

Sheila Roberts has noted that the novel has received surprisingly little critical attention compared to other novels by Coetzee. She asserts: 'Could it be that Magda, the protagonist, is too unattractively baffling for many readers? Or, perhaps her situation as a second-in-command colonizer on an almost empty farm renders her finally uninteresting as a representative of coloniality: after all, she has no real power' (Roberts 1992: 21). Roberts notes that the work of the critic might be further challenged because of how critical Magda is of her own narrative, explaining that she 'performs a continual deconstruction of her narrative, removing another possible *modus operandi* from the critic'

(22). Magda's powerlessness and her invisibility, even to literary critics, will be a focus of this discussion. Magda tries to construct an identity for herself, but she is undermined by her gender and by her position on the farm as a daughter with little agency.

The novel explicitly deals with a daughter resisting the paternal narration of her father through trying to weave her own narrative, as Chiara Briganti discusses in 'A Bored Spinster with a Locked Diary: The Politics of Hysteria in *In the Heart of the Country*' (1994). Briganti looks at the parallels between the relationship of the author and literary critic as compared to the psychoanalyst, represented by Freud, and the patient, classically represented as the hysterical woman. These concerns are interwoven with Magda's struggle to resist the paternal narratives of her father. Briganti explains:

> The novel itself is a process of unlearning this paternal language that has crystallized into a series of uncongenial plots, a process that parallels Magda's re-vision of her master narrative. These plots unfold like a hall of mirrors in which she encounters herself already cast as a fictional character and realizes her own entrapment (1994: 42).

Briganti sees the novel, thus, as an affront to realism; while the novel seemingly presents a realist vision of rural South Africa, it also demonstrates how literature erodes these realist elements and how literature, for Magda, constitutes a vision of the real:

> The literary archives of the past are raided for the fictional possibilities they contain and at the same time help to expose the paternalistic colonizing impulse that underlies narrative realism. The narrative, in fact, stretches the boundaries of realism, on the one hand, by taking the stuff for its story from literature, and, on the other, by creating a narrator who is able to find evidence of her own existence only in her own writing (Briganti 1994: 34).

Stephen Watson clarifies these issues by asserting that the novel is 'on one level, concerned to demonstrate that realism is not real at all, but simply a production of language, a code that people have come to accept as "natural"' (1986: 373). Furthermore, the novel can be linked to the concerns of structuralism in codifying meaning through language, and the breakdown of language, Watson argues, indicates a confrontation with Roland Barthes's conception of structuralism:

> On the one hand, [Coetzee] obviously wishes to register the impact of colonialism not, as is customary in the realist novel, through a series of incidents or events but at the more basic level of language itself. For this purpose, structuralism, with its emphasis on the creation of meaning through relationship, is a useful tool. In the same way that human relations are opaque and destructive in the colonial situation, so, Coetzee would seem to suggest, language itself fails to signify, to mean at all, under the conditions prevailing in such a situation. The only tongue the colonialist can speak is the circular one of tautology (Watson 1986: 373).

Due to the deconstruction of realism present in the novel, it moves to fantasy in the end, with Magda experiencing messages from flying machines. Watson concludes: 'The deconstruction of realism, then, is evidently intended, at the most basic level of language itself, as an act of decolonization and, as such, is very much part of its political meaning' (1986: 374). Magda's quest for freedom from her father is linked to her quest for freedom from language and from the 'Law' (Canepari-Labib 2000: 117), which enshrines the life of every character. Canepari-Labib explains:

> Magda actually enacts a struggle against language itself – the language that, in Lacanian philosophy, is the primal factor of alienation and repression, that which, being a means of thought, consciousness and reflection, poses a distance between the mind and the lived experience – and tries to re-appropriate her essence, the substance that she lost when she entered language, fighting the inauthenticity of her life, her alienation from the real experience and the mediation language provides (2000: 116).

Furthermore, language in the novel is linked to 'authority that the father, as a representative of the Law, speaks, and hence becomes a vehicle of the Law' (Canepari-Lahib 2000: 117). Magda's loss of language is linked to her rebellion against the control of her father's dominance and the 'Law' that he represents.

Briganti also explains that Magda's gender has impacted on how critics have engaged with the novel, as her behaviour and quest for agency is very often linked to mental illness rather than more nuanced readings. She suggests: 'For most of her critics, Magda is simply mad, and she is mad because she is a spinster' (Briganti 1994: 34). These concerns, and Briganti's reading of paternal dominance, will be used in this section to highlight how Magda struggles to realise her own narrative power when she is entrapped in the paternal narratives of her father, psychoanalysis and narrow literary criticism.

The novel has been read as a reflection of colonial anxieties. Attwell explains that it exposes 'the structures of relationship and authority – with their accompanying pathologies – of the settler-colonial context' (1993: 60). Roberts argues:

> [The] emblematic pattern of the irreparably nonhuman interaction between the colonizers and the colonized, between the white farmers in a 'stone country' where their will is law and the brown servants whose only exercise of will can be to run away, an interaction that even Magda in wild fantasies cannot break down and reconstruct (1992: 22).

These conflicts highlight how the novel can be read in terms of paternal narratives of power. Power in the novel is constructed through law, language, gender and race, and through familiar masculine symbols of power, such as money and guns.

Additionally, the novel has been linked to the tradition of the South African pastoral by researchers such as Watson, who compares it to Schreiner's *The Story of an African Farm* by linking the themes of feminism in the setting of the farm: 'There, too, one finds a character (Lyndall) with a frustrated, impassioned hunger for a world with horizons broader than those imposed by the institutionalized mediocrity of the colony' (Watson 1986: 371).

Roberts links the colonial concerns of gender and race in the novel, suggesting that gender 'colonisation' is much more subtle and more powerfully socially encoded than racial colonisation: 'Magda is both colonizer and colonized. Colonization of the female by a masculine culture differs, however, from that grounded in race and geographic exploitation by being more thoroughgoing and more natural-seeming' (1992: 23). Thus, Magda is in a position of being powerful due to her race but powerless due to her gender. In this way, it would be impossible to imagine, for example, the character of Klein-Anna in the novel being able to narrate a tale similar to the one Magda does, as her disempowered position is compounded by both race and gender.

Roberts further highlights how paternal narratives are not merely reproduced by fathers or even just by powerful men, but how others in a social system are complicit in the reproduction of these narratives, which serve as conduits for ideologies: 'Firstly, Magda, like the majority of women since time immemorial, is perforce in unconscious complicity with the Father in creating her condition. Secondly, Magda, like all women everywhere, does not have any memory of a mode of existence independent of the patriarchal one' (1992: 22). This complete encapsulation within the paternal influence could help to explain the disjointed nature of Magda's tale, in which she has little subjectivity to narrate her own life.

## Women and subjectivity

Magda directly questions the power of women to narrate or to provide substance and understanding to their worlds. In her first introduction, she shows a sense of being insular and motionless, and her father is presented as being in motion, pacing as though contemplating the world around him. Magda says:

> I am the one who stays in her room reading or writing or fighting migraines. The colonies are full of girls like that, but none, I think, so extreme as I. My father is the one who paces the floorboards back and forth, back and forth in his slow black boots. And then, for a third, there is the new wife, who lies late abed. Those are the antagonists (Coetzee 2004: 1).

The two women in this first narrative branch are immediately shown to be physically isolated and presented as having less agency than the father. The father is shown as active in contrast with the passive, sheltered women – Magda fighting migraines in her room and her father's new wife sleeping in. This new wife will ultimately disappear from all subsequent narrative branches after she is killed by Magda, again indicating how tenuous her presence is and how she is relegated to silence and absence in the text.

Indeed, in a later narrative branch when Magda realises that she desires the farmhand Hendrik's wife, Anna, she reflects on her womanhood as represented by an emptiness:

> I am not one of the heroes of desire, what I want is not infinite or unattainable, all I ask myself, faintly, dubiously, querulously, is whether there is not something to do with desire other than striving to possess the desired in a project which must be vain, since its end can only be the annihilation of the desired. And how much keener does my question become when woman desires woman, two holes, two emptinesses. For if that is what I am then that is what she is too, anatomy is destiny: an emptiness, or a shell, a film over an emptiness longing to be filled in a world in which nothing fills (Coetzee 2004: 114).

By removing the substance from her being, linking her entire being to the orifice of her vagina, Magda sees herself merely as an object in the world of men, who are able to desire, dictate and control the objects in the world. Her father is the ultimate symbol of this control. Briganti claims that Coetzee is deconstructing the assumed authorial power of men by allowing Magda these questions, suggesting that 'the inscription of the female subject demystifies authorial identity by questioning the legitimacy of the father/author as locus of authority and begetter of texts and makes visible that which . . . was previously invisible, untold, unspoken' (Briganti 1994: 34). Magda's quest for agency, and her ability to be the author of her own existence, deconstructs the way that she herself represents her father as having narrative power.

However, she constantly claims to require the meaning-making of a male influence in order to live, and men as capable narrators are able to create this meaning for her. In fact, Roberts maintains that Magda orders her self-awareness in terms of psychoanalytic and philosophical conceptions constructed by European males: 'Magda herself offers explanations for her predicaments in Lacanian and Hegelian terms' (1992: 21). These philosophical groundings could actually be seen as paternal narratives themselves, especially in a text that deals allegorically with colonialism. Magda asserts: 'I am incomplete, I am a being with a hole inside me, I signify something, I do not know what, I am dumb' (Coetzee 2004: 9). Without the influence of a man, she will remain an 'emptiness', and will be void of meaning:

> I was not, after all, made to live alone. If I had been set down by fate in the middle of the veld in the middle of nowhere, buried to my waist and commanded to live a life, I could not have done it. I am not a philosopher. Women are not philosophers, and I am a woman. A woman cannot make something out of nothing (Coetzee 2004: 119).

Magda dismisses her own narrative power when there is not the influence of men to rely on, even though she already contradicts this assertion by constructing various narratives about her world. In this way, her own narrative uncertainty is constructed as symptomatic of her gendered identity, and as a result of the narrative dominance of her father. Briganti explains: 'In her longing to become "the medium," Magda invokes the death of the subject as culturally constructed by the language of the father' (1994: 45). This demonstrates a psychology of narrative inferiority that Magda seems to struggle to overcome but never truly does, with her narratives always deteriorating into confusing, disjointed and incomplete tales, which she has to continuously restart. Her narrative relies on the influence of men, and at the death of or abandonment by male figures her narrative branches usually end or become extremely unstable, such as her imagining the messages from the Spanish-speaking flying machines. Macaskill says that Magda 'looks to her father for this lead, but how could she possibly find it there? Tautology is the only dowry her father can bequeath Magda. His is the language and the home she must abandon, but he cannot lead her out, and there are no suitors for her hand' (1994: 461).

Within Magda's tale where the paternal influence is so powerfully present, the maternal voice is lost, and this loss is constantly mourned in the novel. Roberts expounds on 'Magda's bondage to and resistance against an inflexible patriarchal culture, a cathexis that includes the seeming simplicities of the Electra plot. But what differentiates Magda from most other "seduced" daughters in literature is her conscious desire and search for the mother – however self-ironic and temporary this may be' (1992: 22). Magda reflects: 'The old [wife] is dead. The old wife was my mother, but died so many years ago that I barely recall her' (Coetzee 2004: 2). She, however, constructs a comforting, loving maternal narrative, and again the entire novel can be seen as an example of the unconventional, dream-like maternal narrative that resists patriarchal control: 'From one of the farthest oubliettes of memory I extract a faint grey image, the image of a faint grey frail gentle loving mother huddled on the floor, one such as any girl in my position would be likely to make up for herself' (Coetzee 2004: 2). In this gendered dichotomy, women are frail but loving, and men are powerful but oppressive. Her constant reference to this frailty shows the strong focus on women as weak, and Magda's tale, in which she seeks to dominate men and her surroundings, can be seen as a rebellion against this identity of frailty, emptiness and the inability to create narratives or construct meaning.

Magda continues by explaining that the mother's death was punishment for failing to fulfil the requirements of providing a son to perpetuate masculine power:

> My father's first wife, my mother, was a frail gentle loving woman who lived and died under her husband's thumb. Her husband never forgave her for failing to bear him a son. His relentless sexual demands led to her death in childbirth. She was too frail and gentle to give birth to the rough rude boy-heir my father wanted, therefore she died (Coetzee 2004: 2).

Magda blames her father's control for the death of her mother, and again reflects this through her own gender as being an affront to the control of the father. The father desires a male heir, someone to perpetuate his power, and since Magda's mother could not provide this, she no longer fulfils her function as an object of the male subject's dominance. She becomes meaningless, and dies. Magda's imaginings of the mother demonstrate that she is able to create counter-narratives to the father's dominance, engaging in the realm of maternal narrative, which gives her the option to see her mother as more than a failed object of male dominance. Roberts explains that 'we may, indeed, read *In the Heart of the Country* in the light of not only nineteenth-century and Victorian novels but of later literature, even current works by feminists, where the voice of the mother is silenced, her body obscured' (1992: 23). Magda resists this by her constant references to this absent mother.

Roberts further highlights how Magda's interactions with other women in the novel might be a reflection of searching for a mother figure, or at least a sister figure, and her desire to be close with these women is often shown sexually. Roberts suggests: 'Magda's imbricated desires – to rediscover her mother, to regain verticality and achieve womanliness, and to break the barrier between herself and the servants – find full expression in her longing, literally, to interface her body and mind with that of Klein-Anna' (1992: 27). Her desire for connection with women is a way of asserting her own narrative power, of giving substance to women and claiming the power to desire, but these attempts all fail as she imagines killing her father's second wife and she is rejected by Klein-Anna. Roberts notes that when Magda fantasises about being closely connected and even merging her body with Klein-Anna, it might again indicate her desire to overcome the patriarchal boundaries of the colonial system: 'It expresses a deep desire for what Magda thinks is the tranquillity of fulfilled womanhood as well as a rejection of coloniality at the most basic level. Magda wants to step through the barrier dividing her consciousness and sentience from that of the "other"' (28). As Teresa Dovey notes, Magda's desire is to be recognised by the Other, but Klein-Anna 'recognizes Magda only from her dependent position as servant, which is, in Hegelian terms, no recognition at all' (1988: 172). Magda is not able to overcome the divide between coloniser and colonised, and, importantly, she is simultaneously not able to connect with other women in a meaningful way, never finding the mother/sister/lover figure that she seeks: 'Magda, locked into the discourse of the Master, has no means of discovering the quality and complexity of Klein-Anna's thoughts. And Klein-Anna, whether real or a phantasm, is herself not able or not interested in Magda's attempts to violate the economies of their master/servant relationship' (Roberts 1992: 28).

Importantly, since Magda is not the son that her father wanted, she becomes invisible, not only to him but also to the world, as he is given narrative priority to dictate her worth. Sandra Gilbert's analysis of literary daughters states that 'if the very structure of patrilineage guarantees that a man's son will inexorably take his place and his name, it also promises that a daughter will never be such a usurper, since she is an instrument of culture rather than an agent' (1985: 361). Magda sees herself as an absence and struggles to assert herself: 'My father pays no attention to my absence. To my father I have been an absence all my life' (Coetzee 2004: 2). She sees herself as having no purpose because she cannot serve her father well, as she thinks that he does not need her. She characterises him as powerful and self-sufficient, and she cannot see herself as the object of his desire since she is of no use to him. She explains: 'If my father had been a weaker man he would have had a better daughter. But he has never needed anything. Enthralled by my need to be needed, I circle him like a moon' (5). Briganti explains: 'Identity is at best provisional in Magda's case, as she assumes a self only to call it into question' (1994: 35). Magda is never able to consolidate an identity for herself. However, Briganti continues that 'her invisibility allows her to traverse the narrative regardless of sex, age, and class and to refuse to endorse the father's vision' (36). By her position as a non-entity, Magda is ironically allowed to negotiate a new, transcendent narrative for herself and to resist her father.

Furthermore, Magda is not only denied her own narrative power, but she is also denied access to the internal narrative of her father's life. Only through the death of her father is Magda able to gain some semblance of access to his interiority. In an extended section she points to all of the imagined narratives that the father has constructed, and how her presence might be stifling to his narratives and passions in the same way that his dominance restricts her from having agency in her life. Many of her anxieties are exposed here as the father's power is variously demonstrated, from his power over money, his ability to desire and his longing for a son:

> The day I compose my father's hands on his breast and pull the sheet over his face, the day I take over the keys, I will unlock the rolltop desk and uncover all the secrets he has kept from me, the ledgers and banknotes and deeds and wills, the photographs of the dead woman inscribed *With all my love*, the packet of letters tied in a red ribbon. And in the darkest corner of the bottommost pigeonhole I will uncover the one-time ecstasies of the corpse, the verses folded three and four times and packed into a manila envelope, the sonnets to Hope and Joy, the confessions of love, the passionate vows and dedications, the postmarital rhapsodies, the quatrains 'To my Son'; and then no more, silence, the vein petering out. At some point on the line from youth to man to husband to father to master the heart must have turned to stone. Was it there, with the advent of the stunted girl? Was I the one who killed the life in him, as he kills the life in me? (Coetzee 2004: 38-9)

Magda is unable to have narrative power because of her gender, but it is also an impediment to the narrative power of her father. There is great irony in this final line of this extract, as Magda has now imagined killing him physically rather than merely killing his ability to narrate or to be passionate, but she sees the latter as more important. This line exposes a narrative power struggle between father and daughter in the text, the presence of each stifling the freedom of the other. In order for Magda to reclaim her power and be more than a frail emptiness, she suggests that she has to kill her father.

### *Magda's transgressive narratives and inhabiting masculine symbols of power*

In many ways, Magda tries to replicate the narrative power of the father, which he uses to make a life of his own and to forge a self-definition. Briganti claims that Magda's 'self-representations also show Magda as engaged in a masquerade that enables her to parody the male gaze and those images that are seen culturally through men's eyes'

(1994: 36). Magda is able to emulate masculine power by engaging in her own narratives and by parroting the symbols of power employed by her father. Helen Tiffin explains that 'the codes of the father have inevitably ensnared the daughter; she cannot escape perpetuating them' (1987: 28).

When the father buys candies shaped like hearts and diamonds for his new wife, Magda says: 'I want a life of my own, just as I am sure my father said to himself he wanted a life of his own when he bought the packet of hearts and diamonds' (Coetzee 2004: 50). This conflation of desire, creation and narrative power contradict Magda's view of herself as an emptiness. Her father is shown to want to reproduce and presumably to father the son that he has always wanted, giving him a sense of hope to create something more than the emptiness that Magda is constructed as: 'My father and his new wife cavort in the bedroom. Hand in hand they stroke her womb, watching for it to flicker and blossom' (2). Through her imagination and narrative power, and by beginning to resent and resist her father's power, Magda manages to make her way into intimate spaces that she is otherwise denied access to, and she is able to move beyond the confines of her bedroom. She gains a similar sense of active and expansive power that her father demonstrates, and this ability to imagine and narrate eventually gives her the power to take control of her situation by killing her father. Through words and narrative, she is able to see herself as powerful. She reflects on how words can liberate her: 'Aching to form the words that will translate me into the land of myth and hero, here I am still my dowdy self in a dull summer heat that will not transcend itself' (4).

Another important aspect of the novel is how Magda is situated within predetermined gender expectations, which she frequently highlights and often blames on her father. She seems deeply dissatisfied with her situation in life, but also seems not to know a way to overcome it. Despite assigning blame to the outside world as well as to herself, she suggests that the only way to find liberation is through constructing her story. She shows this fractured assignment of blame when she explains:

> What automatism is this, what liberation is it going to bring me, and without liberation what is the point of my story?

> Do I feel rich outrage at my spinster fate? Who is behind my oppression? You and you I say, crouching in the cinders, stabbing my finger at father and stepmother. But why have I not run away from them? (Coetzee 2004: 4)

Magda's inability to run away or to take action in her life leads to her remaining within her 'spinster fate'. However, even though she resists this fate, she does not know what other narratives are available for her life:

> But what other tale is there for me? Marriage to the neighbour's second son? I am not a happy peasant. I am a miserable black virgin, and my story is my story, even if it is a dull black blind stupid miserable story ignorant of its meaning and of all its many possible untapped happy variants. I am I. Character is fate. History is God (Coetzee 2004: 5).

She seems to claim that she is choosing her narrative, resisting history and her fate as a woman, even if just in her own imaginings or thoughts. Briganti again highlights how narrative offers her the power to resist this containment through exploring the various literary allusions that Magda makes (1994). She is able to see herself as many different types of women, showing how literature has located her within particular roles, but also showing that she is able to move beyond her roles by her own narrative power. Briganti notes:

> The assumption of different roles, while granting her a sort of invisibility, suggests the self-referential, hyperliterary nature of the universe in which she acts, a universe in which everything has already been said, thus strengthening the tension between imagination and reality and the presence of a strong self-referential element which is typical of post-modernism (1994: 37).

Magda asserts her ability to reclaim her life, stating that she is more than history, fate or the oppression of others:

> I live, I suffer, I am here. With cunning and treachery, if necessary, I fight against becoming one of the forgotten ones of history. I am a spinster with a locked diary but I am more than that. I am an uneasy consciousness but I am more than that too. When all the lights are out I smile in the dark (Coetzee 2004: 3-4).

She has been relegated to one of the limited narratives for women, namely, the obedient spinster, and cannot see a way out of this role. Her assertion that there is more to her than the narrow conceptions that history might frame her within allows her to find power to reshape her own life. She says: 'I am not interested in becoming one of those people who look into mirrors and see nothing, or walk in the sun and cast no shadow. It is up to me' (Coetzee 2004: 23).

In order to become a presence rather than merely an emptiness, Magda needs to emulate the symbols that give men power. There is a strong contrast between the physicality of men and women in the novel, and, as Magda reclaims power, she needs to move towards the rough, active and violent male physicality just as much as she needs to engage in constructing narratives as (white) men are allowed to do. The power of men is located as much in their bodies as in their narratives and ideologies, and Magda has to invade both realms in order to reclaim her identity.

When she refers to the body of her father, it symbolises all male bodies to her: 'When I think of male flesh, white, heavy, dumb, whose flesh can it be but his?' (Coetzee 2004: 9). She contrasts this with a description of her mother as loving, gentle and comforting: 'And mother, soft scented loving mother who drugged me with milk and slumber in the featherbed and then, to the sound of bells in the night, vanished, leaving me alone among rough hands and hard bodies – where are you? My lost world is a world of men' (7).

However, Magda's body is not like either of these; she is neither suited to lovingly caring for children or bearing them, nor for the brusque work of men, as she characterises herself as frail, weak and undesirable: 'But who would give me a baby, who would not turn to ice at the spectacle of my bony frame on the wedding-couch' (Coetzee

2004: 10). Magda seems unable to negotiate an understanding of her body when it does not conform to her gender ideal. Roberts comments: 'Although it gives Magda no pleasure to pore over her reflection in a mirror (which she believes she inherited from her long-lost mother), she does so minutely and critically' (1992: 25). Her body is a site of self-reflection, but it is also the curse that might lead her to the same doomed fate as her mother because of her gender. If she does not meet the expectations of a patriarchal society, as her mother failed to do by not securing her father a son, she will suffer an existential death due to losing the attention and thus the meaning that only the father or husband can provide to the life of the daughter or wife.

This conflict points to another contrast between the roles of men and women, in the motivations for childrearing. For Magda and for her mother, it is a way of fulfilling the desires of men and enacting the ideals of femininity, whereas for men it is a way of perpetuating their own power. Hendrik demonstrates this desire to have children as an extension of his masculinity:

> Hendrik would like a house full of sons and daughters. That is why he has married. The second son, he thinks, the obedient one, will stay behind, learn the farmwork, be a pillar of help, marry a good girl, and continue the line . . . Hendrik has found a wife because he is no longer a young man, because he does not wish his blood to die from the earth forever, because he has come to dread nightfall, because man was not made to live alone (Coetzee 2004: 24).

Hendrik's desire for children, particularly for sons, mirrors that of Magda's father, and reinforces how masculine power is subject to filial perpetuation.

Magda also contrasts the roles of men and women in work on the farm, seeing the work of men as more noble. She describes it as practical and shows how men engage with the world, being able to claim space and work outside whereas women are confined to the kitchen. She begins this reflection by characterising the way that men talk:

> Men's talk is so unruffled, so serene, so full of common purpose. I should have been a man, I would not have grown up so sour, I would have spent my days in the sun doing whatever it is that men do, digging holes, building fences, counting sheep. What is there for me in the kitchen? The patter of maids, gossip, ailments, babies, steam, foodsmells, catfur at the ankles (Coetzee 2004: 21).

By locating herself in the world of men, Magda allows herself to transcend the small, contained domains reserved for women in the novel. She links herself to masculinity, and she says of farmwork later in the novel: 'Given time I can do whatever a man can do' (Coetzee 2004: 90). She takes on her father's position as head of the farm, and, as Berganti states, this is another sign of Magda overcoming her gendered position: 'By flouting the very principle that governs the structure of patrilineage in the taking of the father's place by the son, she turns herself into an agent instead of being an instrument of culture' (1994: 39). Magda is able to negotiate subjectivity and agency for herself in a world where she was relegated to an emptiness and to stereotypical gender positions.

The men in her life use violence to control her, such as her father beating her and Hendrik raping her. Her father's assault comes as a result of her interrupting his lovemaking with Hendrik's wife, Anna. After he hits her, she reflects on it using a sexual connotation, indicating the intimacy and the transformative nature of this violence on her: 'A moment ago I was a virgin and now I am not, with respect to blows' (Coetzee 2004: 58). Violence is a way of enacting power, and, as Magda suggests by the loss of her 'virgin[ity]', it is a form of intimacy as well. There is a sense that her father has at least acknowledged her existence through his violence, and through killing her father it might similarly be an act of fulfilling her desire to be acknowledged by him.

The phallic symbol of the gun is what eventually gives her power over these men, and she responds to the violence with violence, killing her father and threatening Hendrik with the gun. She sees the death of her father as necessary for her own liberation, claiming of her father's body: 'Until this bloody afterbirth is gone there can be no new life for me' (Coetzee 2004: 15). Importantly, the gun belongs to her father, indicating how power has shifted from him to her, but she sees this form of power as insubstantial, giving much more weight to narrative than to violence: 'Am I one of those people so insubstantial that they cannot reach out of themselves save with bullets? That is what I fear as I slip out, an implausible figure, an armed lady, into the starlit night' (59). The power of self-expression through words and ideas is much more meaningful to Magda than the power she can gain from the gun and violence, and the dominance of the physical realm, while the most immediate form of her oppression, does not liberate her from her situation and the role she occupies.

## *The deconstruction of language and paternal narrative power*
The centrality of narrative and language to create an identity and personhood, even above physical concerns, is reflected when Magda remembers her childhood and the bond she shared with their servants. She demonstrates the sense of the external, imposed, learned culture symbolised by her father and the influence of history that is linked to him, and contrasts this with her natural inclination towards the feminine and visceral connection to her mother and to an innocent sense of community with their servants. She explains: 'I grew up with the servants' children. I spoke like one of them before I learned to speak like this' (Coetzee 2004: 6). There is the lost language of youth for Magda, and her movement into a superior position due to her race and position as 'master' robbed her of this. Canepari-Labib says that '[Magda's] father's language of authority clashes in a traumatic way with the language of her childhood – that which, being closer to what Magda romantically considers as the real essence of things, remained in her unconscious as a "lost world," the lost Paradise to which she tries to regain access' (2000: 119). Magda demonstrates this by saying: 'I played their stick and stone games before I knew I could have a dollhouse' (Coetzee 2004: 6). She did not yet understand that she was of a different social class to her servants, and the divisions between them were not as pronounced as they became in adulthood.

She feels more connected to the narrative of an innocent, connected childhood than the one of power differentials she inherits from her father, as she remembers the types of narratives that she enjoyed as a child with her servant friends:

> I sat at the feet of their blind old grandfather while he whittled clothespegs and told his stories of bygone days when men and beasts migrated from winter grazing to summer grazing and lived together on the trail. At the feet of an old man I have drunk in a myth of a past when beasts and man and master lived a common life as innocent as the stars in the sky (Coetzee 2004: 7).

Roberts highlights that this moment of engaging with stories might be seen as linked to Magda's yearning for a mother, for the maternal narrative to rescue her from strict patriarchal structures:

> Women have no memory traces of any Utopian existence of living in equality side by side with men. Magda has no such traces and she can find no trace – not even a clear photograph – of a mother who preceded her on the farm. It is significant that directly after her speculation about a mythic time of innocent communal existence, her thoughts turn to a 'soft scented loving mother' who vanished (1992: 23).

Magda's attraction to Hendrik and Klein-Anna could be seen as symbolic of trying to reclaim this link to a lost innocence, where myths of unity gave her a sense of connection uncontained by her gender or her historical fate. She is able to escape the paternal narrative of the law, explaining of her new situation with Klein-Anna and Hendrik: 'We are outside the law, therefore live only by the law we recognize in ourselves, going by our inner voice' (Coetzee 2004: 90). She is now also able to look past the law of language, which she feels permeates every part of her being, claiming:

> How can I say, I say, that these are not the eyes of the law that stare from behind my eyes, or that the mind of the law does not occupy my skull, leaving me only enough intellection to utter these doubting words, if it is I uttering them, and see their fallaciousness (Coetzee 2004: 84).

She seems to have become aware of her constraints within the history, law and language of her father, and seeks to return to a place of intuition outside of social constraints that separate her from others and from herself. Macaskill explains:

> The language of the law, that nonexchange expected to pass between Magda and the farm servants, 'the old language, the correct language' . . . has been subverted by her father's sleeping with Anna and the postpaternal consequences of this act, under which Hendrik, Anna's husband, comes to share Magda's bed. 'I cannot carry on with these idiot dialogues' . . . Magda confesses under the strain of broken laws which 'no angel has descended with flaming sword to forbid' (1994: 463).

However, even after she kills her father and tries to reclaim this connection, she realises that it is impossible. She cannot reclaim the innocent language that she knew as a child: 'The language that should pass between myself and these people was subverted by my father and cannot be recovered. What passes between us now is a parody. I was born into a language of hierarchy, of distance and perspective. It was my father-tongue' (Coetzee 2004: 97).

Eventually, Magda questions the power of her own narrative, trying to construct a comforting maternal narrative for Klein-Anna but realising that she is only reconstructing the limiting narratives of her father in ways that offer no comfort, perhaps even reflecting the emptiness that Magda imagines herself as:

> This is what she gets from me, colonial philosophy, words with no history behind them, homespun, when she wants stories. I can imagine a woman who would make this child happy, filling her with tales from a past that really happened, how grandfather ran away from the bees and lost his hat and never found it again, why the moon waxes and wanes, how the hare tricked the jackal. But these words of mine come from nowhere and go nowhere, they have no past or future, they whistle across the flats in a desolate eternal present, feeding no one (Coetzee 2004: 114).

It becomes clear that Magda's newfound power does not give her the control that she imagined it would. She is unable to negotiate the financial obligations of the farm or to pay Hendrik, she is not physically strong enough to do the farmwork or even to dispose of her father's body properly, and Hendrik and Klein-Anna do not show her the respect that she tries to demand. Canepari-Labib explains that 'Hendrik now assumes the position of mastery, and as a consequence Magda, instead of experiencing the communal life of her childhood, finds herself in the same submissive position she already had to suffer because of her father' (2000: 118). She also has not completely silenced the influence of her father, and she reflects on imagining him die: '. . . waiting for my father's eyebrows to coalesce, then the black pools beneath them, then the cavern of the mouth from which echoes and echoes his eternal NO' (Coetzee 2004: 16). Characterising the oppression of the father as 'eternal' makes his influence present to her even when she has killed him, and she realises 'he does not die so easily after all'.

At the end of the novel, Magda imagines flying machines sending messages in Spanish to her, among which she recounts: 'It is the slave's consciousness that constitutes the master's certainty of his own truth. But the slave's consciousness is a dependent consciousness. So the master is not sure of the truth of his own autonomy. His truth lies in an inessential consciousness and its inessential acts' (Coetzee 2004: 129).

Magda reflects after this message:

These words refer to my father, to his brusqueness with the servants, his unnecessary harshness. But my father was harsh and domineering only because he could not bear to ask and be refused. All his commands were secret pleas – even I could see that. How then did the servants come to know that they could hurt him most essentially by obeying him most slavishly? Were they too instructed by the gods, through channels we were unaware of? Did my father grow harsher and harsher towards them simply to provoke them out of their slavishness? Would he have embraced a rebellious slave as a father embraces a prodigal son, though his next act might be to chastise him? (Coetzee 2004: 129–30)

This reflection by Magda again recalls Dovey's link to Hegelian recognition of the self by the Other, and demonstrates the impassable distance between those characters constructed as 'master' and 'slave'. Magda imagines that her father desires the conflict that is traditionally constructed between father and son in order to validate his power. The opposition Magda offers, however, ends in the father's death, whether real or imagined, and she is left more confused than before without his influence.

Macaskill highlights that Magda struggles to find a form of middle ground between the authority of her father and intimacy with the black workers on the farm or her lost mother:

> Voiceless under the authority of her father, but in turn forced to inhabit the voice of authority when speaking to the servants (from whom – even after her sexual 'intimacy' with Hendrik – she remains forever isolated), Magda desires a middle locution between active and passive in which she can discourse (or 'do-writing') 'with reference to' a 'self' that rigid strictures of sociolinguistic barriers have hitherto not allowed her to know (Macaskill 1994: 465).

Magda's reflection above thus does not only refer to her father, but also to herself, as she desires communion with the servants by recognising their subjectivity.

Attwell explains that Magda's 'communion with the sky-gods is a substitute for ... human communication and an attempt to find a language not mediated by social division' (1993: 67). Magda has questioned and resisted social divisions throughout the novel, but in her interactions with Hendrik, Klein-Anna and her father, she has discovered that it is impossible for her to transcend them with other people. She will always be either the master or the slave. She escapes into conversations with the flying machines, a moment that Briganti again links to the loss of her father and his paternal control as well as to psychoanalysis: 'The disruption of speech in Magda's narrative is ... a consequence of the fall of the father ... [She] writes the messages in broken language, thus furthering the act of political decolonization already implicit in the narrative disjunctions that challenge traditional realism' (Briganti 1994: 44). Furthermore, Magda overcomes the restrictions of language, which throughout was inadequate to describe her identity, and 'by constructing her speech as a pastiche from several languages, Magda goes beyond the perimeter of any given linguistic system and challenges the patrilinear law which governs its construction' (45).

The climax of the novel is linked to the role of the text in relation to the critic, as Briganti explains:

> Like the novel's critics, the sky-gods ignore her attempt to be more than the protagonist of a political allegory and reduce the specificity of her experience to a case of hysteria. In an effort to respond, she forms gigantic messages made of painted stones, thereby 'encoding' for us the narratorial merging of arid country, sterile spinster, and the language that flows through her (1994: 42).

Briganti also notes that at the end of the novel, Magda claims the story as interwoven with her body (1994: 42), when Magda says: 'I have always felt easier spinning my answers out of my own bowels' (Coetzee 2004: 138). By creating her own narrative, making words out of rocks on the ground, and feeling intimately connected with this story by locating it within her body, Magda reclaims a sense of narrative power and transcends her position as prefigured daughter: 'The medium. The median – that is what I wanted to be! Neither master nor slave, neither parent nor child, but the bridge between, so that in me the contraries should be reconciled!' (132). Macaskill comments on this assertion:

> Here Magda expresses – in writing – her hope of being a middle voice, her desire to write herself into a new existence, to escape the 'old locutions' that have forced her to veer to and from the 'master-talk' between mistress and servants and alternate attempts at intimate chatter with Anna and Hendrik (1994: 465).

Briganti notes that the deconstructionist process in the novel is completed when Magda becomes linked to the country, unlike other novels where the father is usually the one closely linked to the nation:

'The merging of Magda and country is strengthened by allusions to the violation of the country by its colonizers. The country, too, like Magda, is a "jagged virgin," and Magda devises an act of self-exposure that collapses rape and colonization' (Briganti 1994: 43). Magda's position becomes representative of South Africa, not only of its colonial past and the oppressiveness of colonialism, but also of the struggle for freedom and self-narration in apartheid South Africa. In this comparison, in her position as daughter, Magda takes on both roles of coloniser and colonised. Briganti argues that 'she uses the stones to sketch "a woman lying on her back, her figure fuller than mine, her legs parted" . . . thus portraying herself as a violated body stranded in the middle of a violated country as she is stranded in the middle of a postmodernist text' (1994: 43). Becoming conscious of this position and challenging the categories of 'master' and 'servant' allows for Magda to deconstruct her role as voiceless, powerless object in the narration of her father.

At the end of the novel, Magda presents a new narrative branch where her father is still alive and aged, and she finally gains narrative power. Roberts explains this shift clearly in an extended analysis:

> In the final pages of the book Magda's narrative of action and debate is negated as she describes the quiet times she spends with her (now old and invalid) father, their talk largely her reminiscences of the past. If this is a new fantasy, it relates to the earlier ones in that the father is again disempowered. He is now emasculated in his helplessness, as sightless as Mr Rochester and, although probably deaf, condemned to listen to an incessant chatter of 'Do you remember' and 'Do you remember' from Magda. Magda's revenge now takes the form of forcing a past on the father who denied her a necessary rooting in a past that contained a mother (1992: 29).

Magda is able to narrate to the father a past of her own construction, finally gaining a sense of narrative power over him. The novel, allegorically, might suggest resistance against oppressive authority figures, but the complexities of the text allow for this moment to also speak to gender constructions and the quest for self-determination, showing how this process of resistance and reinscribing the self is impossible for Magda as daughter, one of the 'forgotten ones of history' (Coetzee 2004: 3).

Macaskill frames Magda's character and the novel itself as a resistance to dominating frameworks that seek to limit the unique expression of the individual, both Magda and Coetzee as an author. He explains that the novel 'locates its attack against the authoritarian locutions of deconstruction and historicism alike by demonstrating the extent to which structures of language ("the old locutions") do indeed determine and limit individual agency while simultaneously demonstrating the possibility of acting nevertheless "with reference to the self" that commits itself to resisting structural determinism' (Macaskill 1994: 465-6). This framing makes the novel a form of resistance against paternal narratives, albeit imperfect, both highlighting the power of the father figure as well as subverting it. Macaskill continues:

> Coetzee has illustrated the pervasive power of structure (or society) and language (or social fact) in which agents (or subjects) are embedded, but he has also powerfully illustrated the extent to which individual agents may position themselves in such a way as to resist the determinism of structure, just as this text resists the critical orthodoxy that mandates it serve as a supplement to history and serve the interests of a more transitive contribution to the struggle currently under way in the 'South African reality' (1994: 468).

Magda, despite her resistance, is always enshrined within the language, law and history represented by her father; despite this, she transcends the limits placed on her, deconstructing the father's authority and challenging his rules of law and language by finding her own sense of power and constructing her own narratives. Magda's resistance is significant in the historical moment of the 1970s where resistance against paternalistic censorship, resistance against requirements for teaching Afrikaans to school students and an escalating mood of political dissent were sweeping the nation. These trends of resisting paternal narration will be further explored in Gordimer's text, in which the father is a liberation leader.

## Nadine Gordimer's *Burger's Daughter*
### Gendered narrative power

As discussed in the previous chapter, the figure of the father is often tied to existing structures of power, by linking the father to the nation. In *Burger's Daughter* this link to existing power structures is clear. The father is immediately linked to the nation by his name, Burger, which is the Afrikaans word for citizen, and the title of the novel already places the protagonist, Rosa, in the position of being defined by her father, Lionel Burger.

Rosa is raised by her father, who is a white South African struggle leader, after her mother dies in prison when Rosa is only fourteen. Her parents had been members of the South African Communist Party (SACP) and were active in the resistance against apartheid throughout Rosa's life. Rosa's father is eventually arrested for treason when she is an adult, and after his trial he is sentenced to life in prison, but he dies three years into his sentence. Clingman notes that Lionel Burger's 'fictional career has therefore coincided with most of the major developments in the revolutionary opposition in South Africa in the twentieth century' (1986: 171), demonstrating how the figure of the father is tied to broader, national concerns. Rosa then struggles with the legacy of her father, who is seen as a hero by many, and with defining her own life after he dies. She is seemingly unsure whether she wants to be involved in the liberation struggle or whether she wants to leave South Africa, as 'both positively and negatively, Rosa's career is measured out in the novel in relation to that of her father; and her father was a man with a significant . . . personal history'.

Clingman characterises much of Gordimer's writing as constituting 'historical consciousness', explaining that 'dealing with social transformation as it affects the individual is the primary way in which Gordimer's novels develop a consciousness of history' (1986: 171). Gordimer is thus interested in how the individual experiences history, and, by representing it in *Burger's Daughter* through the conflicted character of Rosa Burger, she gives a voice to the anxiety of white liberal subjects. During the tumultuous 1970s, white liberals, as Clingman explains, were unsettled by the Soweto revolt of 1976, which '[thrust] the position of dissident whites into radical ambiguity' (170).

There is an important link to history in *Burger's Daughter* as the novel is in many ways a homage to the life of Abram 'Bram' Fischer, 'one of the most prominent leaders within the SACP' (171) and a lawyer who defended anti-apartheid figures in treason trials, including Nelson Mandela at the Rivonia trial. This link to a historical father figure gives the novel added significance and provides another dimension to its elements of historical consciousness. Clingman maintains that through Gordimer's interviews with those connected with Fischer, she constructs the figure of Burger 'as a bridge in the novel between fact and fiction, and past and present, as the methods of the novelist and a more orthodox historian coincide' (172).

The shift to the focus on a daughter figure in *Burgher's Daughter* and *In the Heart of the Country* might signify the greater awareness of women's roles in the liberation struggle. It might also indicate that the paternal narratives of father figures were unable to be effectively enacted or disseminated within society due to widespread censorship and political oppression of authors. This inability of power to be perpetuated allows for the traditionally under-represented and narratively disempowered figure of the daughter to emerge in these texts. She is, through her gender, unable to effectively perpetuate the narratives of the father. Clingman notes, in his assessment of Gordimer's novel:

> One striking motif is that of the revolt of children against parents; this occurred in Soweto and this is what Rosa Burger goes through in relation to her father. An added dimension is the feeling in the novel that new forms of struggle are required for new circumstances . . . The heritage of the fathers must be evaluated, modified and reformulated (1986: 182).

The daughters in these two novels, wrestling with the legacies and power of their fathers, but struggling with their own relative powerlessness and inability to narrate, demonstrate a moment of ambivalence, especially for whites in South Africa, as Clingman explains: 'The explosion of the Soweto Revolt of 1976 indicated just how tortuous the path of change was going to be . . . The easy mood of celebration of just a few years earlier was dramatically displaced'

(1986: 170). Clingman further claims that Gordimer's project in *Burger's Daughter*, as well as her next novel *July's People*, was to 'assess whether there can be a role for whites in the context of Soweto and after, and what the practical implications of such a role might be'. These many disjunctures between fathers and children create the context for the daughter figure to take up the role of narrator.

Lorraine Liscio suggests that Rosa's development in Gordimer's novel is to identify with the personal realm, represented by the feminine, rather than the public realm, represented by men and particularly the father. This can be achieved by engaging in maternal rather than paternal narratives, which Rosa eventually realises by breaking free of the ideology of her father and finding her own narrative voice:

> Having inherited a well-defined, paternal, public role of commitment, Rosa seeks to fill in the present form with meaning, that is, the feminine, the personal, the maternal, the concealed life. She must get in touch with her self, body, voice, and modes of perception in ways that are similar to a child who learns how to walk before crawling. She must at some time regress to go through that step. For full coordination it is necessary to return to the feminine/maternal, which coincides not surprisingly with childhood (Liscio 1987: 249).

Ironically, even though Rosa is essentially narrating the legacy of Lionel throughout the novel, seemingly giving her a sense of narrative power, she always gives him prominence and power in this narrative and struggles to define herself in relation to his overwhelming presence. Dimitriu explains how the 'national narrative in *Burger's Daughter* is in many ways qualified by a personal narrative, the traumatic evolution of Rosa Burger's identity . . . So far, Rosa has led a "simplified" life, in which the political struggle for which her father stood has been foregrounded at the expense of any form of meaningful private life' (2000: 35).

Additionally, Rosa's narrative power in relation to her father is undermined since he is often remembered through the reflections of others like Conrad, and his story is eventually told through a male biographer and not by Rosa herself (Gordimer 2000: 84). Indeed, the lack of a son to carry on the paternal legacy is even referenced in the novel, firstly in the fact that Rosa's brother, Tony, Lionel's only son, dies by drowning in their swimming pool, and secondly in the way that Conrad, Rosa's lover, becomes a substitute son for Lionel. When she discusses her brother's death, she imagines that Conrad must have been a substitute son for Lionel in order to enact his own fatherhood and meaning-making, which is often only reflected through the son. She wonders if Lionel tried to recruit him to his political cause:

> Lionel Burger probably saw in you the closed circuit of self; for him, such a life must be in need of a conduit towards meaning, which posited: outside self. That's where the tension that makes it possible to live lay, for him; between self and others; between the present and creation of something called the future. Perhaps he tried to give you the chance (Gordimer 2000: 82).

Rosa could never constitute this 'closed circuit' for Lionel because of her gender and thus her inability to maintain and perpetuate paternal narratives. She is not given the same narrative power as men in the novel.

The son, even though he is given the power of constructing his own narrative, is shown to be necessary for the success of paternal narratives as it is his responsibility to maintain them. This is shown when Rosa reflects on Brandt Vermeulen, a prominent and conservative political figure who eventually helps her to get a passport. In an extended passage she demonstrates how the son maintains social power:

> The sons of distinguished families also often move away from the traditional milieu and activities in discordance with whatever their particular level of frontier society has confined them to. Just as the successful Jewish or Indian country storekeeper's son becomes a doctor or lawyer in the city, or the son of the shift-boss on the goldmine goes into business, Brandt Vermeulen left farm, church and party caucus and went to Leyden and Princeton to read politics, philosophy and

economics, and to Paris and New York to see modern art. He did not come back, Europeanized, Americanized by foreign ideas of equality and liberty, to destroy what the great-great-grandfather died for at the hands of a kaffir and the Boer general fought the English for; he came back with a vocabulary and sophistry to transform the home-whittled destiny of white to rule over black in terms that the generation of late-twentieth-century orientated Nationalist intellectuals would advance as the first true social revolution of the century (Gordimer 2000: 174).

Importantly, even though the son might seem to choose a new path, the text argues that he is always in service of the paternal narratives that he is situated within, and Vermeulen demonstrates this when he returns to South Africa to reinforce the project of apartheid.

The image of parenting and of caring for children is given prominence throughout the novel, both in perpetuating paternal narratives through children as well as in caring for vulnerable children who are disenfranchised by social conditions. Politics is framed as a discourse of filial succession and spreading ideology to offspring, through Brandt Vermeulen as well as Lionel's influence over Rosa's life. As Rosa explains: 'Children and children's children. The catchphrase of every reactionary politician and every revolutionary, and every revolutionary come to power as a politician. Everything is done in the name of future generations' (Gordimer 2000: 339). The struggle itself is a form of parental narrative, as the political struggle will allow for future generations to live under a different political paradigm. These many dynamics construct Rosa as both defined within the paternal narrative of her father and his political influence, as well as unable to adequately perpetuate this paternal narrative due to her gender and her lack of a narrative voice.

The role of gender on narrative power finds expression in the symbol of the body. The power of the father is shown through his link to ideas and politics, and this is contrasted with the link of women and children to the body and to physicality. When the father is at his most powerful, there is a strong distancing from the body in favour of ideology. Clingman characterises Lionel Burger as 'a charismatic figure – doctrinaire, but first and foremost full of what Rosa at the end of the novel considers to be his "sublimity"' (1986: 172). Clingman shows how Lionel is almost a metaphysical figure, sublime in his charm and his commitment to his ideology. For most of the novel, Lionel is also literally disembodied as he is dead, and yet his presence remains. Dimitriu notes that 'the figure of Lionel Burger . . . though physically absent, hovers like a presence over the novel' (2000: 36).

Rosa's own femininity and her relative powerlessness are shown through her link to her body. Once her mother is taken to prison after a political rally, she menstruates for the first time. In front of the prison, surrounded by many other visitors, she reflects: 'I am within that monthly crisis of destruction' (Gordimer 2000: 10). At the moment of potentially losing her mother, in the chaos of the political tensions outside of the prison, she enters an important rite of passage into womanhood, but she also begins to question her own body and womanhood and uses negative descriptions of her menstruation. Her femininity and her body are linked to crisis, chaos and destruction, the opposite of order and reason, which her father embodies. Judie Newman also notes that only by distancing herself from her body is Rosa able to gain a sense of liberation at the end of the novel. During a scene after Rosa vomits when confronted with her childhood friend Baasie/Zwelinzima, she refers to herself as ugly, soiled, filthy and debauched, and Newman comments: 'Disfiguration is an essential step in Rosa's progress toward autonomy, an autonomy which depends upon confrontation with her real body, repugnant as well as beautiful, a body which cannot be split into good, clean, white or bad, dirty, black' (1985: 83). Linking both blackness and womanhood to the image of the body constructs this as a site of relative weakness, under the control of the white men who occupy the realm of ideas.

Rosa's mother, Cathy Burger, is also linked to her body and to her physical attractiveness in one of the few passages that describe this elusive character. She is described as attractive, but her political concerns seem to remove her from the body:

> There is supposed to be a particular bountiful attractiveness about a woman who is unaware of her good looks, but if, as with my mother, she literally *does not inhabit them*, lives in

purposes that are not served in any particular way [by her looks] . . . these beauties fall into disuse through something more than neglect (Gordimer 2000: 78).

She is able to transcend the feminine realm of the body through inhabiting the ideas of the struggle, linked to the paternal narratives. As Liscio notes, Cathy 'seems subsumed in the political ideals and image of the father' (1987: 249). Liscio also explains Cathy's assumed absence in the novel: 'It would be telling to note how many readers ignore the fact that in the title, *Burger's Daughter*, Burger can apply equally to Cathy and to Lionel.' This absence of Cathy is reflected through her neglected body, as Dimitriu notes that 'neglected bodies and neglected families are offered as sacrificial lambs on the altar of the cause' (2000: 67). The politics, in essence, becomes a part of her body, as also happens to Rosa when she begins to inhabit the politics of her father. She reflects to Conrad: 'You didn't want to believe that at twelve years old what happened at Sharpeville was as immediate to me as what was happening in my own body' (Gordimer 2000: 112). She links her puberty and her physical changes to political movements in the country. Her body becomes the property of the country, located within the narratives of her father and the nation.

In relation to the gendered construction of her elusive mother, Gordimer herself, in an interview with Gardner, explains how the political voice of women might have been silenced in favour of a traditional paternal narrative, where the father is granted power within the narrative. Gardner suggests that many characters construct Rosa's mother as the more prominent revolutionary, and Gordimer responds: 'The question of who was the more important person in party work would very often be covered up, in the eyes of the world, with the façade of the marriage. So that one would conveniently make use . . . of the convention that Papa is the master' (Gardner 1990: 163). Her gender does not allow her to be a fully realised political, powerful subject, but instead only locates her within the broader power of the father.

Clingman identifies another woman in the novel who is tied to her body, Marisa Kgosane, the wife of an imprisoned African leader and an activist herself. He suggests: 'Rosa recognizes just how much the strictly political dedication of her family was mediated by the sensuality and warmth that Marisa both embodies and represents, acting as an unconscious physical and emotional attraction for whites' (Clingman 1986: 175). By locating Marisa's political activism in her body instead of in her ideas, the symbolic, objectified nature of female characters is highlighted, and Rosa's own position as located within and limited to her body because of her gender is reinforced. Dimitriu adds: 'While Katya lives in her body as a dancer, Marisa worships hers by paying great attention to cosmetics and outfits, and by taking lovers despite a residual loyalty to her imprisoned husband' (2000: 69).

In contrast, the father is distanced from the body, as Rosa reflects when she imagines a conversation with Lionel: 'I didn't ask them for your ashes . . . After all, you were also a doctor, and to sweep together a handful of potash . . . futile relic of the human body you regarded as such a superb example of functionalism' (Gordimer 2000: 339). The father's body is merely functional in order to accomplish his political aims.

Despite the father's distance from the body, Rosa finds a link to the father through the physical realm, as she notices that she has 'a mouth exactly like her father's' (Gordimer 2000: 4), but her eyes were light: 'Not at all like his brown eyes with the vertical line of concern between them that drew together an unavoidable gaze in newspaper photographs' (5). In this reflection of Lionel's physicality and of their connectedness, she already frames him as a figure who is represented and interpreted through media and external voices, not through her own intimate understanding. This is a theme that will be returned to later.

Conrad also constructs Lionel as powerful and in control, and in the process creates another link between Lionel and Rosa when he says to her: 'You're always so polite, aren't you. Just like your father. He never gets rattled. No matter what that slimy prosecutor with his histrionics throws at him. Never loses his cool' (Gordimer 2000: 17).

Lionel's sense of rational control constructs him as the distant father figure who practises his power and authority without emotion. His position as linked to ideas and the dissemination of these ideas through the voice is contrasted with Rosa's link to the body. His certainty and self-assuredness are in opposition to her sense of not belonging and questioning her own power. These aspects are linked to both the generational and the gender dynamics of this father-daughter relationship.

Indeed, Lionel's distance from the body is also highlighted in his career as a medical doctor. During his final testimony at his trial, Lionel recalls:

> When as a medical student tormented not by the suffering I saw around me in hospitals, but by the subjection and humiliation of human beings in daily life I had seen around me all my life – a subjection and humiliation of live people in which, by my silence and political inactivity I myself took part, with as little say or volition on the victims' side as there was in the black cadavers, always in good supply, on which I was learning the intricate wonder of the human body (Gordimer 2000: 19).

Lionel demonstrates a sense of culpability with the deaths of these black bodies through not using the power of his voice, through his 'silence'. Once he is able to master this narrative tool, he is also able to exert some control over the fate of those black bodies. Rosa recalls the power of this broken silence as Lionel gives his final testimony:

> She heard him speaking aloud what she had read in his handwriting in the notes written in his cell. Nobody could stop him. The voice of Lionel Burger, her father, was being heard in public for the first time for seven years and for the last time, bearing testimony once and for all (Gordimer 2000: 19).

However, when he loses this power to narrate and to use his voice, and he is about to be sentenced to life in prison, he becomes weakened and this leads to Rosa linking him to his fragile body. His heroic status becomes secondary to his human, physical presence for Rosa:

> He – her father was led up from cells below the court into the well, an actor, saviour, prize-fighter, entering the realm of expectation that awaits him. He was, of course, more ordinary and mortal than the image of him as he would be on this day

had anticipated; a spike of hair stood away from his carefully-brushed crown, her hand went up to her own to smooth it for him (Gordimer 2000: 19).

She notices the disparity between the public figure that her father had become and the fact that he was merely a man. He is refigured as unkempt, and located within the body. Rosa finds the physical link to her father by smoothing her own hair in an attempt to smooth his, showing that in these moments of vulnerability, when he becomes situated within his body instead of in the ideas and ideologies that he represents, Rosa feels closeness to him. The voice, the power to speak and to create meaning with words and narrative, is the father's power, and Lionel's voice is being silenced. Importantly, after he is sent to prison he begins to have throat infections, again focusing on the organ of his voice and how this has been destroyed. His voice is tied to the body, which now suffers the same destruction as he loses his power and influence. Dimitriu notes: 'While the prison represents public confinement, the *tomb* – the body – and the *womb* – the intricate private space – are recurrently composite in their symbolism' (2000: 84). The body symbolises a type of death and confinement simultaneously, in Dimitriu's symbol of the tomb, and is also linked to the individual existence rather than the national, or the privacy and femininity of the womb. Once his sentence is announced, he is the only one in the courtroom who is located in the physical body, and he becomes vulnerable and weak and is even explicitly linked to femininity:

> The newspapers reported a 'gasp through the court' when the judge pronounced sentence of imprisonment for life. [Rosa] did not hear any gasp. There was a split second where everything stopped; no breath, no heartbeat, no saliva, no flow of blood except her father's. Everything rushed away from him, drew back, eclipsed. He alone, in his short big-headed body and his neat grey best suit, gave off the heat of life. He held them all at bay, blinded, possessed. Then his eyes lowered, she distinctly noticed his eyelids drop in an almost feminine gesture of selfconscious acknowledgment (Gordimer 2000: 22).

Importantly, he loses a sense of power here, and immediately the descriptions shift to focus on his body and on the 'feminine gesture' of lowering his eyes.

His body continues to deteriorate in prison, and Rosa witnesses this as a loss of his power. When she sees him in the prison she wants to ask him about his political convictions, but is unable to due to witnessing the decline in his physical state:

> I could not have found the way to ask him . . . Do you still believe in the future? The same Future? Just as you always did? And anyway it's true that when at last the day of my visit came I would be aware of nothing except that he was changing in prison, he was getting the look on those faces in old photographs from the concentration camps, the motionless aspect, shouldered there between the two warders that accompanied him, of someone who lets himself be presented, identified (Gordimer 2000: 113).

He is now being situated within the narratives of others, and does not have his own narrative power, and this is shown through detailed descriptions of his body and its deterioration. Rosa shows a sense of mourning at witnessing her father's state, again focusing on the deterioration of his mouth, which situates his voice and thus his power:

> His gums were receding and his teeth seemed to have moved apart at the necks; I don't know why this distressed me so much. In the cottage I used to see that changed smile that no one will know in the future because the frontispiece photograph I've been asked for shows him, neck thick with muscular excitement, grinning energy, speaking to a crowd not shown but whose presence is in his eyes (Gordimer 2000: 113).

He is no longer able to narrate to the 'crowd not shown' and is not located in the powerful narrating public persona, but simply becomes a weakened man located in his physical body. He has lost the masculine power that he was linked to.

In the end, his body is claimed as well as his voice: 'The prison authorities did not consent to a private funeral arranged by relatives. His life sentence was served but the State claimed his body' (Gordimer 2000: 32). His body is destroyed and his voice is silent, and through this loss he is displaced from the masculine, paternal power that he inhabited.

### The legacy of the father and the name

There is, however, another way in which the paternal narrative is maintained when the voice is silenced, and that is through the power of legacy. Lionel Burger becomes legendary and is linked to the engrossing power of narrative. This legacy of the father is constantly stifling for Rosa, as she is forever captured within and negotiated in relation to the narrative of the father. She wonders whether she should study medicine just as he had: 'Why not in the field of medicine, my father's daughter' (Gordimer 2000: 59), and eventually becomes a physiotherapist; she narrates his story to his biographer; and she is not allowed to have a passport because of her link to her father: 'I have no passport because I am my father's daughter.' Her life becomes dictated by the narrative of her father, and she is unable to escape it. Her quest in the novel is to try to find a narrative voice of her own.

Rosa is constantly shown to be silent. She reflects: 'My silence hammered sullen, hysterical, repetitive without words: sick, sick of the maimed, the endangered, the fugitive, the stoic; sick of courts, sick of prisons, sick of institutions scrubbed bare for the regulation endurance of dread and pain' (Gordimer 2000: 66). She is always shown to be contained within the narratives of others. Conrad says to Rosa: 'The day somebody said look, that's Rosa Burger . . . from the first time . . . I have the impression you've grown up entirely through other people. What they told you was appropriate to feel and do. How did you begin to know yourself?' (41). The newspapers also cannot report on what she says; only her name is reflected in papers:

> Using the courts as the only political platform I could get at, getting my name in the papers, starkly eloquent of the gag on my mouth I've inherited in the family tradition, since only my name – Lionel Burger's daughter, last of that line – can be reported, not my 'utterances'. That's how they perceive her,

people who read the name. I am a presence. In this country, among them. I do not speak (Gordimer 2000: 202).

Rosa is unable to have her own voice heard in the media due to her connection to her father. She links her silence and inactivity directly to her physical connection to her parents after her father's death. She reflects on her inability to move on and defines her own life as being passive: 'When I was passive, in that cottage, if you had known – I was struggling with a monstrous resentment against the claim – not of the Communist Party! – of blood, shared genes, the semen from which I had issued and the body in which I had grown' (Gordimer 2000: 58). Her resentment towards her parents, and especially her father, continue to haunt her, and she resents the physical link to them as her body and genes locate her as a woman, voiceless, and surrounded by the narrative of Lionel Burger.

## *Women and the voice*

The constant references to Rosa not having a voice and not being able to narrate her own life or engage in paternal narratives is indicative of the position of women in Gordimer's novel. Femininity is linked to political and personal silence, and for the most part only men are shown to have real political power or voices. Rosa attends a gathering hosted by one of Lionel's friends, Flora, assembling black and white women in her community after Lionel's death to discuss the political situation. At this gathering, Rosa notices the 'respectful silences for the weakness of our sex' (Gordimer 2000: 205). The realm of women is always linked to the body, and not to the voice, as one white women at the assembly reflects: 'We don't need to bring politics into the fellowship of women', again distancing the feminine from the paternal narrative of politics. In addition, the aspects of class and race further rob some women of their voices, as Rosa observes of the black women at the assembly:

> They didn't know why they were there, but as cross-purpose and unimaginable digressions grew louder with each half-audible, rambling or dignified or unconsciously funny discourse, clearer with each voluble inarticulacy, each clumsy, pathetic or pompous formulation of need in a life none of us white

women (careful not to smile at broken English) live or would know how to live, no matter how much Flora protests the common possession of vaginas, wombs and breasts, the bearing of children and awful compulsive love of them – the silent old blacks still dressed like respectable servants on a day off (Gordimer 2000: 206).

The inadequacy of language and the inability to communicate in this feminine realm is shown through the various references to broken speech: 'half-audible', 'rambling', 'inarticulacy', and 'broken English'. Again in this passage women are linked to the body and to children, which is given as their common binding force, and they are unable to engage in the narratives of politics or to express themselves articulately. They are also separated by class and race despite their commonalities as women. The women are unable to narrate a new ideology that binds them despite their differences.

The dialogical nature of the novel means that Rosa is often given some narrative power in being able to reflect on and describe her world, but in an interesting line at the start of the novel Rosa says: 'If you knew I was talking to you I wouldn't be able to talk. But you know that about me' (Gordimer 2000: 11). In this passage she is ostensibly referring to her father, and claims again that only because he doesn't know that she is talking to him is she able to talk at all. There is a sense that the presence of the father limits the narrative power of the child. This links to a discussion that Rosa has with Conrad where he retells a story about Carl Jung: 'One day when he was a kid Jung imagined God sitting up in the clouds and shitting on the world below. His father was a pastor . . . You commit the great blasphemy against all doctrine, and you begin to live' (42). Jung defies his father and defies God, engaging in an imaginative narrative in order to challenge the paternal narrative of his stifling father, and thus gains his own narrative power. Conrad seems to be offering the story as a suggestion for Rosa to abandon the narrative of her father, but Rosa is unable to transcend the paternal narrative. In the same conversation Conrad refers to 'the tension between creation and destruction', which exists in trying to create a narrative while under the influence of the paternal narrative. The personal, creative voice is stifled by the paternal narrative. Indeed,

Dimitriu suggests that Conrad might be a part of Rosa's consciousness, which allows her to construct different narratives, imaginatively refiguring her own father out of the role that he is afforded as a father figure:

> Whereas the parental relationship has led to Rosa's psychological constriction, her relationship with Conrad is characterised by highly articulate self-expression . . . Conrad inhabits a space, prior to dying in a space that resembles his deeper self: amorphous, open-ended, committed to nothing but its own inclination. Within the design of the novel, it is from this 'non-committed' space and through Conrad's non-political eyes that the stature of the committed Lionel Burger is placed under qualificatory scrutiny. More precisely, it is through conversations between Rosa and Conrad, or else through Rosa's own inner dialogues with Conrad, that Lionel Burger emerges for the reader as a more complex point of reference than a liberation hero to whom one is expected to pay unqualified obeisance (Dimitriu 2000: 59-60).

Once her father dies, Rosa finally hints at a sense of freedom:

> Now you are free. The knowledge that my father was not there ever, any more, that he was not simply hidden away by walls and steel grilles; this disembowelling childish dolour that left me standing in the middle of them all needing to whimper, howl, while I could say nothing, tell nobody: suddenly it was something else. Now you are free (Gordimer 2000: 58).

The passage again references her inability to speak, but now, once her father is dead, she finds 'something else': a sense of freedom. She immediately begins to feel a sense of distance from the stifled part of herself that existed under the influence of her family and mainly of her father, saying: 'Everything that child, that girl did was out of what is between daughter and mother, daughter and brother, daughter and father' (Gordimer 2000: 58). She refers to herself as 'that child, that girl', showing that she no longer feels stifled by her generational position or by her gender as she has gained distance from this persona.

She starts to imagine leaving South Africa, the country she associates with her father and his legacy, and considers 'taking off for another country: always in Africa, of course, because wasn't that where my father had earned the right for us to belong?' (Gordimer 2000: 58). However, her freedom of movement is prohibited, and, importantly, her sexual freedom, academic freedom and freedom of career are limited, as she shows when she reflects on her father in prison:

> My mother is dead and there is only me, there, for him. Only me. My studies, my work, my love affairs must fit in with the twice-monthly visits to the prison, for life, as long as he lives – if he had lived. My professors, my employers, my men must accept this overruling (Gordimer 2000: 59).

She wishes to escape the fact that she is always situated within the influence of her father, and that her life is dictated by the name that she inherited from him, as well as his enduring legacy. She says after Lionel's death: 'I knew I must have wished him to die; that to exult and to sorrow were the same thing for me' (Gordimer 2000: 59), a moment reminiscent of Magda's desire for her father's death in order to secure her own power. Rosa now begins to show signs of her own freedom to choose her narrative, gaining sexual freedom, which symbolises her control of her own body and how this is no longer situated within the link to her father or to her position of disempowerment as a woman, and eventually leaving South Africa for her trip to Europe. As she prepares to leave, she again links the father to the nation, saying: 'I don't know how to live in Lionel's country' (213). The father is intimately tied to the nation, even though he challenges the dominant apartheid ideology, and by leaving South Africa, she is leaving the influence of the father and his legacy.

## *Symbols of masculine power*

Throughout Gordimer's novel, many familiar symbols of masculine power and paternal narratives are used to highlight the influence and control of the father, including references to religion, political ideologies and, as shown earlier in *Cry, the Beloved Country*, the power of the voice, which allows the father to construct his narratives of power. The ideas of ethnic culture, money or possession, risk-taking and sexual freedom, sport and freedom of movement are also used as symbols of masculine power, which serve to perpetuate paternal narratives. Each of these aspects offers a perspective into how the characters are located within paternal narratives as well as how they try to resist them.

Firstly, even though Lionel is not religious, he is constructed within religious narratives in order to show his paternal narrative power. He is seen as a religious figure by many, including Rosa. When Rosa is having coffee with Conrad, they are approached by someone who praises Lionel: 'The government calls him a communist but your father is God's man, the holy spirit of our Lord is in him, and that's why he's being persecuted' (Gordimer 2000: 12). Rosa is an extension of the father here, and, by acknowledging his greatness to her, these comments are honouring her father. Rosa also refers to those who admire her father as the 'faithful' (339). She explains in an earlier passage, when she is surrounded by her father's friends at his lawyer Theo's home:

> There was bravado and sentiment in the confidence of the room full of people at Theo's that they were behaving as Lionel Burger would expect, as he would do himself in their situation. That was how they saw themselves. Strong emotion – faith? – has different ways of being manifested among the different disciplines within which people order their behaviour (Gordimer 2000: 28).

By following the way Lionel would expect or would behave himself, they are demonstrating the power of his paternal narrative in influencing those around him. Dimitriu claims that this scene 'is reminiscent of the apostles' gathering after Jesus' crucifixion' (2000: 42). This is framed by Rosa as 'faith', and demonstrates that even with the subversive narratives that Lionel is trying to weave, the traditional structures of power are used to demonstrate respect for the narrative power of the father. He is framed as an extension of the original Father God's power. Dimitriu explains that 'in symbolic fashion', Lionel is constructed as a Christian in order to idealise his character, and his political convictions in light of his role within a national narrative, even further (41).

In fact, even Rosa becomes one of the faithful eventually when she becomes a revolutionary when returning to South Africa at the end of the novel. Gordimer says that one of her critics, Connor Cruise O'Brien, sees *Burger's Daughter* as a profoundly religious book (Gardner 1982): 'In the book was the idea of redemption being entered into through suffering. Taking it on in one way or another, politically or religiously motivated, that is the only choice you have . . . [which is] the reason why Rosa goes back to South Africa and, ultimately, to prison' (Gardner 1990: 172). Rosa's conversion to a true revolutionary, represented in religious terms under the paternal figure of Lionel, is finally completed when she meets the same fate as he does.

This focus on religious symbolism is echoed when Rosa's mother lets her see one of the letters that arrives at their home addressed to her father: 'It said her father was a devil and a beast who wanted to rob and kill, destroying Christian civilization' (Gordimer 2000: 13). Here Lionel is framed within religious myth in order to conceptualise his narrative influence, this time as a threat to religious hegemony. However, it is also linked to 'rob[bing]', hinting at the protection of possessions, which a democratic country, in the minds of many conservative whites, would threaten, as well as to the role of the father as protector and provider of these possessions. The Marxist references become clearer in the rest of the novel, but they are obviously drawn to show the link with communist Lionel, and the religious framing shows the mythical status that he had obtained through his views and political activism. Conrad explicitly compares communism to religion, saying to Rosa: 'Being brought up in a house like your father's is growing up in a devout family. Perhaps nobody preached Marx or Lenin . . . They just lay around the house, leather-bound with gold tooling, in everybody's mind – the family bible. It was all taken in with your breakfast cornflakes' (Gordimer 2000: 46). Political ideology, like religion, consists of narratives of influence and control, which the father uses to frame the lives of others. Clingman claims that this religious framing of communism does not undercut the text's commitment to its ideology, but rather demonstrates a fracture between performance of communism and its doctrine: 'Where

Rosa rehearses the "litany" (her word) of Party dogma, the mood is frequently – though not stridently – ironical; on the other hand, it is demonstrated in the novel that the historical record of the SACP is a proud one' (1986: 173).

While Lionel is often constructed within the framework of religious devotion, he is critical of religion itself and the power structures that it justifies. During his final testimony, he criticises religious hypocrisy:

> I am talking of the contradiction that my people – the Afrikaner people – and the white people in general in our country, worship the God of Justice and practise discrimination on grounds of the colour of skin; profess the compassion of the Son of Man, and deny the humanity of the black people they live among. This contradiction that split the very foundations of my life, that was making it impossible for me to see myself as a man among men, with all that implies of consciousness and responsibility (Gordimer 2000: 19).

Indeed, even justice, which is framed within religious doctrine, is linked to masculinity here in order for Lionel to be defined as a 'man among men'. Lionel uses this construction to criticise the masculinity of the religious hypocrisies he points towards. The national political and religious narratives are shown to be contradictory, but these contradictions are ignored in favour of maintaining power. These ideologies are justified again by Brandt Vermeulen, who claims: 'Communism, accusing the Afrikaner of enslaving blacks under franchise of God's will, itself enslaved whites and yellows along with blacks in denial of God's existence' (Gordimer 2000: 174). Communism contradicts religion, but Vermeulen is ignorant of Lionel's point that racial exploitation contradicts it as well. By advocating the primacy of religion, and using it to justify political ideologies, the power of this paternal narrative is highlighted, and its ability to serve structures of power is demonstrated. The manipulation of religious doctrine serves the narrative power of the father, and it demonstrates his masculinity. Because Vermeulen is able to construct religious doctrine to suit his political agenda, he demonstrates his own narrative power.

By constructing the father as a religious symbol, his link to patriarchal power structures is highlighted. The father is able to debate, construct and renegotiate political and religious doctrine, and to shape public thinking, while women and children are merely offered the ability to follow these beliefs. This public power is how the father extends his being beyond himself, and in order to successfully fulfil the role of father he has to have the control over his sons and daughters, maintain the tradition of his own father, as well as shape the thinking and identity of a wider community. Robert Boyers explains this succinctly when he says: 'Lionel Burger is at once an activist and a patriarch, a sower of the seeds of disorder and a stable centre around which numbers of people gather to discover where they are to go' (1984: 69). Hence, he encapsulates the father figure, who is also the arbiter of his own form of paternal narratives.

This idea of public power finds expression in the idea of 'nationhood', which was a popular construction of identity during apartheid. For Rosa, the idea of the Afrikaans 'nation' or ethnic grouping is one that she has an ambivalent connection to. There is the sense of a familial link with other white Afrikaners, such as when she visits Vermeulen:

> There might be some distant family connection between Brandt Vermeulen and Rosa Burger. It was not on record in Bureau of State Security files. Her mother had been vague about it. Brandt Vermeulen's mother and Rosa's mother could have been third or fourth cousins on the maternal side; he had no need to acknowledge the possibility, nor would Rosa have much ground to claim kinship in the collateral of Afrikanerdom where, if you went back three hundred years, every Cloete and Smit and van Heerden would turn out to have blood-ties with everyone else (Gordimer 2000: 182).

Rosa acknowledges her link to Vermeulen despite their ideological differences. There is a sense of shared identity, and Rosa acknowledges that her father, in his legendary, powerful status, is still claimed as an Afrikaner:

> She and her father and mother belonged with him even though they disowned the volk – nothing could change that, Lionel Burger who died an unrepentant Communist jail-bird also died an Afrikaner. Brandt Vermeulen did not need to tell her her father could have been prime minister if he had not been a traitor. It had been said many times. For the Afrikaner people, Lionel Burger was a tragedy rather than an outcast; that way, he still was theirs. They could not allow the earth of the fatherland to be profaned by his body; yet, that way, they were themselves absolved from his destruction (Gordimer 2000: 186).

In this reflection of the common bonds of 'nationhood', Rosa sees how her father's legacy is still configured within the simplistic nationalist ideology. Treason is a betrayal of the national identity, and in a way it is a denouncement of nationalist fatherhood. However, by refiguring Lionel as a tragic hero, he is reintegrated into the nationalist narrative. Dimitriu argues: 'Afrikanerdom has to be strictly protected against the intrusion of external influences, especially revolutionary influences, and its defence justifies extraordinary measures, including the abrogation of the rule of law' (2000: 69). This tumultuous link between Lionel and his ethnic identity is echoed in Brandt Vermeulen's impassioned speech about apartheid, the ultimate paternal narrative of maintaining power structures, into which he tries to locate Lionel. He says to Rosa:

> You'll see – I hope. What we are doing here may frighten the world, but what is bold and marvellous is always a little terrible to some. Your father had the same reaction to *his* ideas, né . . . ? Of course – we who are most diametrically opposed understand each other best! If things had been different – well . . . If your father had lived longer, I think he would have overcome his despair – you see, I think his living as a Communist was an expression of despair. He didn't believe his people could solve the problem of their historical situation. So he turned to the notion of the historically immutable solution . . . yes, he didn't trust us: his own people; himself . . . that's how I see it. But if he had lived a

bit longer – I honestly believe a man of his quality – a great man . . . (Gordimer 2000: 187).

Lionel is still understood as a 'great man', having the power to wield great power and influence, and his betrayal of nationalist narratives enshrined in apartheid is simply seen as a form of 'despair' or a lack of trust in 'his people'. Interestingly, Vermeulen tries to refigure the apartheid project as a form of a new narrative, something 'bold and marvellous'. Lionel is made to be a stubborn reproducer of a stifling narrative, and the apartheid project is seen as a type of dynamic counter-narrative. However, Lionel's narrative resists traditional forms of power, and indeed his betrayal is against the economic and social power of the 'nation' that he belonged to, as he points out in his final testimony when he explains: 'I saw that white Marxists worked side by side with blacks in an equality that meant taking on the meanest of tasks – tasks that incurred loss of income and social prestige' (Gordimer 2000: 20). These potential losses of power are what apartheid resists, reinforcing racial hierarchies.

The contrast between Lionel's narrative and traditional masculine, nationalist power structures is shown when Lionel, accused of various crimes earlier in his life, has his indictment quashed: 'In the Burger house there was a party, then, more . . . triumphant than any *stryddag* held by the farmers of the Nels' district in celebration of the white man's power, the heritage of his people that Lionel Burger betrayed' (Gordimer 2000: 57). He is clearly constructed as a figure resisting traditional power structures, and this contrast with a sporting event linked to 'white man's power', which Lionel betrays, shows his own narrative as working counter to that of traditional power, and working against the nationalist narratives of his 'people'. Indeed, even though Lionel is often constructed in a way that reinforces masculine, paternal power, his narrative is one that fits into the maternal structure of shared power and resisting traditional power, where he sees whites and blacks 'sharing policy-making and leadership. [He] saw whites prepared to work under blacks. Here was a possible solution to injustice' (20).

## Rosa's assertion of narrative power

Lionel maintains his ideologies up to his death as Rosa sees him 'dying for his beliefs in a prison hospital' (Gordimer 2000: 75). Rosa reiterates this when Conrad asks her: 'Why d'you talk about him as "Lionel"?' (77). She reflects: 'It's true that to me he was also something other than my father. Not just a public persona; many people have that to put on and take off. Not something belonging to the hackneyed formulation of the tracts and manifestos that explain him, for others. He was different'. She sees him as intimately tied to his politics, and she negotiates many different relationships with him, as a father, political persona and as merely 'Lionel'.

Rosa's own personal identity is similarly always linked to politics. Rosa was born in May 1948, as the Afrikaner nationalist government took office (Gordimer 2000: 90). Conrad also remarks to Rosa: 'Personal horrors and political ones are the same to you. You live through them all. On the same level' (37). In the same way that Lionel's identity and personal life are tied to his political life, so Rosa's life is a narrative of the political tensions in South Africa. The personal identity as shaped by the political is shown when Rosa eventually leaves South Africa and finally feels a sense of freedom to define herself. Clingman explains that 'the keyword Rosa uses to describe her reason for going is that of "defection". Quite simply Rosa Burger goes to Europe to learn how to "defect" from her father and the historical legacy he has handed on to her' (Clingman 1986: 177). On her trip to Europe she meets Lionel's first wife Katya, who was also involved in the resistance movement. Katya explains that within South Africa, being white necessitated a political identity based on power. She explains that the binary of either traitor or supporter demanded a political identity that could not be escaped, within the narrow Afrikaner identity and by extension the racial identity of whiteness:

> If I'd stayed . . . at home, how will they fit in, white people? Their continuity stems from the colonial experience, the white one. When they lose power it'll be cut. Just like that! They've got nothing but their horrible power. Africans will take up their own kind of past the whites never belonged to. Even the Terblanches and Alettas – our rebellion against the whites was also part of *being white* (Gordimer 2000: 257).

Whiteness is given power in many senses, constructing white characters as those who are able to either perpetuate or resist power structures. Black characters are divorced from this narrative power. For Katya, as well as for Rosa, this power is stifling. Europe offers a sense of release of responsibility, as Katya describes:

> Nobody expects you to be more than you are, you know. That kind of tolerance, I didn't even know it existed – I mean, there [in South Africa]: if you're not equal to facing *everything*, there . . . you're a traitor. To the human cause – justice, humanity, the lot – there's nothing else (Gordimer 2000: 256).

Katya's explanation links to why Rosa was unable to negotiate an identity for herself within South Africa that went beyond these simple binaries: not only was she voiceless on account of her gender, but she was ambivalently connected to her ethnic group and constructed as politically prefigured by her race. In addition, she was also immersed in the narrative of her father and his legacy, unable to form a self-definition.

Rosa is always the observer, rarely being shown to have narrative power in the novel, as Conrad points out when he says to her: 'You never got beyond fascination with the people around Lionel Burger's swimming pool; you never jumped in and trusted yourself to him, like Baasie and me, or drowned, like Tony' (Gordimer 2000: 114). By contrasting Rosa with the three son figures, Conrad the substitute son, Baasie, the black child who lives with their family while Rosa is growing up after his own father is arrested, and Tony, her drowned brother, Conrad shows that Rosa is always at a distance to the narrative power of Lionel, unable to truly embody it. She cannot narrate her own life, always existing within the confines of Lionel's narrative, but she is never truly able to engage and embody it herself.

Only once she leaves South Africa, 'Lionel's country' (Gordimer 2000: 213), is she able to find some semblance of a narrative voice. When the father is intricately linked to the nation state as well as to the 'nation' or ethnic group, only by distancing herself from these is she able to find her own narrative power. She imagines a narrative for herself through those who subscribed to the narrative of her father, 'the faithful' (196), which gives her a sense of agency and which counters her 'inactivity' (197):

> After I had taken the passport, after I'd gone – I don't know what they said: the faithful. They would surely never have believed it of me. Perhaps they got out of believing it by substituting the explanation that I had gone on instructions, after all, instructions so daring and secret not even anyone among themselves would know. So my inactivity for so long would present them with a purpose they had always hoped for, for my sake. And by what means I had managed to get papers – that was simply a tribute to the lengths a revolutionary must go (Gordimer 2000: 196–7).

She imagines she is seen as a revolutionary, as following the narrative of her parents, but finally creating a narrative for herself as well. This marks a shift as Rosa sees herself as the protagonist of her own story instead of simply a secondary character in the story of her father.

John Cooke links this sense of power and freedom to her control over her own body and sexuality, both in her mobility in finally being able to leave South Africa, and in taking on the role of mistress in France to her lover Bernard Chabalier (1985). Before, the father was shown to be in control of the bodies of those who are relatively disempowered, as seen in Lionel Burger's description of black corpses and the fact that Rosa participates in a false engagement with Noel de Witt, a fellow revolutionary, so that she can further her father's cause by giving him access to Lionel. In this way Rosa even sacrifices her own romantic and sexual being in service of the father. Cooke notes:

> The development of the latent desire for pleasure in the sensual world of the present comes through a love affair with a married French professor, Bernard Chabalier . . . Rosa is beginning to see herself as the focal point of her world; and for the first time in her life she finds no disparity – no threshold – between what she is and what her appearance shows her to be, as she so painfully had when posing as de Witt's fiancée . . . Only through her private time in France, Gordimer stresses at the

close of part two, could Rosa sever the hold of her father and feel herself as the place at the center of the world (1985: 92-3).

However, even when she finally has the chance to step out of the narrative of her father, she is drawn back into it by encountering her childhood friend, whom she knew as Baasie but who now insists on being called by his real name, Zwelinzima Vulindlela. When she runs into Zwelinzima in London, he constructs his own paternal narrative and questions why whiteness affords Lionel such a powerful narrative. He tells her:

> Everyone in the world must be told what a great hero he was and how much he suffered for the blacks. Everyone must cry over him and show his life on television and write in the papers. Listen, there are dozens of our fathers sick and dying like dogs, kicked out of the locations when they can't work any more. Getting old and dying in prison. Killed in prison. It's nothing. I know plenty of blacks like Burger. It's nothing, it's us, we must be used to it, it's not going to show on English television (Gordimer 2000: 328).

In Zwelinzima's critique, the power to be represented and to have narrative power is thus reserved for white fathers. He explains that his father also died in prison, but that he did not receive the reverence that Lionel did. The idea of race thus also presents an interesting contrast with masculine and paternal power, with whiteness seeming to be the ultimate symbol of dominance. Rosa recognises this power of whiteness to narrate and control when she drives through a township and sees a man abusing a donkey, and reflects that she could have stopped him: 'I had only to career down on that scene with my white authority' (Gordimer 2000: 211). When Zwelinzima calls Rosa in the middle of the night and she calls him Baasie, his Afrikaans nickname, he reclaims his identity and his power by asserting: 'I'm not "Baasie", I'm Zwelinzima Vulindlela' (326). Clingman links this to the Black Consciousness movement by demonstrating how it is a powerful moment of realisation for Rosa: 'Whereas blacks had never been truly "other" for her, by the end of the novel Rosa has reached the point where they are objects neither of mental projection nor of displacement, but exist fully in their own right. This allows for her own authentic political re-engagement' (1986: 176).

At the end of the novel, Rosa returns to South Africa, locating herself again within the tumultuous prefiguring of her race and the legacy of her father. She becomes a parental figure herself when she works in the physiotherapy department of a hospital for children with deformities, taking on a role of relative power to the black patients who make use of the hospital: 'She was white, she had never had a child, only a lover with children by some other woman. No child but those who passed under her hands, whom it was her work to put together again if that were possible, at the hospital' (Gordimer 2000: 357). She is framed here as a carer for black children, and her whiteness, although placing her at a distance from them, also affords her the narrative power that she speaks of earlier. By taking on a parental role, she is affirming another form of power to change her surroundings and reshape South Africa, but this time in the caring, maternal role instead of perpetuating the ideologies of her father. Cooke notes about her new position as a physiotherapist that 'in this calling she has found a means of alleviating the paralysis she had felt as a child under parents' demands. She can act when faced with the inexplicable suffering of crippled and wounded children' (1985: 86). This power over black bodies also reshapes her into a similar paternalistic role as her father. Newman explains: 'As a physiotherapist, Rosa (like her doctor father) restores feeling to the nerves of injured black people. Rosa's return is to a world of repugnant bodies – horribly mutilated in the Soweto riots – but she is now able to face these bodies and act in their world' (1985: 97). Her profession does give her a measure of control, and importantly it signifies that she is no longer merely subject to the legacy of her father but can be an active agent to care for these children.

She witnesses the Soweto uprising of June 16, 1976 as a way for children to reclaim their power over their own lives, echoing her ability to reclaim her life as well as signalling an ambivalent despair and a sense of hope for South Africa. Her active role in caring is a part of equipping these children to take up the struggle. She reflects: 'Our children and our children's children. The sins of the fathers; at last, the children avenge on the fathers the sins of the fathers. Their children and children's children; that was the Future, father, in hands not foreseen' (Gordimer 2000: 360). While the influence of the 'sins of the father' is highlighted in this section, leading to the horrors of apartheid South Africa, Rosa sees the children as reclaiming their power over the fate that seemed inevitable for them. In the same way, she rediscovers her own narrative power, gaining a sense of generational power through her new motherly, caring role, and is made to question the power afforded to her and her father by race. These influences all echo a conflicted relationship with paternal narratives, which seem inadequate to make sense of the South African apartheid reality. Clingman clearly frames this maturation of Rosa through the lens of psychoanalysis:

> The basic organizing motif of the text is that of the family; we see Rosa not only in relation to her father, but also in relation to her surrogate mother, Katya, in France; and the relationship between Rosa and Conrad is presented in what are finally incestuous terms, as if they were brother and sister. The Communist Party itself is presented as if it were a 'family' . . . but it is one in which Rosa is always regarded as a 'daughter'. *Burger's Daughter* might then be regarded as a *Bildungsroman* with a difference, in which Rosa is eventually expelled from the womb-like infantilization she is subjected to from so many sources into the mature acceptance of her own life history (which of necessity leads her into another kind of womb, the prison cell) (1986: 175).

Rosa needs to overcome all of these limiting familial relationships, mostly to see herself as an agent of her own life instead of subjugated to the father figures of Lionel and the Communist Party. Gordimer herself explains this movement: 'What is certain is that in taking up the burden of other people's suffering through revolutionary political action, she has acted in her own name and her own identity, rather than the family tradition' (Gordimer 2003: 152).

In the end, Rosa is imprisoned, her fate remaining a mystery. The narrative ends elliptically, with Rosa unable to complete her story and being robbed of her voice in the same way her father had been. Clingman explains that the reader's access to Rosa's thoughts and feelings 'is now sealed off; even what Rosa has done in the underground [which led to her being taken into solitary confinement] remains undisclosed' (1986: 192). Clingman links this silencing of Rosa to the role of literature in representing history: 'It may be suggested that this withdrawal embodies a recognition relating to Gordimer's own position; if the novel cannot speak what Rosa has done, this is because fiction cannot do what Rosa might speak.' The novel offers a powerful display of the conflict between father and daughter even when they share political ideologies, and how symbols of masculinity prevent the daughter from claiming narrative power in many ways. Rosa is finally able to attain a level of resolution to her conflict with Lionel's influence, but she does not escape his legacy as she meets the same fate as her father.

CHAPTER 4

# Paternal Narratives in the Transition from Apartheid
## *The Smell of Apples*, *Ways of Dying* and *The Quiet Violence of Dreams*

The end of apartheid saw an explosion of diverse literature in South Africa. Sam Durrant argues that this period was potentially transformative for the nation:

> Post-apartheid literature might be described as exemplary postcolonial literature not simply in the chronological sense of literature written after the release of Nelson Mandela in 1990 or the democratic elections of 1994 but in its transformative potential, its ability to grapple with legacies of oppression and imagine new states of being and even new beings of the state (2005: 441).

In the literature following the end of apartheid, national narratives and, by extension, the identity of the nation could be redefined. Marius Crous highlights that ideas of gender, race and politics were being confronted in new ways, through both social shifts as well as shifts in literature, as white men were unseated from their assumed positions of power:

> In the aftermath of apartheid, white men, and in particular Afrikaner men associated with the National Party apparatus of the state, have lost their privileged positions. In the new dispensation a distinct loss of political power (but not necessarily a loss of economic power) is experienced, especially

by older members of this group and the younger generation of white males tend to feel threatened by affirmative action and gender equality (2007: 18).

By unsettling identities of empowered/disempowered, especially in terms of gender and race in South Africa, paternal narratives were also unsettled and fathers were often represented as distant to the landscape of a 'new South Africa'.

Pumla Dineo Gqola, writing on Njabulo Ndebele's conception of how apartheid reflected the 'spectacular', explains that 'the spectacular permeated various institutions and structures of meaning in South Africa's past. Such meanings have material effects that are racialised, economic, gendered and spatially designated' (Gqola 2009: 64). Gqola follows Ndebele by arguing that the extreme violence and poverty, the excessively lavish lifestyles of those in power and the assumed impenetrability of the horrific apartheid system constituted the 'spectacular', and that there was an imperative to represent these realities through literature during apartheid. Literature, in Ndebele's analysis, often represented the spectacular during apartheid, pointing broadly to social realities. Gqola notes that post-apartheid literature saw a shift from a political drive and writing of the 'spectacular' to more intimate storytelling:

> Even when many of these texts revisit apartheid it is not to the macro-political that the reader's attention is drawn, but to the opening up of the possibilities and the daily preoccupations that characterize human life. South African literature has veered away from a preoccupation with the spectacular contest between dominant and disempowered to a textured exploration of emotion, possibility and entanglement (2009: 62).

The writing of intimate, diverse stories thus saw the possibility to confront these social realities in more nuanced ways in post-apartheid South Africa, removing the impetus to write broadly political fictions.

However, it could be argued that the Truth and Reconciliation Commission (TRC) saw another showcase of the spectacular in post-apartheid South Africa. The commission allowed for marginalised, repressed narratives about trauma during apartheid to be aired, with the promise of amnesty for those who had committed crimes based on political motives. The narratives were framed, under the guidance of the spiritual and political father figure Desmond Tutu, as restorative justice for South Africa. Tutu's paternal narrative power is shown in his assertion that South Africa is the 'rainbow nation of God' (Myambo 2010: 94), and William Gumede notes that 'Tutu, democratic South Africa's moral conscience, bestow[ed] divineness on South Africa's ethnic diversity' (2007: 242). The discourses surrounding the TRC and the influence of Nelson Mandela and other political leaders indicated that these father figures could shepherd the nation towards new national narratives.

Some literature dealt specifically with the TRC, most famously Antjie Krog's *Country of My Skull* (1998), a non-fiction text with journalistic, personal narrative, poetic and analytical features. Gillian Slovo, daughter of anti-apartheid activists Joe Slovo and Ruth First, published her novel *Red Dust* in 2000, exploring the impact of TRC hearings in a fictional town. These texts reflect how history has been confronted in the transitional South Africa.

A new popular national narrative also emerged during the transition period, that of the rainbow nation, and Annie Gagiano notes that this narrative created the danger that 'the rich variety of cultural expressions, political preferences and social formations in a "national" territory might be subordinated to a legitimised, "official" and reductive master narrative' (2004: 814). Gagiano adds that this shift did not necessarily lead to black writers gaining equal prominence in South Africa or multivocal representations being recognised widely. However, Gagiano does add that novels, such as those by K. Sello Duiker (*The Quiet Violence of Dreams*, 2001), Zoë Wicomb (*David's Story*, 2000) and Mandla Langa (*The Memory of Stones*, 2000), have received critical attention and have contributed profoundly to the South African literary landscape: 'Although a text profoundly centred in white perspectives, such as *Disgrace*, has been allowed to dominate the national imaginary, these three novels, nevertheless, have attracted notice and their literary and social sophistication has been recognised by reviewers' (Gagiano 2004: 815).

Crous highlights that masculinity has been threatened by the end of apartheid and the disruption of established power relations. He points out that in 'the modern patriarchy of South African society, where African men have acquired political power, African women are faced with new difficulties, in particular assumptions relating to the maleness of African power' (2007: 18). Gqola adds that 'assertions of African masculinity can be expressions of both freedom and patriarchal power. Under colonialism and apartheid, adult Africans were designated boys and girls. It is therefore important to be attentive to the layered meanings of asserted manhood' (2009: 66). Raymond Suttner elaborates on this point:

> The infantilisation of Africans and men in particular links to or seeks to justify political domination by designating Africans as a race of children . . . In reading African assertions of manhood, therefore, we need to understand it as a challenge not only to a childlike status but as symbolising wider rejection of overlordship . . . The assertion of manhood is in this context a claim for freedom (2007: 197).

Gqola claims that these nuances of masculinity require careful reading, and she asserts that in many ways 'apartheid was always a gendered project. Consequently, anti-apartheid initiatives were also gendered in precise ways' (2009: 66).

Crous maintains that rape has become increasingly part of the public discourse, which is reflected in the literature published during this period (2007). Lucy Graham notes that 'a factor that has characterized post-apartheid South Africa is a proliferation of media and cultural texts on sexual violence. From local news media to novels, theatre, film, television drama, and the visual arts, rape is one of the issues that has moved to center stage' (2012: 133). Meg Samuelson explains that racial tensions were often represented through the image of rape during the transition period, explaining that 'race [is inserted] into the scene of rape by focusing almost exclusively on interracial rape' (2002: 88), as can be seen in the case of Tshepo in *The Quiet Violence of Dreams* being raped by his Coloured roommate Chris. Importantly for this book, rape is committed against women, children and even other men, but the perpetrators are always male and often fathers, as is the case in Wicomb's *David's Story*, J.M. Coetzee's *Disgrace* (1999), Phaswane Mpe's *Welcome to Our Hillbrow* (2001), Achmat Dangor's *Bitter Fruit* (2001), as well as all three of the novels discussed in this chapter.

The recasting of men, and often fathers, as predatory and dangerous, indicates that fatherhood is stripped of its moral and narrative authority. Many fathers become symbols of the violence and oppression of the apartheid state, such as Johan Erasmus in *The Smell of Apples* (Behr 1995), demonstrating distrust of traditional father figures and the oppressive control they represented.

Many texts during the transition represent a sense of powerlessness and emasculation through the imagery of failed or threatened fatherhood. Ndebele's *Death of a Son* (1996), Zakes Mda's *Ways of Dying* (1995) and Rayda Jacobs's *My Father's Orchid* (2006) offer some examples of this disrupted fatherhood, and demonstrate attempts to repair paternal relationships or negotiate fatherly roles as reflective of a country in healing. Following the end of apartheid, fatherhood is represented as linked to violence, oppression and absenteeism. Fathers are no longer represented in idealised or hyperbolised political terms, but in many cases even became antagonistic to their sons and daughters and, by extension, to political change. Fathers are unable to negotiate the realities of a changing social and political climate, and they are shown to feel threatened by how these changes constitute an affront to their power. The loss of the father's idealised role in post-apartheid representation can be linked to the fact that the father is no longer necessary as a symbolic leader towards liberation. It could also be linked to disillusionment with leadership, both in the form of leaders who perpetuated narratives that maintained apartheid structures, as well as leaders who are not adequately addressing current problems in South Africa. The reality of unstable fatherhood in the light of widespread unemployment and the link of fatherhood with violence are reflected in these novels. The subjectivities of fathers become unstable and anxious; whereas once fathers were represented as uncritically dominant or oppressive, now these roles become uncertain. The sons and daughters, who are now shown to be much more critical of the influence of their fathers, are also uncertain of their identities when confronted with unstable father figures.

The three novels under discussion in this chapter, *The Smell of Apples*, *Ways of Dying* and *The Quiet Violence of Dreams*, present the stories of three sons who negotiate their relationships with their fathers. In these novels, there is even greater distance from the fathers than in the texts discussed in the previous chapter, distance that is never reconciled due to the introduction of dangerous, oppressive or even cruel fathers, who present challenges to the simplistic adoption of paternal narratives. This could signal a distancing from the history and protection that the father traditionally represents. It could also indicate a disillusionment with the new African National Congress (ANC) government, which was already showing signs of corruption and complicity with economic exploitation during the early years of transition. As Rita Barnard notes: 'The literature of the transition, responsive to such matters, seems increasingly to record a sense of the vulgarity of power' (2004: 292). This power is often represented metonymically by father figures. The father's narrative is shown to be oppressive and damaging in all of the texts, and the sons are still interpellated within it while struggling to find their own narrative voices.

## Mark Behr's *The Smell of Apples*
### *Perpetuating apartheid ideology*
In Mark Behr's novel, *The Smell of Apples*, the son figure and protagonist of the novel, Marnus, is shown to adore and admire his father. The novel is primarily set in 1973, in apartheid South Africa, and it focuses on a few months in Marnus's life when he is an eleven-year-old boy living with his family in the coastal town of Muizenberg. By presenting the narrative through Marnus's perspective, the novel demonstrates his indoctrination into apartheid ideology through the ideas shared by his parents and the narratives he is told about South Africa, race and his grandparents' exodus from Tanzania, called Tanganyika before its independence. Barnard explains that 'Behr's novel offers a veritable compendium of the sayings, stereotypes, and justifications that made up the everyday banality of apartheid' (2000: 207), offering an intimate portrayal of how apartheid ideology affected those who were its main beneficiaries. Marnus's father, Johan Erasmus, is an army general in the South African Defence Force (SADF) and is

often referred to as appearing strict and masculine. Marnus idolises his father and tries to emulate his ideas and his behaviour at various points, seeming to neatly fit into the narrative power of the father figure. As Barnard explains:

> The narrative traces a closed circle. It starts with a list of the names and nicknames the young protagonist's parents have given him ('Marnus,' 'my son' or 'my little Bull,' 'my little piccanin'); it ends with the narrator's acceptance of these identities and of his position in the racist, hyper-masculinist society that these names simultaneously construct and express (2000: 207-8).

David Medalie notes that the novel 'emphasises the extraordinary power of indoctrination' (2000: 50), referring to Marnus's words as demonstrative of this central concern: 'You never forget the things you were taught or the things that happened to you as a child. Those things make up your foundation for the future' (Behr 1997b: 184-5). Medalie also notes that the confluence of war and family life indicate that 'the power of the male at home and the power of the man at war are presented as intimately related, for a pervasive masculinist ethos will not spare the family, and certainly not the women and children' (1997: 513). The father's power is represented at home in the same way that he is able to practise militaristic power in order to defend apartheid ideology.

Marnus's childhood narrative is interspersed with the recountings of an adult Marnus fighting in the war on the Angolan border in 1988 and seeming to die in conflict. Being a part of the armed forces and dying for this cause could be seen as the ultimate integration into the paternal narrative, linked to a national narrative of maintaining power structures and enacting violence. The son is completely encapsulated within the narrative dominance of the father, and 'any hope that he might come to reject the lessons he ventriloquizes so cleverly is thus foreclosed' (Barnard 2000: 208). Medalie adds that 'Behr's novel is the opposite of a *bildungsroman*: it is an investigation of the origins of warped understanding and behaviour, one that locates the monstrosity of later years, as it were, in the distorting influences that prevailed in formative years' (1997: 512).

Marnus's admiration for his father is later undercut in the novel by the revelation that his father raped his young friend Frikkie. The sexual dominance, violence and sexual taboo cast the father as similarly violent and dominant as Tshepo's father in *The Quiet Violence of Dreams*, explored later in this chapter.

It is important that in Behr's novel, in contrast to many of the other novels under consideration in this book, there seems to be a successful reproduction of the paternal narrative with little resistance from the son, and the influence of the father is almost complete over the son, who unquestioningly accepts the authority and narrative dominance of his father. Michiel Heyns notes that the novel demonstrates that 'the child is implicated in the structures which guarantee the privileged childhood' (2000: 53). Behr, in 'Living in the Fault Lines', explains that his choice to use a child narrator was to demonstrate how this indoctrination takes place and how paternal ideologies are reproduced:

> The child's voice could, I felt, succeed in accusing the abusers while at the same time holding up the mirrors. I hoped, and doubted, that the text would show how one is born into, loved into, violated into discrimination and how none of us were, or are, free from it. But to do so I needed a voice that would seem not to seek pardon or excuse, in a language different from the adult's which invariably contains in it whether it wants to or not, a corrupt and corrupting formula, always an attempt to justify or frequently to demand absolution (1997a: 116).

This complete indoctrination, and what Barnard refers to as the novel's 'closed circle' (2000: 207), could be linked to Marnus's death in the novel, as he is eventually unable to forge his own identity and is instead led into violence and defending the nation. Through many symbols of masculinity in the novel, Marnus is positioned as a replica of the father, over-identifying with his powerful and dominant ideology. The novel criticises Afrikaner apartheid ideology, which unflinchingly reproduces the oppressive system. It could also be linked biographically to Behr's own role as a spy for the security police while he was a student at Stellenbosch University in the 1980s, being unable to break free of the apartheid ideology in which he was raised. This biographical parallel gives the novel added resonance, indicating that it might be, as Barnard puts it, 'some sort of carefully masked confession' (2000: 211). As Behr himself expressed in the conference where he admitted to his role as a spy:

> As an act of creation, *The Smell of Apples* represents, for me, the beginnings of a showdown with myself for my own support of a system like apartheid . . . [If] the book's publication has assisted white people in coming to terms with their own culpability for what is wrong in South Africa, then it has been worthwhile (1997a: 115).

### *Symbols of masculinist dominance and power*

Various symbols of masculinity are employed in Behr's novel in order to demonstrate the ways in which the father asserts his dominance and constructs his narrative power. Early in the novel, Marnus is mesmerised while watching his father prepare for a celebratory dinner as he has just been promoted to be the youngest major general in the history of the SADF. The ideas of violence and sport, as well as a paternal legacy that links to Johan's father as well, are mentioned in the grooming rituals as Marnus observes his father preparing for the dinner:

> Dad was using Oupa's old shaving brush to lather his chin in quick little circles. The handle of Dad's shaving brush is inlaid with ivory from the bottom ends of tusks of an elephant that Oupa shot next to the Ruvu in Tanganyika. The tusks are mounted on either side of the fireplace in our lounge (Behr 1997b: 14).

There is a confluence of masculine imagery linked to this moment of being named a major general, and Marnus's admiration for his father is clearly demonstrated. The father is immediately constructed as hypermasculine by being linked to images of the military, hunting and the legacy of his own father.

Later in the text, these masculine images are again tied to sport in the form of a boxing match, and the father is shown to be intimately connected with these images, as well as to symbols of nationhood through the national anthem and patriotism:

> We sometimes go to the boxing in the Good Hope Centre, or at other times we listen to the matches on the radio. When Arnold Taylor knocked out Romeo Anaya of Mexico and became the world champion, it was an almighty big day for the Republic. We listened to the fight on the radio, and when they played 'Die Stem', Dad had tears in his eyes (Behr 1997b: 44).

The father is shown to have a strong connection to the masculine symbol of sport and its link to national narratives of patriotism, and bonding over this masculinist activity demonstrates the closeness between father and son. These moments allow for the reproduction of subtle messages about national pride and allow the father to demonstrate an idealised masculinity to the son.

An interest in sport and a deep connection to the narratives surrounding the symbol of sport seem to be requirements for the father figure to enact his masculinity. Marnus reflects this again with an interracial boxing match:

> Just before the General came, we also listened when Pierre Fourie fought against Bob Foster in Johannesburg. It was the first time in the Republic that a non-white fought against a white. The referee let Foster win because he's black, even though Pierre should have won the match. But overseas they're bringing politics into sports, and they discriminate against us white South Africans (Behr 1997b: 44).

The irony of this statement is of course lost on Marnus, who is merely echoing the sentiments of his father while trying to defend the racial superiority of whiteness. Sport has power in reinforcing paternal narratives and maintaining strict power relations within the South African setting. Sport is a connection between the father and the son, especially when the paternal narrative is as effectively reproduced as it is in this novel. Marnus comments: 'The other big hero for Dad and me is Gary Player. Dad always says that Springboks may come and go, but the one Springbok that will always wear the green and gold is Gary Player' (Behr 1997b: 44).

Marnus also variously refers to a physical resemblance to the father as reflective of the influence that his father has over him, similar to how this literary device of family resemblance was used in *Burger's Daughter*, for example. Marnus observes that he has light hair and his father dark, but says: 'Even though my hair is still fair, I know it will go dark like his when I get older, because on Uncle Samuel's photographs and slides of Tanganyika, where Dad is still a boy, you can see his hair also used to be light' (Behr 1997b: 15). Later, the general from Chile, who Marnus is instructed to simply refer to as Mr Smith, says to Marnus: 'You are a carbon copy of your father' (35). The physical link to the father emphasises their closeness as well as the ideological links that are being reinforced gradually by the father. Barnard explains that in going to war: '[Marnus] formally accepts the identity to which he has been "recruited" all along. The subject comes to reflect the Subject, as Louis Althusser might put it . . . The novel concludes, in other words, with a scene of specularization, dramatizing the boy's doubling of his father' (2000: 212).

The father's body in itself becomes a very important symbol of masculinity, and Marnus's reaction to Johan's body demonstrates his admiration for his father in the same way that his physical resemblance demonstrates how he will echo the paternal narratives. When Johan has prepared for his promotional dinner, Marnus looks at him and says: 'Dad looks just as pretty as Mum' (Behr 1997b: 17). This gendered construction, feminising his body as 'pretty', is resisted by Johan, and he responds: 'Handsome is probably a better word.' Marnus's mother, Leonore, also constructs Johan's physicality as linked to his military position, as Marnus explains: 'Dad's chin is almost completely square and Mum says you can know by just looking at it, that a man with a chin like that should be in uniform' (15). The gendered body of the father constructs him as a paragon of masculine power and authority.

The father's body also becomes important in passages where Johan and Marnus share showers. The phallus becomes central in these moments, and the father also uses showering as opportunities for sexual instruction. Marnus reflects on the body and phallus of his father in one of the showering scenes and uses it as a way to reflect on his own body:

> Dad's whole chest and stomach are covered with hair and his John Thomas hangs out from a bushy black forest. Once, after we heard that hair down there grows quicker if you shave it, Frikkie used his father's razor to shave off all the fluff around his John Thomas. I almost shaved off mine as well, but then Frikkie got a terrible rash that made him walk around scratching like a mangy dog, so I decided not to. And, anyway, Dad might have seen it when we took our shower and he would have had a good laugh at me for being so silly (Behr 1997b: 62-3).

The father's body is made to be the ideal, and Marnus considers shaving his pubic hair to make it grow as thick as his father's. However, he fears being shamed for this by his father, reinforcing his position as a boy who relies on his father's approval. His father then introduces a sexual element to the showering, and seems to be offering a form of sexual initiation to Marnus:

> Between soaping and washing our hair, Dad asks: 'So tell Dad, does that little man of yours stand up yet sometimes in the mornings?' Whenever Dad asks me that I get all shy, so I just laugh up into his face without really answering. I saw Frikkie's standing right out of his pyjama pants one morning, but mine doesn't really do it yet (Behr 1997b: 63).

The phallus becomes the focus of these moments between father and son. This can be seen as another grooming ritual, which signifies the enactment of masculinity and a site of masculine performance. The father is able to use the body and the phallus as sites of instruction to initiate the maturation of the son. In the light of the father raping Marnus's friend Frikkie later in the novel, these moments also offer some foreshadowing of the father's ominous and threatening sexuality. Barnard comments that the moments of sexual instruction and hints at maturation are undercut by the lack of moral knowledge or change evinced in the text: 'Knowledge – sexual knowledge in particular – is the very warp and woof of power and offers no thread by which to escape the labyrinth' (2000: 209-10). In this way, the novel can be contrasted with Duiker's novel as sexuality is never a means to liberation from the paternal narrative for Marnus as it is for Tshepo, but rather another form of oppression.

Immediately following this passage, Marnus again reflects on his penis as an adult in one of his reflections when he is at war. He gives a great deal of detail in his description of his penis, looking at the wrinkles and veins. He thinks after urinating: 'When I look down again, I realise I'm still holding my dick. The head, enfolded by the soft foreskin, is half flattened from the pressure of thumb and index finger. Curling through the opening of my fly, are long dark hairs' (Behr 1997b: 64-5). Seeing the long dark hairs now, the hairs he admired in his father when he was a child, shows how he mirrors his father physically and has matured through the phallic symbol to resemble what he looked up to in his father. This image is contradictory, however, as Cheryl Stobie explains: 'The dark hairs connect him to his father-line, but the lighter hairs are reminders of his childish self' (2008: 82). Mervyn McMurtry adds to this by showing that the symbol of the penis here also indicates a sense that Marnus is powerless in relation to perpetuating the paternal narrative or, indeed, resisting it: '[Marnus] examines his penis: it is no weapon, not the "mister" of a man, but a flaccid "dick" . . . suggestive of powerlessness and impotency, and therefore the futility of perpetuating the contaminated seed and sins of the father' (1998: 103). The penis indicates that Marnus is tasked with the masculinist imperative of perpetuating paternal narratives, but its weak, almost revulsive description here indicates that this process will not take place; Marnus will die, and he will be free from the history he has inherited.

Implicit in this construction of masculinity is the requirement for heterosexuality. Heterosexuality is important to the construction of paternal narratives and patriarchal power because it symbolically calls for the dominance of men and fathers in traditional family systems, and they are able to exercise their power more directly within these systems. In the novel, Marnus tries to link heterosexuality to violence and war, and when his limits of heterosexuality are breached, he defends the heterosexuality of his grandfather who could be seen as transgressing these limits: 'Frikkie and I have decided to join the army when the war comes. The army is better than the air force or the navy where all the poofters go. Well, I said, everyone who goes to the navy isn't a poofter, because Oupa Erasmus was in the navy' (Behr 1997b: 71). When a father figure is linked to homosexuality, like his grandfather being in the navy, he immediately defends this and expands his definition of the limits of sexuality.

Later, he reflects this required heterosexuality through singing as well. He and Frikkie were in a choir when they were younger but no longer wanted to be part of it. He explains the link between singing and homosexuality: 'We called everyone who sang poofters. Except when Mum's around, because she says it's disgusting to call someone that just because he sings. She says you aren't a poofter just because you sing, but Dad just laughs and says he's not so sure' (Behr 1997b: 104). Johan laughs when considering men who sing as being homosexuals, even though he commits same-sex rape against Frikkie. This demonstrates that the sexual practice is not as important in the construction of masculinity as the performance of symbols of masculinity are. Johan can safely maintain his status as not being a 'poofter' because he is seen as masculine, and he distances himself from men who do not practise these symbols of masculine dominance.

Similarly, the patriarchal framework of religion is employed to reproduce the dominant narratives in the novel, especially about race and the power of the father. Marnus reflects about Coloured people, using a religious framework to make a racial argument:

> More often than not, they're criminals who won't ever get to see heaven. St Peter, who stands at the portals of eternity, will pass out stone-cold when he smells their breath. But Doreen, she's a good girl and she might go to heaven. In heaven she'll live with other Christian Coloureds in small houses and the Lord will reward her for never boozing it up like the rest. Also because she never nabs Mum's sugar like Gloria does from Mrs Delport. Gloria, the real flooze with the purple lips who fancies herself to be a real madam – her type will *never* inherit the Eternal life (Behr 1997b: 39).

Marnus implies that there is apartheid in heaven as well, extending his racist conceptions to metaphysical realms. Again, when these narratives are insufficient at encapsulating those he cares about, he finds ways to extend them, such as finding a way for his Coloured housekeeper to also be accepted into heaven despite his racist conceptions of it. However, his use of the term 'girl' to refer to Doreen shows how patriarchy is linked to race, and Marnus is able to infantilise Doreen because of his position of power. Medalie explains that the novel evinces 'the reliance upon religion, particularly Calvinist doctrine, to mystify and present as inevitable or predestined an act which has no etiology other than the political situation in South Africa and the widespread inculcation of racist doctrines' (2000: 52). Religious narratives are used to obscure or explain away the underlying racist ideologies.

Later, the link between the symbol of religion and paternal narratives becomes strongly reinforced. Marnus looks at oil paintings, which the pastor's wife hangs at his church's entrance. One painting catches his attention:

> One of the big paintings in the foyer is of a father and his children on the beach. It could be somewhere along Muizenberg, because the beach is long and flat with dunes in the distance, and far in the background it looks like the Hottentots-Holland. The man in the picture is speaking to his children, and in the bottom of the painting, written in big letters in the sand, it says: 'Honour Thy Father and Mother'. When I look at that painting, I sometimes wonder why only the father is there (Behr 1997b: 52).

The construction of the father as disciplinarian and the figure to be honoured by children in this painting shows how religion becomes a tool for perpetuating paternal narratives. The father's voice can be reflected through religious narratives, and ideologies such as racism and patriarchy are perpetuated, as in Marnus's conception of apartheid in heaven. The father is given ultimate authority, fulfilling the role of both parents to be honoured in these paintings.

## The father reflects the nation

One of the most striking ways in which the paternal narrative is linked to patriarchal power is shown through linking the father to the nation, as has been demonstrated in previous discussions. McMurtry explains that in Behr's novel 'the hegemonic power of the individual father is extended into and reinforced by the patriarchal structures of the state' (1998: 102). Marnus's father thus comes to represent the nation to him, and the national narrative of apartheid is perpetuated through him. Mark Gevisser comments that the 'general [Johan] is the patriarch, the father(land) to whom the son (citizen) must prove himself' (1995).

Marnus alludes to this conflation of the father and the nation by referring to political leaders in the apartheid government in familial terms, showing the close bonds that he feels with these leaders. He refers to 'Uncle PW Botha' (Behr 1997b: 45) and 'Uncle John Vorster' (70) at many points throughout the text. These symbolic familial bonds with political leaders show how ideologies are reproduced in both the real and the symbolic family structures, with older male figures always given the authority in these settings.

The ideas of nationhood, ethnicity and racial identity are highlighted by Johan when he recounts the history of Tanzania to Marnus to foster pride in his national and ethnic heritage. The political aspects are clearly highlighted by the demonising of 'Communists' and 'blacks' by Johan in this narrative, constructing a positive self-identity through othering. Importantly, Johan links this to his identity as an Afrikaner, showing the link of this paternal narrative to power relations within apartheid South Africa. Marnus says:

> [Dad] says he'll *never* forget what the Communists and the blacks did to Tanganyika. And Dad says we *shouldn't* ever forget. A *Volk* that forgets its history is like a man without a memory. That man is useless. Dad says the history of the Afrikaner, also the Afrikaners from Tanganyika and Kenya, is a proud history. We must always remember that and make sure one day to teach it to our own children (Behr 1997b: 38).

The gendered construction of ethnic history, a 'man' maintaining his 'memory' in order not to be 'useless', constructs the father's stories as symbolic of reinforcing the strength of the entire ethnic group. By telling Marnus these stories of Tanganyika, Johan is practising paternal narration in order to maintain the power associated with his ethnic identity. Spreading this history to children and requiring them to transmit it to their children demonstrates the perpetuation of the paternal narrative and its use in constructing a cohesive national narrative. This narrative, uncontested, serves to show Marnus that he is entitled to a position of power just like his father.

The ironies of history are easily negotiated within these paternal narratives. Even though the Afrikaner history that Johan shares is one of victimhood and struggling to be free of oppression, paternal narratives are able to navigate the obvious inconsistencies when apartheid serves to oppress other groups. Marnus relays one answer to these ironies:

> Even the Prime Minister, Uncle John Vorster, said something similar in Pretoria the other day when someone asked him about the Coloured question. Uncle John said that the Coloureds will never be able to say that we did to them what the English did to the Afrikaners. The Afrikaners' struggle for self-government, and for freedom from the yoke of British Imperialism, was a noble struggle (Behr 1997b: 38).

There is no logic in this narrative, but it is still powerfully adopted by Marnus here and presumably shared by his father. The narrative and its symbols, namely, religion, ethnicity, race, sport and the various gender disparities, all demonstrate that these narratives are employed for maintaining structures of power. Johan reinforces this, and what he sees as the rightful power of white people, by using Tanzania as a cautionary tale and thus justifying apartheid in South Africa. He explains:

> But now the blacks are trying to do to the Republic exactly what they did to Tanganyika. They're trying to take over everything we built up over the years, just to destroy it as they destroy everything they lay their hands on. Of all the nations in the world, those with black skins across their butts also have the smallest brains (Behr 1997b: 38-9).

## The daughter's counter-narratives

The final important aspect of the paternal narratives present in Behr's novel is how they maintain, and simultaneously are maintained through, gender binaries. Gender is performed in various ways throughout the novel, and gender dynamics clearly construct men, especially fathers, as those with power and women as subordinate. This is undercut by the sister Ilse's rebellion against her parents and the systems of power she encounters, and, indeed, Ilse, just like the two daughters discussed in the previous chapter, is the only one who seems to challenge the paternal narratives and seeks to find a narrative voice of her own. Stobie explains that: 'Like Karla [Ilse's liberal aunt], Ilse goes overseas, although briefly, and here she too gains a wider perspective on the univocal message of her ideological background' (2008: 83). Ilse is able to escape the paternal and national narratives in order to assert dissidence. Daughters seem to be given more licence in these South African texts to challenge patriarchy as sons are expected to be perpetuators of paternal narratives and power structures. This is accomplished in the novel by linking Marnus to his father and distancing him from his mother, as McMurtry notes: 'Marnus'[s] passage into social maturity begins with the severance of the mother-bond, for renunciation of the feminine and affirmation of the masculine difference are central to patriarchal power' (1998: 101). This is demonstrated through Marnus's resistance to any signs of femininity or traits that fall outside of the heterosexist ideal. While these trends are powerfully challenged in later texts, especially those discussed in Chapter 5, they are already beginning to unravel in texts such as *The Quiet Violence of Dreams* and *Ways of Dying*, where sons challenge the power of their fathers. However, *The Smell of Apples*, set during apartheid and detailing a conservative family, uses the familiar trope of the daughter challenging the father's power.

Leonore's sister, Karla, is shown to be liberal and has left South Africa to work in London. Ilse is influenced by Karla in many ways, and it is implied that Ilse has adopted liberal politics and has been excommunicated by her father at the end of the novel. Leonore has given up her successful career as a singer in order to be a housewife, and Karla writes a letter to challenge her by stating that Johan is controlling her. Leonore refuses to read the letter, but Ilse and Marnus read it secretly in the bathroom. In the letter Karla writes:

> Why are you afraid of hearing me explain *why* I say Johan is the master of your life? Why do you refuse to listen to *why* I say he has stolen your life from you? Leonore, don't you see – it is not *your* marriage that I want to criticize – it's *every* marriage where the potential of a woman is lost because it is the man's imagined *right* to be the leader (Behr 1997b: 111).

This letter demonstrates the gender dynamics of the novel, which are necessary for paternal narratives to be successful and for patriarchy and its ideological offshoots to be perpetuated. In order for the conservative apartheid ideologies to be reproduced, women have to be held in positions of subordination within marriages. By challenging this, Karla loses her relationship with her sister. Medalie notes that Leonore, 'a singleminded ideologue who defers to her husband in almost every respect, seems nonetheless to make available a space for small disobediences, tiny cracks in the ideological carapace, as, for instance, when she shows herself capable of appreciating a slightly wider cultural ambit and introduces the children to jazz' (2000: 52). These moments indicate that there is always potential for the paternal narrative and patriarchal power to be resisted, which is shown through the female characters in the novel, but Medalie claims that 'nothing ever comes of these small and discreet rebellions: the mother never steps out of the narrow confines of her beliefs, and when Marnus's sister Ilse begins to show signs of a more enlightened political consciousness . . . she suppresses this very firmly'.

Ilse is shown throughout the novel to be facing great tension, and it is often implied that this tension arises from the injustices in South Africa. Ilse struggles to understand how people can be so violent when it is discovered that white men burned Doreen's son for trying to steal from them. She questions the simplistic narratives of her parents when they tell the general that bobotie is traditional Afrikaner food. She is also angry at her mother for breaking off ties with her aunt Karla, to whom she was close. All of these aspects construct her as a character who challenges the paternal narratives that most other characters easily adopt.

At the end of the novel, in a letter that Leonore writes to Marnus when he is at war, there is the intimation that Ilse has betrayed the father in some way, and that they have cut off ties as well: 'Ilse visited for a week last month while Dad was away' (Behr 1997b: 134). Ilse challenges the patriarchal gender dynamics that underscore paternal narratives, and thus her relationship with the father becomes strained.

The role of women in racial narratives is also highlighted in Marnus's reflection on the rape of white women. He says: 'In one week two white women were raped by Coloureds at Salt River Station. It's the most dreadful of dreadful disgraces if a woman gets raped' (Behr 1997b: 45). The target of this disgrace is not clarified here, and it could be seen as a disgrace for the woman herself, for the man who raped her, or, in light of the racial politics of the novel, a disgrace for white people to have women violated by Coloured people. This reflection is also ironic since sexual assault is at the heart of the story, but in this case it is the assault of a male child by the highly respected white father, and thus the disgrace does not seem to be as apparent for Marnus. The reflection rather seems to imply the danger posed by Coloured people in threatening vulnerable white women. The attachment of shame to this moment, as well as Marnus's inclusion of the aspect of race, highlights the underlying ideological argument for racial separation, which informs the world view of the characters in the novel.

These gender dynamics have rigid requirements for men as well, and they need to perform their masculinity in various ways. One such incident occurs when Marnus is scolded by his father for not being able to reel in a shark. Men are required to exhibit power and stoicism. Marnus explains a single moment when he saw his father's veneer of masculine power crack when he cries at his mother's funeral. Marnus says: 'That was the first time I saw Dad cry. At Ouma's funeral Sanna Koerant said men always cry when their mothers die, but only the men themselves know why. The mothers aren't there to see their tears anyway' (Behr 1997b: 25). There is an implied closeness between men and their mothers, which allows for this expression of vulnerability, but the implication remains that men generally perform their masculinity by not showing this form of emotion.

### Performing masculinity through violence

In the final few sections detailing Marnus at war, he demonstrates another aspect of masculine performance in the form of violence. He asks a black soldier why he is fighting in the border war, essentially serving the apartheid system and the colonial propaganda underpinning the war:

> I stopped myself from asking why he is fighting against his own freedom. I waited for his answer, I waited to hear him say that theirs is a form of economic conscription, that he was here only because he was unable to find a decent job on account of the system. Eventually he shrugged and answered: 'To make war, Captain. We are not like the Cubans who take women to fight. It's men that must make war' (Behr 1997b: 119–20).

War and violence are forms of masculine performance, and for this black soldier this serves as enough justification for him to fight in the war that essentially serves his own oppression.

By fighting in the war, Marnus has become the embodiment of these ideologies. The novel seems to suggest, as Medalie states, that 'boyhood turns out to have been a preparation for war' (2000: 49). Barnard explains that Marnus's death represents the fact that he is never able to escape from his father's influence: 'Closed off, as it were, by that weighty patriarchal hand, the novel conveys a kind of moral airlessness that may be new in South African writing' (2000: 208). He has maintained the legacy of his father, clearly never sharing the fact that his father has raped his friend. There are slight signs of conflict within Marnus in these reflections on war, such as how he examines his penis in an almost disparaging way and how he questions the black soldier, but these do not clearly make him question or deny the paternal narratives that he operates under. Medalie notes that the novel ends in a way that indicates Marnus's dissatisfaction with his position, explaining: 'Behr's Marnus Erasmus, whether he survives physically or not, has no legacy other than of disenchantment, of the corrosion of belief and value, to leave behind. He is indeed like an erstwhile believer fallen into disbelief, into sour apostasy' (2000: 49). Marnus reflects on his link to history and how his death is the only way he is able to escape his position in society: 'Death brings its own freedom, and it is for the living that the dead should mourn, for in life there is no escape from history' (Behr 1997b: 198). Marnus's final words hint that he had been living with friction caused by 'history', which in death he is finally able to escape. Medalie explains that this moment 'implies an unmitigated existential despair whereby life itself becomes something to mourn, a nihilism of such depths that it seems impossible to recover from it' (2000: 49).

One of the sections in the text links to the title of the novel and how this impacts on the paternal narratives. The smell of apples is shown to be pleasant and comforting when Marnus is driving home with his father from his uncle's farm, when they are transporting crates of apples given to them by Uncle Samuel. Johan shares with Marnus a sense of ownership of South Africa linked to their position as white people. As they look over False Bay from the top of Sir Lowry's Pass, Johan reminisces about how Uncle Samuel and his family left Tanzania for South Africa, and Marnus reflects: 'When Dad and I stood up there, watching the red sky, Dad said that that was why we can never go back. The blacks drove the whites away and all we have left is here, Dad said, sweeping through the air with his arm' (Behr 1997b: 124). There is a sense of closeness that Johan and Marnus share in this moment, with each other and with South Africa. Johan continues by explaining: 'And this country was empty before our people arrived. *Everything, everything* you see, *we* built up from nothing. This is our place, given to us by God and we will look after it. Whatever the cost.' The narrative of religion is again employed by referring to God to reinforce the assumed legitimacy and even righteousness of this position of power. As it gets dark and they re-enter the car, the smell of the apples becomes an important symbol of this colonial myth: '"Dad, do you smell the apples?" I asked in the dark. "Ja, Marnus," Dad answered as he turned the Volvo back on to the road. "Even the apples we brought to the country."' The apples become a symbol of South Africa being the Afrikaner home in the narrative that Johan constructs. Heyns explains that 'the eponymic apples are obviously the apples before the fall' (2000: 51), referencing the biblical fruit that led to the expulsion of the first humans from Eden. The apples thus symbolise the loss of innocence for Marnus as he is indoctrinated into his father's narratives, but also indicate the approaching undoing of apartheid.

However, the harmony evoked by this reference to the smell of apples is undercut by Frikkie on the day after he is raped, taking an apple from a bowl in Marnus's house and saying that it smells sour. In fact, his hand has a strong odour from the sexual acts that he was forced to perform with Marnus's father. The apples, symbols of Afrikaner dominance and the unrelenting belief in the paternal narrative, are undercut by the sins of the father and the stories that are untold in this ideal narrative, stories of violence and oppression, which, for Marnus, are shown through the rape of his friend. Barnard explains that the rape symbolises 'generational violence perpetrated against apartheid's ostensible beneficiaries' (2000: 208). Heyns notes that Marnus's reaction to Frikkie and his father, attempting to ignore the rape that he has become aware of, 'dramatizes the process by which a young boy is co-opted into the system to the extent that he eventually tacitly condones his father's rape of his little friend' (2000: 53-4). Medalie adds to this by noting: 'In *The Smell of Apples*, patriarchy is abusive, corrupt, but seemingly invincible in that it never seems to lose its power, even when its corruption is exposed' (2000: 58). The smell of these apples is sweet and pleasant, but also sour and ominous when linked with the abuse of Frikkie and the underlying horrors that apartheid ideology created and obscured.

## Zakes Mda's *Ways of Dying*
### Mourning after the fall of apartheid

Zakes Mda's *Ways of Dying*, published in 1995 and set during the end of apartheid and the early transition period in South Africa, presents a conflicted father-son narrative with the son struggling to break free from the oppressive power of his father. The son, Toloki, is focalised in the narrative, leaving his rural home to work in the city after being beaten by his father Jwara. In the city, Toloki works as a professional mourner, travelling to funerals and accepting money in order to mourn for the deceased. This role as professional mourner is particularly striking during the transition period, as it signals not only a moment of confronting the violence and deaths of the past, but also the violent struggle still ongoing during the transition. As Durrant notes in his reading of the novel, mourning rites are important sites of negotiating the meaning and cohesion of communities, but in the case of the extreme violence that led up to and continued during the transition, the meaning of these rites and how they were enacted became destabilised, allowing the space for Toloki's role as a 'professional mourner':

> What anthropologists term mortuary rites usually relate to so called 'good' deaths, where the death can be anticipated, preparations made and relatives gathered round. It is under the pressure of dealing with what anthropologists call 'bad' deaths, those which happen outside the home, in unexpected or unknown circumstances, that mourning rites undergo their most radical reinventions (2005: 442).

The process of mourning is affected by the political shifts in the country, where political killings or 'bad' deaths were often shrouded in secrecy during apartheid. Mark Sanders adds that through withholding information about deaths and the bodies of those who have died, apartheid was guilty of 'a systematic prohibition on mourning and a withholding of condolences' (2002: 72), but the TRC ostensibly could shift this by unearthing silences. Mda's novel confronts the process of mourning within this changing political climate where death was no longer something abstract and political, but could be recognised more as a personal tragedy.

The city is represented mostly through the squalor of the townships, and the rural village is shown to be a place of economic exploitation and deprivation, even as the text seems to be representing a historical moment of transition. This indicates how, according to Melissa Tandiwe Myambo, the ideology of the 'rainbow nation' became abstract to the material concerns of poverty and the racial and economic divisions spatially in South Africa:

> Was the multiculturalism advocated by Archbishop Desmond Tutu to end the endemic epistemological and literal racial violence of the apartheid system ever anything other than a nation conceived as ultimate abstraction? Yet, coming from a historical context in which most of the country was/is literally owned by whites, is a feeling of metaphorical ownership of

> the abstract Rainbow Nation enough for the disenfranchised masses crammed together in overcrowded townships and unsanitary 'squatter camps'? (2010: 95)

Mda's text confronts the great material concerns of a transitioning country by representing the '(formerly illegal) rural-urban migration and life in the "squatter camps," those "unofficial" shanty towns that sprang up in the 1990s alongside "official" townships as apartheid power waned' (Myambo 2010: 100). Grant Farred explains that the novel is 'set in an era that appears to belong in equal measure to the past, present, and future . . . It captures the entangled and uncertain tenor of an historic(al) era – a moment in which these different epochs are difficult to distinguish, complexly bound up in each other' (2000: 184). The transition era, the liminal moment at the dawn of a 'new country', presents the possibility for reinvention, such as the two protagonists, Toloki and Noria, undertake in the novel.

Early in the novel Toloki mourns at the funeral of a young boy, Vutha, the son of Noria, who also came to the city from Toloki's village. Noria was very close to Toloki's father, acting as Jwara's muse and inspiring him to create beautiful figurines whenever she sang to him. Later, Noria also becomes Toloki's muse and they begin to form a close relationship, demonstrating how the son echoes the narrative of the father, albeit in complex new ways. Toloki's confrontation with the memory of his oppressive and abusive father is paralleled with the reality of a young nation finding an identity after the 'paternal' influence of the apartheid government and liberation leaders is no longer given authority. Essentially, sons and daughters are rendered 'fatherless', and need to discover identities separate from the father figures of the past: 'In order for the postapartheid future to be manifestly different, the novel suggests, it has to distance itself from the political atrocities and the (anti-apartheid) radicalism of the past' (Farred 2000: 184). Barnard explains that the novel 'is "post-anti-apartheid" not only with respect to its thematic preoccupations, but with respect to its form: a multilayered, fantastical plot, which decisively breaches the generic constraints that the culture of resistance, with its demand for realist immediacy, had for years placed on the black writer' (2004: 280).

Similarly, by resisting the material realism espoused during apartheid, the novel is able to find new forms of representing South African realities, and *Ways of Dying* has frequently been understood as forming part of the magical realist mode.[1] Marita Wenzel explains the role of magical realism in South Africa's transition narratives:

> [Magical realism] illustrates the essential duality of existence by illustrating the possibility of different interpretations of reality and contests the simplistic, orderly interpretation foisted on the reader by historical documentation. As subversive strategy, magical realism reflects the postcolonial identity crisis resulting from an oppressive colonial past and captures the reality of a postcolonial and multicultural society within the South African context; a position that Toloki occupies in *Ways of Dying* (2003: 325).

The subversive nature of Toloki's character is highlighted through his role as a professional mourner during the transition from apartheid. Myambo explains that Toloki's occupation can be seen as ironic within the discourse of the rainbow nation as 'the reader is led through the many ways of dying in these difficult days of senseless violence. At the moment of the Rainbow Nation's birth, it seems odd that Toloki is not a Professional Celebrator; instead he "was a Professional Mourner who mourned for the nation"' (2010: 103). The implication here is that the nation has suffered a death worthy of mourning rather than facing a simplistic rebirth. The beginning of a democratic South Africa is thus represented as a sombre, challenging time, where the nation has died as many father figures do in the text; however, this creates the space for Toloki to negotiate his own identity and to become politically engaged.

---

1. Mda explains that his use of 'magical realism' is a product of his cultural background, and he seems uncomfortable with the label as it signals a distinction between the magical and the real: 'I wrote in this manner from an early age because I am a product of a magical culture. In my culture the magical is not disconcerting. It is taken for granted. No one tries to find a natural explanation for the unreal. The unreal happens as part of reality' (Mda 1997: 281).

### The father's creative dominance

Through long sections in the text detailing his memories of his home village, Toloki refers to his strained relationship with his dominant, cold father, and how he managed to build a life that he is proud of, away from his father's cruelty. However, there is irony in this simplistic ideal of reaching a better life after he escapes the paternal influence, since he still lives in poverty and is not respected by others in the township. Only by replicating the creativity of his father, and relying on his father's creative power when he sells the figurines that his father made, is there any hope for Toloki to overcome his hardships. The novel seems to present a conflicted representation of the paternal influence, being something oppressive and harmful but also something that could be redemptive and useful for the son. Through the novel's linking of fathers to the role of political father figures, the implication seems to be that forms of creativity and political resistance also need to be refigured and adapted to the new political landscape in South Africa.

The first description of Jwara presents him as a powerful and creative force:

> His father, a towering handsome giant in gumboots and aging blue overalls, was a blacksmith, and his bellows and the sounds of beating iron filled the air with monotonous rhythms through the day. Jwara, for that was his father's name, earned his bread by shoeing horses. But on some days . . . he created figurines of iron and brass. On those days he got that stuck-up bitch, Noria, to sing while he shaped the red-hot iron and brass into images of strange people and animals that he had seen in his dreams (Mda 1995: 23).

Jwara is inspired by Noria's song and is able to create because of it. Noria is described as a 'stuck-up bitch' initially because of her influence over Jwara, inspiring him to spend his time creating his figurines and thus neglecting his paternal duties: 'The earliest reference to Noria as a stuck-up bitch was first heard some years back when Toloki's mother was shouting at Jwara, her angry eyes green with jealousy, "You spend all your time with that stuck-up bitch, Noria, and you do not care for your family!'" (Mda 1995: 24). Jwara is obsessed with the figurines and seems to become possessed when Noria sings for him.

The creative impulse is so overpowering for Jwara that he and Noria spend days on end with Noria singing and Jwara creating his figurines. They become so distracted by this work that they do not eat or sleep during this time. There is a spiritual dimension given to these encounters that seems to entail something beyond either of their control:

> Xesibe, Noria's father, came to the workshop, stood pitifully at the door, and pleaded with Jwara, 'Please, Jwara, release our child. She has to eat and sleep.' But Jwara did not respond. Nor did Noria. It was as though they were possessed by the powerful spirits that made them create the figurines (Mda 1995: 24).

Toloki's own creative power is shown early in the novel. He wins an art competition as a child and wants to share this news with his father:

> After school, filled with excitement, he ran home with his new books, and went straight to his father's workshop. 'Father, I have won a national art competition. I got all these books.' 'Good.' Jwara did not look at Toloki, nor at the books. There were no horses to shoe, no figurines to shape. He was just sitting there, staring at hundreds of figurines lined up on the shelves where they were fated to remain for the rest of everybody's lives. And he did not even look at his son (Mda 1995: 27).

This section shows a strong fissure between father and son, and also reveals the creativity of both father and son as being meaningless. Neither Toloki nor Jwara's work is acknowledged; Toloki tries to gain his father's interest and respect through his accomplishment, but Jwara is not interested. Jwara also realises that his figurines would amount to nothing, fated to remain on a shelf in his workshop. Farred argues that a contrast can be seen in the types of creativity that Toloki and Jwara engage in: 'Toloki's greater sensitivity, as opposed to that of his neglectful father, is displayed through the medium of his art. While the hard, unfeeling Jwara worked in iron and brass, the always malleable son prefers the softer, childlike crayons' (2000: 190). While the creative pursuits demonstrate a relative sense of power for father and son, and their ability to assert masculinist power over others, Toloki's greater sensitivity allows him to later become a nurturing father figure to the township children and encourage their creativity, unlike Jwara who ignores and tries to quash Toloki's creative power.

In a later discussion with Noria, she reminds Toloki about winning the art competition and he remembers that his picture would appear in a calendar, indicating that Toloki would have had much greater influence with his art than his father ever could. He remembers being proud of this as a child, still trying to use his accomplishments in the creative realm to impress his father:

> Even though Jwara had not shown any appreciation of the books that his son had won as a prize, Toloki hoped that he would be happy about the calendar. After all, it was going to grace the walls of homes and offices throughout the land. In April, everyone would know who Toloki was, for his name was printed just below the picture . . . (Mda 1995: 60).

Toloki gains a sense of self from his creativity, and is proud of what he has done. However, Jwara does not react with pride as Toloki had hoped, demonstrating the conflict at the heart of many father-son narratives as a struggle for more narrative power:

> When he got home he ran excitedly to the workshop, and found his father brooding over his figurines. 'So, now you think you are better? You think you are a great creator like me?' 'I want to be like you, father. I want to create from dreams like you.' 'Don't you see, you poor boy, that you are too ugly for that? How can beautiful things come from you?' (Mda 1995: 60-1)

Jwara quashes Toloki's confidence by insulting him and insisting that he is unable to create at the same level. He introduces the idea that their creative expression is a form of competition, referring to himself as a 'great creator' and challenging Toloki for supposedly thinking that he is 'better' than Jwara. Creative power is a form of narrative power in the text, reinforcing the 'greatness' and 'beauty' of the creator, and Jwara attacks Toloki's sense of self by saying that he cannot create beautiful things. Toloki abandons his own creativity and submits to the dominance of the father here. He does not draw again for many years, until he is able to find a sense of self and gain some narrative power in his life by becoming a professional mourner and leaving the oppressive influence of his father: 'From that day, Toloki gave up trying to impress his father. And he gave up drawing pictures. He even – tearfully and with great bitterness that gnawed at him for a long time afterwards – destroyed his precious calendar' (Mda 1995: 61).

Farred explains that Toloki's creativity might be a reference to creative individuals, or indeed the author, in post-apartheid South Africa where texts are no longer required to be in service of political change, and Toloki, like the post-apartheid writer, needs to discover creativity anew; he can be seen as a

> creative individual who transcends context and political strife even as he or she is surrounded by the tumultuous workings of history. *Ways of Dying*'s artist represents Mda's attempts to carve out a new space for black writers in postapartheid South Africa, a mode liberated from the incessant political demands placed upon disenfranchised authors in the anti-apartheid struggle (Farred 2000: 187).

Breaking free from his father's control is Toloki's attempt to abandon the stifling authority that rejected his creativity, and symbolically it is related to Mda abandoning the politically motivated creativity that characterised apartheid-era authors and finding a voice that reflects the changing country.

Jwara's dominance is also linked to gender when he asserts his position of power over his wife. She tries to argue with him to allow Toloki to attend a funeral of a schoolmate, but Jwara insists: 'You know I don't argue with women, Mother of Toloki. If you want to be the man of the house, take these pants and wear them. Can't you see that this child of yours is so stupid that he will get lost in the city?'

(Mda 1995: 36). Instead of allowing Toloki to attend the funeral, Jwara buys Noria sweets for her trip, and as justification for this he says that she is not ugly or stupid like Toloki. Noria is not a threat to Jwara's dominance, and she does not try to create for herself, instead merely supports his creativity. For this reason, he favours her and is closer to her than his own son, highlighting the gendered nature of the struggle for narrative power.

Toloki later admits to Noria why he left home, saying: 'I fought with my father' (Mda 1995: 51). Noria questions him: 'Fought? Actually fought with Jwara? No, Toloki explains, his father beat him up, so he ran away and vowed never to return while his father was alive. He did not have any money. He walked all the way from the village to the city.' Physical violence, one of the most common masculinist and patriarchal symbols explored in this book, becomes the factor that severs the son's ties to his father and his village. Finding Noria again offers Toloki a chance to renegotiate his link to his father and thus his link to his past, as well as giving him the possibility to rediscover his creative power. In addition, it gives Toloki the opportunity to engage with political realities that Noria is concerned with, and he can use his creativity to become a father figure himself to the dispossessed children of the township. As Farred explains: 'These two protagonists, the father [Jwara] and the sister/lover [Noria], are closely connected in Toloki's psyche; they both belong, in different ways and measures, to Toloki's past and his future' (2000: 189).

### The destruction of the father figure

Toloki traces his journey from his rural village to the city, exploring the factors that lead him to discover himself and to become a professional mourner. When he first leaves his village, he works at a mill, and meets a father and son who work there as well. The relationship he witnesses between this man and his father is surprising to Toloki, immediately striking a contrast with his relationship with Jwara, and indicating the potential for loving father-son relationships. Toloki notes: 'These companions were like family to him. He envied the cosy relationship that his new friend enjoyed with his father, and wanted to be a part of it. They were indeed more like mates, and shared everything. Theirs was the closeness of saliva to the tongue' (Mda 1995: 56). He gravitates towards these two men who share such a father-son bond. This idealised state is however short-lived; Toloki leaves the mill when the young man is burned to death by a white man who claims that the killing was part of a game, and this encounter frames the racial and political injustices that become the focus of the rest of the novel. This idyllic father-son relationship is destroyed because of forces of racial inequality. The white man is not prosecuted and others also defend him by saying that this is part of a game. This man is given narrative power through constructing the murder as part of a game as well as through practising the masculinist symbol of violence. The death of Toloki's friend and the destruction of the only close father-son relationship in the novel could be seen as a part of what inspires Toloki to become a professional mourner. As Yogita Goyal suggests, the fact that the death of this man, similar to the death of Vutha, is erased and not mourned due to it being a 'game' or framed politically means that these deaths are haunting and unsettling, without any closure in the text. Goyal says: 'Violent deaths, Mda suggests, continue to haunt people till they have been properly mourned . . . How does one continue to live with the memory of atrocities committed, either by oneself or by others?' (2011: 149). Toloki struggles to reconcile the harsh realities of South Africa and notices the injustices inherent in the systems of inequality. He mourns not only the deaths but also what they symbolise, severing familial relationships and destroying the loving bonds between father and son. The novel suggests that such bonds are not possible or sustainable in the version of apartheid and transitional South Africa constructed in the novel, and all of the father-son relationships are destroyed by violence or death: Napu neglects the first Vutha and he dies, Toloki is unable to reconcile his relationship with his father who is violent with him, and the one loving depiction of a father-son bond, between the men at the mill, is shown to be destroyed by racist violence.

Toloki goes to the city and starts a business selling food. When this business fails, he turns to another father figure, Jwara's friend Nefolovhodwe, who came from his village but had since become extremely successful selling coffins in the city. Barnard explains that 'insofar as he makes a living out of death . . . Nefolovhodwe is Toloki's counterpart or alter ego. But while Toloki remains identified with the netherworld of the ragged and ugly people, Nefolovhodwe tries to elevate himself' (2004: 287). Nefolovhodwe pretends not to know Toloki, but due to his persistence in asking for a job Nefolovhodwe hires him to watch over graves and see if the coffins that he sells are being dug up to be resold. Toloki notes that Nefolovhodwe has changed since he left the village. After Nefolovhodwe scolds him and echoes Jwara's words by saying that Toloki is ugly and stupid, Toloki reflects: 'Toloki was beginning to hate this new Nefolovhodwe. In many ways he reminded him of his father, Jwara' (Mda 1995: 122). Nefolovhodwe becomes a new oppressive father figure to Toloki, using the masculine symbol of money to enact his power over Toloki. He reflects again about how Nefolovhodwe refused to acknowledge him: 'How was Toloki to know that homeboys who did well in the city developed amnesia?' (124). Barnard suggests: 'The dangerous failings of the rising black bourgeoisie are most obviously satirized in the caricaturish Nefolovhodwe, with his ballooning figure, his fleet of cars, and his bevy of girlfriends' (2004: 295). Thus, the power that Nefolovhodwe wields is still shown to be oppressive towards son figures, even though he has managed to overcome the barriers of the apartheid system and become rich.

The job of watching for grave robbers proves fruitless, and Toloki is left destitute in the city when he is fired from his job. He eventually manages to secure a costume and becomes a professional mourner, living on the streets and taking donations whenever he mourns at a funeral. When he meets Noria again he feels ambivalent towards her since she symbolises a connection with his past. However, they have both become distanced from Jwara as the father figure as well as from all of the other father figures in the novel, giving both characters the opportunity to renegotiate their identities in the township.

Noria's story since leaving the village has been one of tragedy, and she is often linked to the familiar feminine narrative constructs represented in many other South African novels, namely, her body and sexual desirability, maternal narratives of closeness with her son as well as her relative powerlessness in relation to men. She is blamed for the death of Jwara when she leaves the village, since he no longer has his muse, and once his creative power fades he eventually dies:

> Jwara's obsession could not be quenched, so he sunk deeper and deeper into depression. He could not create without Noria. Yet his dreams did not give him any respite. The strange creatures continued to visit him in his sleep, and to demand that they be recreated the next day in the form of figurines (Mda 1995: 93).

Noria's absence is also the reason for Jwara attacking Toloki, which eventually leads to Toloki leaving the village. Noria does not come to sing for Jwara one day and he is enraged. On the same day he hears about an incident when Toloki was drunk and collapsed at a church service, and this leads to him beating Toloki.

> Throughout his long journey of many months he harboured a deep bitterness against his father. And a hatred for Noria. It was all her fault. The quarrel was not because he had disgraced his family. Jwara didn't even know what it was exactly that his son had done in church. He couldn't care less for the church. The source of all the trouble was Noria (Mda 1995: 96).

Toloki blames Noria for the tension between his father and him since she no longer provided a calming influence and inspiration to Jwara. Eventually, when Noria leaves the village to marry Napu, the father of Vutha, Jwara refuses to leave his workshop and no longer eats. He is later found dead in his workshop. By losing the supportive influence that allowed him creative power, he is unable to continue living.

Farred explains that, for Toloki, finding Noria again leads to the construction of 'a complicated oedipal scenario in which the son wants to gain the approval of the woman who was, as a young girl, his father's artistic inspiration' (2000: 190-1). Farred also notes how Toloki's attraction to Noria is interwoven with his negotiation of his identity as well as with his past: 'Having overcome the debilitations of his relationship with Jwara (rather than the metaphoric slaying of the father), Toloki recognizes that he can only win Noria's assent by being emotionally different from his father, but artistically similar – in terms of talent, and not temperament, that is' (191). This dynamic allows for their relationship, and the creative lifeblood that Noria represents, to become a way for Toloki to confront the memory of his father and to lay his resentments to rest.

Noria's experiences once she leaves with Napu sees her discovering the failings of fatherhood emblematic of post-apartheid literature. Napu is also a disempowered father in the novel, struggling to financially support his family and unable to pay lobola. This is seen as a great source of shame by Xesibe, Noria's father. She considers getting a job, but Napu refuses to allow her to work and suggests that working might lead her to be unfaithful to him. In this way he seems to be controlling her body and her actions, exercising his narrative power over her.

Napu later becomes domineering and drinks heavily. He stops working and does not provide for Noria and her son, and is unfaithful to her. Napu's failure as a provider and his inability to live up to the masculine expectations of paying lobola or caring for his family cast him as a figure who loses his power due to the economic hardships he faces. When Noria leaves Napu and returns to the village, she begins to work as a sex worker in order to support herself and her son. Throughout the novel there are references to Noria's sexual desirability. She recognises that she has a form of power in giving pleasure to others, with the intimation of this being sexual pleasure: 'She knew that her influence came from her ability to give others pleasure. She could give or withhold pleasure at will, and this made her very powerful' (Mda 1995: 65). Brenda Cooper explains that 'Noria represents many of the stereotypes of gender depictions, such as woman as goddess or as virgin and whore combined; she moves from pleasuring men to an immaculate conception and reincarnation of her son, only to have him die again in the relentless cycle of political violence' (1996: 229). Noria could thus be seen as representing a wide range of stereotypical roles afforded to women, and her political activism later is a sign that she seeks to overcome these stereotypical roles and attempts to finally assert her power, demonstrating how the novel confronts traditional power relations.

Napu later kidnaps Vutha while Noria is at work, and she never sees him again. Napu takes Vutha to the city but does not have money to care for him, and uses Vutha to help him beg during the day so that he can spend the money on drinking at night while chaining Vutha to a pole under a bridge where they live. He goes on a long drinking binge and leaves Vutha chained to the pole for many days, and when he returns Vutha is dead and his corpse is being eaten by dogs.

Napu is questioned by some people at the shebeen about where he has left his son, and he responds that he has forgotten where Vutha is. Napu demonstrates the distance of paternal figures in the novel when he responds: 'I don't have time for children. His mother will take care of him' (Mda 1995: 129). Even though Napu has taken Vutha away from his mother, he dismisses his responsibility in caring for his child. When Napu returns to the bridge to find that Vutha is dead he ironically exclaims that someone has killed his son and begins to run aimlessly:

> He ran for many miles, without even stopping to catch his breath. He did not know where he was going. He kept on repeating that they had killed his son, and he was going to chase them until he caught them. He was going to kill them and feed them to the dogs as they had done to his son. He had taken his son away, he howled, to get even with cruel Noria. But she and her wicked mother had now murdered the poor boy. People gave way hastily as he approached. He ran until he reached the big storage dam that was part of the sewerage works of the city. He dived into the dam, and drowned (Mda 1995: 129).

Napu represents the cruel, distant and dangerous father in a similar way that Jwara does. Fathers and father figures in the novel are shown to be uncaring towards their children, especially sons. The death of Vutha in his first incarnation is an indication of the failure and refusal of fathers to care for their sons, and the psychic distance that exists between them.

## *Maternal narratives*
When Toloki meets Noria again, she is burying her second child, also named Vutha and it is implied that he is the same child reincarnated. Toloki asks who the father of this child is: 'She smiles and says the child had no father' (Mda 1995: 139). There is a similar allusion

to figures visiting her in dreams as with Jwara, again showing a connection between them, and she uses this to explain the conception of the second Vutha:

> She explains that she had not slept with any man, except for the strangers that visited her in her dreams, and made love to her. Some of these dream figures began their existence on top of her as strangers, but by the time they reached their fourth ejaculation, they looked and acted like a youthful Napu (Mda 1995: 140).

This spectral younger Napu is taken as the father of the child, and Noria tries to recreate the family that had been destroyed: 'When the child was born, he looked exactly like the original Vutha. He even had the same birth marks. Noria decided to name him Vutha' (Mda 1995: 140). By reproducing the family in an idealised version, redeeming Napu and reincarnating Vutha, Noria demonstrates the power of maternal narratives of imagination. Whereas the traditional familial power structure relied on the father's presence, here Noria simply claims that a dream of Napu acted as the father. By eliminating the physical father in this reimagining of her family, Noria is able to reproduce the son she had lost to the cruelty of his father. She sees this second child as Vutha returned to her: 'So, homeboys and homegirls called him Vutha The Second, or just The Second, so as not to confuse him with his dead brother. But to Noria, he was the original Vutha who had come back to his mother.'

Noria's closeness to children is shown in the fact that she is pregnant with both her sons for fifteen months. She has a corporeal closeness to both of her sons, whom she imagines as the same person, and she also shows a deep spiritual connection to them. She is able to have this connection despite the evils of the father figure, and eliminates him altogether in the conception and raising of the second Vutha. Noria does not take another partner, and rebuffs the advances of men who are attracted to her, such as the taxi driver Shadrack. She finally asserts her power to narrate her life without the influence of men like Jwara, the men she had sex with for money, or Napu. When she reconnects with Toloki, it seems to be a relationship of mutual respect and shared creativity, and, importantly, a platonic relationship without the implied subordination of women present in the many romantic relationships in the novel. Toloki respects her narratives and she respects his career as a professional mourner.

Noria's closeness to children is maintained after the death of her second Vutha. This time, Vutha is killed because of political tensions in the township, as he is seen as a traitor by talking to workers in the local hostels, who are thwarting the political plans of the resistance movement and attacking those living in the township. She works with abandoned children in what is called the dumping ground. She has also become active in the political organisation in the township.

Toloki notices the gender disparity within this organisation: 'Toloki wonders further why it is that the people who do all the work at the settlement are women, yet all the national and regional leaders he saw at the meeting were men' (Mda 1995: 165). Farred also comments in reference to the political organisation's efforts to silence Noria about Vutha's death that it 'shows how resilient patriarchal authority is: Noria is compelled to hold her tongue because the men in power decree it' (2000: 199). Noria responds to Toloki by explaining that many women are moving past their traditional roles as mothers and are gaining identities of their own: 'Yes, when we were growing up, women had no names. They were called Mother of Toloki or Mother of Noria. But here women are leaders of the people' (Mda 1995: 165). By taking a role as a political activist and recognising the power of women to shape their worlds, she is confronting the traditional paternalistic power structures. Noria is resisting the paternal narrative by resisting the invisibility associated with her gender and by confronting father figures like Napu and her own father. Margaret Mervis notes: 'Just as Noria has evolved into a proud individual who values her independence, life is changing for all the women in the transitional period in South Africa as they move from the old deference towards a new authority' (1998: 54).

Toloki becomes more conscious of the political realities because of his relationship with Noria. They challenge the paternal narratives and symbols of paternalistic power structures, which they see as limiting and harmful, such as race, ethnic divisions, money, violence and gender expectations. Importantly, Cooper, in her review of the novel, says that the depictions of violence indicate culpability and skepticism of many different father figures, including the ANC government about to take power as the novel 'suggests that the new leadership about to assume power has elements that are elitist and corrupt, that both the hostel-dwelling migrants and the Young [Tigers] of the movement are twisted by a heritage of violence and power hunger. Even the little children are drawn into battle and forced to take sides' (Cooper 1996: 229). The children are thus manipulated by political father figures, linking to Toloki's role as rejecting not only politics broadly but also rejecting his father.

Toloki further challenges these structures when he takes on a more nurturing role than his own father. Children gather outside of the shack that Toloki and Noria build in the township and sing a mean song about him, and Toloki encourages their creativity in a way that his father never did for him: 'At one stage they sing the song that they composed about Toloki yesterday. Noria angrily tells them that it is naughty of them to sing rude songs about adults. Toloki says, "Let them sing, Noria. Never stifle the creativity of children"' (Mda 1995: 62). Creativity is a symbol of power and individuality in the novel. Toloki allows the narrative power of children to be practised in a way he was never allowed, even if their song frames him negatively. Barnard explains that this scene can be contrasted with the militarisation of children by the Young Tigers and how the young friend of Vutha's is the one instructed to kill him: 'The novel's narrative desire, as these two contrasting scenes suggest, is to transform fighting children into playful ones: to replace a sober militancy with gaiety and laughter' (2004: 280). Toloki becomes the new form of father figure, a mostly apolitical artist, giving children the chance for change.

Toloki and Noria furthermore use imagination and creativity to escape their limited surroundings, employing what resembles a maternal narrative that allows them to feel powerful despite their disempowered positions. They cut out pictures from magazines of beautiful homes and paste them around the tiny shack that they have built, as Noria's previous shack was burned down due to political intimidation. They imagine that they are living in the homes depicted in the pictures. Myambo notes that 'rebuilding is emblematic of the will to rebuild the nation amidst all the turmoil and destruction of apartheid's last gasp during the struggle to the death that characterized transition' (2010: 107). She adds that 'Noria's new shack symbolizes the rebuilding of the new nation'. However, it becomes ironic that Toloki and Noria, like the many people in the township, will likely never move beyond their material deprivation despite their ability to rebuild, and that the pictures are their only means of escape. As Myambo states, 'This shack can only be made inhabitable, as the realistic depiction of its penury, its concrete materiality, becomes transformed into a magical abstraction.' Toloki uses his creativity again as a sign that he has rediscovered a sense of power in his own life, as Wenzel points out: 'Toloki, freed by the boundless realm of the imagination, is able to transcend the barriers and boundaries imposed by apartheid and abject poverty, by creating and "living" his dream of the ideal "home"' (2003: 320). He buys crayons and draws again, just like his father discouraged him from doing when he was a child:

> Toloki remembers the crayons and paper that he bought from the city. He takes them out and starts drawing pictures. He draws flowers, and is surprised to see that his hand has not lost its touch. He draws roses that look like those he bought Noria, the roses that are still very much alive in the bottle that is filled with water inside the shack. He also draws the zinnias that he bought her the other day. 'I was not able to bring you any flowers today, Noria. But you can have these that I have drawn with crayons' (Mda 1995: 186).

Noria acknowledges the power that Toloki is practising by drawing again, telling him: 'I love these even better [than real flowers], Toloki, for they are your own creation' (Mda 1995: 186).

Toloki then mirrors his father by being inspired by Noria: 'Noria jokingly says that maybe she should sing for him, as she used to do for Jwara. After all, Jwara was only able to create through Noria's song. Noria sings her meaningless song of old. All of a sudden, Toloki finds himself drawing pictures of the children playing' (Mda 1995: 187). It is important here that Toloki's drawing is of happy children, as he has become a father figure himself to the children of the community and through his resistance to stifling paternal narratives. Toloki seeks to offer the children freedom and their own creativity, a shared power linked to maternal narratives that Noria represents. By taking on the role of a supportive father figure, Toloki, just like Tshepo in *The Quiet Violence of Dreams*, ushers in a new South Africa by seeking to challenge patriarchal paternal narratives and introduce loving and nurturing maternal narratives. This disruption of gender expectations constructs Toloki as a different form of father figure from the others in the novel, one who is able to acknowledge and encourage the power of children.

Noria still shows an affinity and link to the past, represented by Jwara as the stifling father figure, and makes a comment that suggests that Toloki will have to negotiate his relationship with the past and with his father in order to navigate his sense of self:

> Sometimes [Toloki and Noria] do not see things in the same way. For instance, at one stage Noria says that Jwara was a great man, a great creator who was misunderstood. Toloki chooses not to comment on this. His views on the matter are very different, but why spoil the moment by bringing up contrary opinions about a past that is dead and buried forever? (Mda 1995: 153)

Of course, for the characters and the changing South Africa that they represent, the past is never 'dead and buried forever'. Toloki is left negotiating his sense of self in relation to the oppressive father, who has since died but whose presence and creations are still important.

The past returns to Toloki in the form of another father figure, the character Nefolovhodwe who earlier denied Toloki a decent job. He comes to the township to bring Toloki the figurines that Jwara had created. He says that he had been visited by Jwara in his dreams, and that Jwara cannot rest until the figurines are given to Toloki. There is the suggestion that this might offer some reconciliation between Toloki and Jwara. The past and the present, represented by the spirit of the father and the living son, can be reconciled by finding new use for the old symbols of the father's power. Toloki has to confront the power of his father, shown through his creations, in order to discover his own identity and to truly move forward. Farred explains:

> It is only once Toloki decides to sell his father's art that he comes to a kind of psychological closure with Jwara. The future can then be confronted because the past has been addressed; difficulties have been negotiated, emotional debts have been settled; the past can be laid to rest in the ways that Toloki officiates at funerals (2000: 190).

As representative of a country in healing during this transition period, Toloki needs to reconcile his relationship with his father and with the past before he is able to truly create something new. By selling the figurines, there is finally hope that Toloki and Noria might be able to escape the poverty they are subject to.

This process of being cognisant of the past and creating something new is a part of the project that Mda undertakes in the novel. Durrant maintains that 'the allegorical message could not be clearer: the role of the artist, in an era in which "our ways of dying are our ways of living" and vice-versa, is precisely that of the professional mourner' (2005: 443). Toloki allows for the process of mourning to be removed from political concerns, highlighting the loss that apartheid and the struggle against it have wrought. His own apolitical nature is telling, as he is the artist moving away from his material realist imperative towards art that speaks to personal human grief. The novel is able to imagine the son finding his own voice, now divorced from the political concerns of his symbolic father, but always influenced by history, as Toloki is by the figurines his father created.

## K. Sello Duiker's *The Quiet Violence of Dreams*
### New South African identities

K. Sello Duiker's *The Quiet Violence of Dreams* was published in 2001 at what was to be the end of the TRC process in South Africa. The novel presents the tale of Tshepo, a young, black, gay man struggling to make sense of his identity as he suffers under the oppressive and violent presence of his father and the memories of childhood trauma. The novel also focalises his pregnant friend Mmabatho, meditating on her struggles with her white partner's reluctance to be a father to their unborn child. Shaun Viljoen argues that Duiker's project can be seen as striving towards non-racialism, explaining that Duiker 'desires to live in a world beyond questions of "race" but the racism of the reality constantly intrudes and pushes thinking in the fiction about "race" towards the more radical sense of nonracialism' (2001: 46). Viljoen notes that even though ideas of race are not the central focus of the novel, 'Tshepo and his young female friend Mmabatho constantly interrogate "race" and encounter racism in one form or another' (50). These ideas of race in relation to the ideology of a post-apartheid South Africa will be explored through Tshepo's self-discovery and his narrative power in the novel.

Duiker's novel is often compared with Phaswane Mpe's *Welcome to Our Hillbrow*, another novel dealing with the lives of young black adults in the post-apartheid city. Michael Green notes that these two writers, along with Mda, constitute 'what has now become something of a regular triumvirate forming the kernel of a new canon for the new nation' (2008: 334). The novels are seen as representing black masculinities in dynamic new ways that confront the changing South African landscape. Green observes, rather sardonically:

> The criteria for the post-apartheid canon are clear. In terms of content, no concentration on race and little mention of apartheid – instead, engage with one or more of AIDS, crime, xenophobia, homosexuality, returning exiles, urbanisation, new forms of dispossession, and identity displacement. In terms of style, take as much latitude from the standard realism associated with struggle literature as possible – association with 'magic realism' is acceptable, as long as it is made clear that this is drawn from African tale-telling traditions rather than any particular international influence (2008: 334).

Green points out that 'novels identified as representative post-apartheid works are uniformly written in English. To use any one of the indigenous languages would risk being identified with the years of apartheid-inspired social (and linguistic) engineering aimed at creating stereotypes of racial and ethnic separateness' (2008: 335). Green's analysis identifies how English becomes a medium for counter-colonial literature, even as it echoes the colonial heritage. Within the myth of a 'rainbow nation', English serves as a universalising language. Green elaborates: 'English signals alignment with the avowed nation-building, antitribalist strategy of the new government, and also makes it possible, of course, to gain for the novel something of the international acclaim garnered by the miracle of the new nation.'

Gagiano notes that Duiker's novel recognises that 'the primordialist type of nationalism is responsible for the persistence of patriarchal power in South Africa's "new nation" [and] the modernist (or globalised) kind of nationalism is at work in powerfully persistent class hierarchies' (2004: 815). She adds that Duiker's novel and other fictions published at the time are hopeful signs of shifting representation as they 'depict (particularly black) South Africans as having agency, perhaps most importantly in their storytelling roles as they speak of the ways in which they are beginning to question, reshape or at least re-imagine the local contexts and communities' (816). In other words, young, black South Africans are asserting their narrative power, both as authors and as characters within fiction. Neil ten Kortenaar explains that despite this progressive stance, the novel is not free of problematic gender relations, as it 'expands the repertoire of images available to black men even as it problematically confirms patriarchy and misogyny' (2008: 188).

These concerns reflect conflicts in literary identity formation at the end of the transition period. Whereas ideas of gender, race, language and ethnic identity are confronted and deconstructed, there are remnants of apartheid, patriarchal and colonial ideologies that stunt or complicate this process.

*The Quiet Violence of Dreams* is highly meditative, with the characters spending long passages reasoning through their situations and describing dreams and experiences. This process of maturation can be linked to the time period of political uncertainty, where the confusion of the characters reflects a country still searching for a new identity when the oppressive apartheid regime, represented by Tshepo's oppressive father, is a dying presence but one that is being transcended. Michael Chapman explains that Tshepo's rejection of his father can be seen symbolically as the young South African who 'ditches the Father figures of the struggle years for . . . harrowing adventures' (2003: 3). Chapman sees the novel as indicative of a trend of 'postindependence disillusionment'. Viljoen notes that 'Tshepo's quest is to make sense of the present and the past (Tshepo's narration often contains strings of questions)' (2001: 50). These analyses all highlight the process of individual identity formation within changing national systems.

*Nurturing maternal narratives*
Tshepo's friend, Mmabatho, is expecting a child with her wavering German lover Arne, and she decides to keep and raise her unborn child even if she must do so without Arne's involvement. Mmabatho's pregnancy and Arne's ambivalence towards it are echoed in the concern articulated elsewhere in the novel of the 'danger' of women and how men need to find refuge from them. These dangers are most clearly expressed by Sebastian, one of the men working at Steamy Windows, who tells Tshepo about a brotherhood of men that the sex workers at Steamy Windows are part of: 'The thing about women is that they kept us in fear, because they can reproduce, they can have babies . . . This knowledge alone about what women could do emasculated men. That's why I think the rise of patriarchy, subordination of women and things like genital mutilation have been attempts by men to undermine the uterus' (Duiker 2001: 302). Forms of violence and patriarchy are tied, by Sebastian, to this mythical fear of women's ability to bear children and of men succumbing to this danger and becoming fathers.

Fatherhood thus is constructed as something harrowing and emasculating, which Arne seems to echo through his resistance to becoming a father, saying that he '[does not] want to have babies with [Mmabatho]' (Duiker 2001: 195). For Arne, the danger of becoming a father might be a loss of his agency, as Mmabatho suggests when she says: 'It would have been nicer if he didn't feel obligated to me because I was pregnant, if he wanted to stay for me and no other reason . . . Have I taken him prisoner?' (321). Women are also portrayed as natural mothers, whereas for men it seems much more difficult to assume the role and title of father. Mmabatho recounts about Arne: 'He is kind and loving, a little impatient sometimes but I can train him. He can learn to be a father' (323). Earlier she pre-empts this assessment by placing herself as 'mother' and Arne as 'the provider, the bread winner' (322), seeming wilfully resistant to giving him the title of father. The ease with which Mmabatho accepts the title of 'mother' highlights motherhood's corporeal connection with children and the assumed emotional closeness between mother and child.

However, much later in the novel Mmabatho admits that she 'want[s] [her] child to have a father' (Duiker 2001: 421), but by now the reader notices that Mmabatho's expectations of what fatherhood entails would never allow for Arne to fill that role. Mmabatho seems to expect from Arne the same devotion that her own father demonstrates towards her, and she reacts angrily when he does not commit to their child in the same way that she does. Indeed, Mmabatho's descriptions of her father offer a rare example of a loving father in the novel, possibly indicating the different experience between a father and a daughter. It is unthinkable within the framework of the novel to hear a son speak of his father the way Mmabatho does of her father: 'I cry as though I'm grieving, gentle sobbing that fills me with longing for my father and the comforting embrace of his big arms' (130). Her general disappointment with men is counterpointed by her closeness and comfort with her father, as she recounts to her unborn child: 'But can't you see the marathons I've run, the arseholes who've left me scrounging around for my dignity after they disrespected me? My father loves me. He did not pick me from a fruit tree so that men could devour me' (131). Later, Mmabatho says: 'The only real love from a man a woman gets to know is from her father' (132). At times, Mmabatho seems to sabotage her relationship with Arne because his form of love is not as ideal as her father's, even when he seems willing to assume the role of father to their unborn child.

Viewing the discourse of narrative power through focusing on Mmabatho offers a glimpse at the types of stories that mothers are associated with in the novel. Whereas fathers narrate didactically, in the service of upholding power relations, and they can distance themselves from their narratives, maternal narratives offer fluidity and alternative voices, they are self-created instead of imposed, and they serve as forms of resistance against established patriarchal power relations. These maternal narratives are not necessarily innocent or ideal, since they seem often to encompass an escape from and unwillingness to accept reality. Arne initially seems to take on the role of alternative storyteller when he tells Mmabatho a story that runs counter to the forms of fatherhood found in the novel. The story is about a travelling man who hears the cries of a baby and follows the sound to find the lost child. But Arne immediately distances himself from the story and instead turns to reality, saying: 'It was just a silly story that caught my attention. I don't want to have babies with you now' (Duiker 2001: 195). Mothers, however, are linked to narratives that are used to gain self-awareness, and they narrate artistically and imaginatively. They are also seen to be encompassed within the restrictive and didactic stories that men create, such as stories about patriarchy, but they are able to transcend and resist these restrictions through creativity.

Mmabatho evidences this maternal form of creativity through her conversations with her unborn child, imagining that the child will be a boy and expressing her love for him through a monologue: 'When I think of you I imagine such beautiful things that I have decided that you are a love child. I will name you Venus first, whether you are a boy or a girl' (Duiker 2001: 398). Gagiano explains that 'Mmabatho seems to turn progressively inwards in her dreams for the child she is expecting, even though she bravely and proudly leaves her child's father . . . for being insufficiently committed to her and their child. Mmabatho dwindles, in the latter part of the text, into a state of mystical maternity' (2004: 819). Her myth is unrealistic since it places expectations on Arne that he cannot live up to, and does not allow him to be a father in his own right. She seems to create these dream-like narratives in a similar way to the dreams Tshepo experiences about his late mother, drawing a parallel between these two unconventional mother-son relationships. Both of these relationships are founded on dialogues with the self, disguised as mythical maternal dialogues with an as-yet-unborn son, in the case of Mmabatho, and an absent mother, in the case of Tshepo. Maternal relationships are shown to constitute a natural bond where fluidity exists between the mother and child, echoing the corporeal connection, similar to the longing for an idealised mother in Coetzee's *In the Heart of the Country*. The absence of Mmabatho's unborn child and Tshepo's mother seems to belie a spiritual connection. The narratives that are created in these conversations are foundations for self-awareness precisely because the mother and son are inextricably connected – a conversation with the mother is a conversation with the self. These conversations are pathways to self-knowledge for Mmabatho and Tshepo and create a mythical and dream-like space for happiness in place of the harsh realities that most men represent to the two characters.

Tshepo shows this when he imaginatively speaks to his mother about his father's disapproval and the alternative that his mother offers: 'He has never expressed any emotion towards me other than indignation, disapproval. That is why I find refuge in the dreams you weave for me, Mother' (Duiker 2001: 379). Reality, as represented by his father, becomes overwhelming for Tshepo, and he immerses himself in dreams that allow him to reach self-love and acceptance: 'Perhaps I knew you during kinder days when it was okay to love myself. That myth, it is growing inside me, nourishing questions that make me wonder and keep me awake at night. I read interesting truths from its narrative.' Tshepo uses the maternal narratives to reach a sense of self, as in the way he creates a myth of sexuality in order to come to terms with his own homosexuality. Gagiano notes that 'Duiker's text, like Tshepo's life, depicts a courageous, violence-threatened search for new myths, for a new frame of identity' (2004: 819). Whereas the fathers in the novel are always absent from their sons in many ways, the mothers are ever-present in that they are indivisible from the sons. The maternal narratives offer a means for Tshepo to imagine himself outside of the oppressive authorship and stifling disapproval of his father.

## *Trauma and the paternal legacy*

The most prominent consequence of the controlling paternal authorship in Duiker's novel is the psychological distress of sons. This is most clearly demonstrated by Tshepo who finds himself in Valkenberg mental hospital suffering from 'cannabis-induced psychosis', but through his introspection and interaction with other characters one learns that his mental scars are more directly related to his troubled relationship with his father, or, as Gagiano puts it, 'actually the bitter fruit of much earlier trauma' (2004: 818).

The novel seems to place much emphasis on childhood experiences and poor parenting and how this impacts on the psychology of characters in adulthood. Mmabatho demonstrates this when she says to her unborn child: 'I had one bad parent. I won't subject you to the same. It is hellish, you spend your life in therapy, trying to regurgitate the anger and hatred' (Duiker 2001: 399).

Tshepo's relationship with the past and the psychological scars that his trauma has caused him demonstrate a trend that Dobrota Pucherova finds in South African novels from this period, a sense that 'the past continually inhabits the present, and that it is only by looking back that one can continue to make sense of it' (2009: 930). Pucherova sees Duiker's novel as confronting the violence of the past through narrative; however, 'the past is "always already" inaccessible; it is available to us only through narratives that are based on other narratives or "sites of memory", such as monuments, symbols, or rituals' (930-1). The past is a constant burden for Tshepo, which haunts him and which he struggles to reconcile. Pucherova further explains:

> 'Forgetting' the violence involved in establishing a nation is a prerequisite for beginning a national narrative. The other problem with the insistence on looking back to theorise the present is that, as the . . . [TRC] hearings have made clear, it perpetuates old traumas, producing identities that are continually split between the past and present (2009: 931).

Tshepo's personal journey can thus be seen as paralleling the national transition to moving past apartheid. Pucherova emphasises the role of narrative in reconstructing the past, a state that is only possible because these novels give much greater narrative power to sons in comparison to their fathers, explaining that in '*The Quiet Violence of Dreams* it is possible to come to terms with a traumatic past precisely because the past is only available to us as narrative and can never be recalled in full, but must be re-invented around its own blind spots and repressed silences' (2009: 931). Tshepo is narrating his past in a way that reflects and affects his own identity, constructing himself through these narratives and finding ways to deal with his trauma in post-apartheid Cape Town.

Tshepo also links his childhood experiences with his father to the difficulties he faces in adulthood, when he thinks of his tumultuous relationship with the character Chris. Chris is Tshepo's flatmate before

Tshepo begins working at Steamy Windows. He is a member of a gang, and Tshepo is initially attacted to him, but he eventually betrays Tshepo by robbing and raping him. Crous maintains that 'there is a strong pecking order within their domestic sphere, which is reversed in the outside world, as there, Tshepo is the one who manages to get a better job and earn more money than Chris. Yet their sense of both being outsiders is constantly emphasized' (2007: 29). Chris represents masculinity to Tshepo, as Crous holds that Tshepo has a 'strong preoccupation with [Chris's] virility and physical attributes'. Even though he finds Chris's dominance intriguing, he is again reminded of his father. Crous also notes that 'Chris, like Tshepo's father, is preoccupied with whether he is homosexual or not' (31), further indicating how Tshepo's sexuality is a barrier to a connection with these hypermasculine men and, by extension, to his own sense of masculinity. Tshepo compares Chris's constant criticisms of him to memories of his father:

> I can't do things properly when someone is angry with me. It is intimidating. It makes me think about my father. And how he would be scolding me while instructing me to do something. Sometimes he would just get annoyed and take over what I was doing himself and leave me with tears and feelings of inadequacy. It is hard to outgrow childhood memories (Duiker 2001: 169).

By raping Tshepo, Chris re-enacts the violence of Tshepo's childhood rape and when his mother was also raped and murdered. Pucherova asserts: 'By focusing on male rape in a country with perhaps the highest per capita rate of rape of women in the world, *The Quiet Violence of Dreams* asserts that both men and women are oppressed by a patriarchal, heterosexist society' (2009: 937). Chris becomes an embodiment of the violence and control that Tshepo associates with his father, who orchestrated and benefited from the attack on Tshepo and his mother. In this way, Chris reproduces the paternal narratives of violence and control in Tshepo's father's absence, a link that is drawn through Tshepo's memories. By associating these actions with masculinity and the many oppressive males he encounters who enact similar violence, Tshepo questions his own gendered identity.

Tshepo's father takes on the role of provider yet is emotionally and physically absent, a position that causes Tshepo distress. Despite financial aid and the fact that his father tends to show up when he is in challenging positions, arriving to 'protect' and 'rescue' him in Valkenberg and in prison, Tshepo still heatedly protests when he is visited by his father: 'You're not really my father. Your contribution was a sperm' (Duiker 2001: 190). Tshepo positions his father's influence as a removed corporeality only, and negates the influence of their bond. It is, however, significant that only after his father's death does Tshepo truly feel the rift between them solidify, saying near the end of the novel: 'I'm an orphan. I always felt like an orphan after my mother died, but now it's official' (405). Tshepo seems to acknowledge that his father can now no longer narrate his life, but he still suffers from being unable to see himself as free from the influence of his father. He understands himself within the boundaries of his bond with his father, even when his father dies.

This conflicting closeness and separation from his father manifests in the form of scapegoating, not only for his psychological distress but also for general bad luck. He says to the character Nasuib about losing his keys: 'This is my father's doing . . . My father was evil. He died recently' (Duiker 2001: 443). Tshepo seems to become unable to understand his reality outside of the influence of his father. He positions himself within the control of his father, and struggles to take ownership of his ability to narrate his own reality because of his dependence on the narration of his father. He says: 'Your mind holds you prisoner. But somebody controls it all. Who is it? Why are they doing this to me? Who is the prince of darkness?' (427). Tshepo seems to still need someone to blame when his already absent father has become more absent through death, and yet the underlying psychological effects of this relationship become central at this point when he needs to negotiate a sense of self and an understanding of his masculinity separate from being merely a victim of his father's malevolence and absenteeism.

The paradoxical relationship between masculinity and fatherhood is highlighted by absenteeism: fatherhood both reinforces masculinity since it provides a space where paternal narratives can be reproduced, and also threatens masculinity, since it stifles the masculine ideal of sexual freedom and independence. One of the other sex workers at Steamy Windows, West, speaks of his own gender identity in relation to his father: 'Who knows really what it means to be a man? I'm still learning. My father left me no clues, no answers. His departure was complete' (Duiker 2001: 326). Earlier, he says: 'My father . . . left for a life of adventure, travelling through Africa and other continents far away. I never heard from him again' (293). In this extract the masculine ideal of independence is favoured over paternity, similar to Arne's trip to Germany after he finds out that Mmabatho is pregnant.

## Symbols of masculine power and male bonding

A realm where gender modelling is shown to have great impact for sons is that of sport. West says:

> At school I was bullied and taunted by boys who boasted of having a father to watch them play in rugby matches. I hated those matches because I missed my father the most when I played . . . The other boys bragged about going on fishing trips with their fathers, holidays spent in the Transvaal where they saw Naas Botha score excellent drop kicks at Loftus Versfeld . . . They never forgot to remind me that it was a man who was supposed to teach me how to ride a bike, to buy an air pistol for me or to give me a hiding when I got out of hand (Duiker 2001: 294).

Kopano Ratele et al. claim that 'researchers of masculinities assert that sports provide men, young and old alike, the opportunity for exercising many of the aspects of hegemonic masculinity, such as competitiveness, discipline, physical strength and courage' (2007: 123). Of interest are the sanctions from other boys who try to maintain a space of father-son bonding through sport, reproducing sport as a realm of paternal narration and masculine gender modelling. West begins to internalise this and feels his masculinity implicated by his father's absence: 'I knew why I was drifting. I felt incomplete, hardly a man. Some people feel like that if they grow up without the active involvement of a man in their lives' (Duiker 2001: 294). Even though West's mother and his Uncle Sarel try to fill this role for him by attending his rugby matches, he claims that without the involvement of his father his gender is somehow incomplete. With absent fathers, sons like West and Tshepo need to negotiate gendered identities around other males, as well as through self-narration and maternal narratives.

For Tshepo, re-narrating his own identity begins long before the complete absence of his father through death. Through his reflections in Valkenberg it becomes clear that he struggles with his sexuality and his masculinity, seeming to feel fear and hatred towards men. He reflects on this through the symbol of his penis: 'I must confront the worst in myself, the things I loathe about myself like my small shy penis and my debilitating fear of men' (Duiker 2001: 91). This fear seems to stem mostly from his relationship with his father and at his emasculation at being already narrated. Linking his 'small shy' penis to his masculinity serves many functions: it links his fear and hatred for men with his self-hatred; it reverberates with the idea of masculinity as performed through the use of symbols and of the penis as a symbol of masculinity; and it again links to the Oedipal complex, which Tshepo seems to personify in some respects throughout the novel.

A brief encounter with a man during his walk through the township at the end of the novel provides an example of how the oppressive narratives of masculinity rest on the symbol of the penis: '"Kwedini [boy]," an older man says to me with disrespect. I get irritated and flash my circumcised penis to him. Xhosa men can be full of shit' (Duiker 2001: 430). The circumcised penis is a physical representation of a social and spiritual state of manliness, and Tshepo is proving his masculinity to the older man by showing this physical representation to him. In this moment, Tshepo's gender is tied to a cultural marker of masculinity, which the older man defines as authentic manliness. Kizito Muchemwa explains that 'phallic symbols are . . . deployed to describe the creative process and the stories [which the father figure employs]. The phallus, the gun and pen are often conflated as instruments of writing these texts in articulations of violence and masculinity' (2007: 2). This can relate to how Marnus, the betrayed son in *The Smell of Apples*, examines his penis in a lengthy passage while at war in Angola. Marnus, like Tshepo, is in many ways circumscribed in the narratives of his father and becomes powerless to narrate his own existence. These reflections on their own masculinity through the phallic symbol become ways that sons can engage with their masculinity and the expectations of being male. Tshepo commits to this engagement in Valkenberg and pre-empts the reconstructive events of the novel when he says: 'I must wonder why I always surround myself with women, why I can never look another man in the eye, why I won't allow my own masculinity to blossom. For surely just like a flower a man can blossom' (Duiker 2001: 91).

Interestingly, this blossoming is achieved through adopting a new identity in a place where masculinity is highly valued: the massage parlour Steamy Windows. Tshepo adopts the name Angelo in this space, but only once he begins to question the hegemonic white masculinity that still seems to pervade Steamy Windows does he fully take on the self-authoring identity of 'Angelo', signalled by the use of this name to introduce the sections of text that deal with his point of view. The only section that interrupts the introduction of his point of view as 'Angelo', where he is again called 'Tshepo', is when he is confronted with racism at a bar and when West is fired from Steamy Windows. Tshepo begins to notice the patriarchy that exists in Steamy Windows through the manager Shaun's role as an all-controlling father figure, and he is forced to realise that he cannot completely author an unproblematic self or escape from paternal narration. When he is able to incorporate an awareness of sexuality into his past he becomes Angelo-Tshepo, and, finally, after he leaves Steamy Windows and Cape Town for work in Johannesburg he again becomes simply Tshepo.

Steamy Windows seems to primarily become a space where masculinity can be unproblematic and self-determining, and where Sebastian's ideals of a brotherhood of men can exist. Initially Tshepo is intrigued by these ideals. However, he realises that reality requires a more textured view of masculinity and fatherhood, and that he cannot avoid this through his new identity as Angelo. Through the racism that he experiences and his walk through a township, he reaches a compromise between reality and myth, arriving at an understanding of fatherhood that incorporates paternal as well as maternal narratives, with a clearer understanding of the psychological effects that fathers can have on children. He says: 'Our children are fragile, they inherit everything we leave for them, good and bad' (Duiker 2001: 453). He also reflects on this during his walk through the township:

> Three kids are torturing a dog. They have tied some wire around its throat and are poking it with sharp sticks, its shanks bleeding ... Children are cruel because their parents are also probably cruel ... I want to catch them and beat them senseless. But this is how grown-ups always speak to them. Beating them will only shut them away further from reason and compassion (Duiker 2001: 431).

The moment recalls a scene from Gordimer's *Burger's Daughter* explored in the previous chapter, when Rosa is confronted with a black man abusing a donkey and imagines that she could stop him by asserting her narrative power. Tshepo, similarly, resists becoming a controlling and violent father figure to the children in the township and in the orphanage, and tries to find alternative ways of narrating 'reason and compassion' to these children. The model of masculinity that Tshepo learns from his mostly absent father is reinterpreted and not merely reproduced when he becomes a father figure himself. Only by allowing for alternative narratives does Tshepo transcend oppressive paternal narratives.

### *Paternal control of money*

An important element of the paternal relationships portrayed in the novel is the role of money and how the father figure becomes responsible for the economic education of the son. Money and ownership are associated with men and masculinity in various ways. Money is also linked to the central concern with self-awareness in that it is initially considered a substitute for awareness by Tshepo, but shown to be unfulfilling for him. For father figures, such as Shaun, money again highlights power relations and exposes the patriarchy in the myth of the brotherhood since it is used to maintain these power relations. In this way, money and control over money become part of the oppressive paternal narrative.

Money becomes a signifier of masculinity and also a way of attaining a sense of agency for sons in narrating their own lives. One of the earliest references to this link between fatherhood and money in the novel is a reflection by Tshepo about an allegorical family suffering in poverty during apartheid. He says of the imaginary mother whose eleven-year-old son has been killed by officials: 'Who will listen to her cries when the father walks Jo'burg in search of work, secretly crying over his crumbling pride because he cannot afford a loaf of bread for supper?' (Duiker 2001: 98). Tshepo reiterates the familiar narrative about fathers as providers of material needs and how a failure to perform in this regard seems to be a failure of masculinity. The allegorical father in Tshepo's story leaves the home in search of work, physically distant from his grieving wife, highlighting the way that fathers are shown to be emotionally and physically distant despite providing for their families financially. One such father in the novel is Peter, a man who frequents Steamy Windows as Tshepo's customer. He says: 'A person like me should have never gotten married. I don't even think I make a good father. I'm just a provider' (266). Two similar examples are Tshepo's father who provides him with money but not the type of fatherhood he requires, and Mmabatho's reference to Arne as potentially 'the provider, the breadwinner' (322) but not the 'father' of her unborn child. All of these cases demonstrate how inadequate the role of being merely a provider proves to be. Money is constructed as a symbol of patriarchal masculinity, but not a factor that defines authentic fatherhood.

Money, financial literacy and self-sufficiency seem to symbolise the hope of sons to transcend the stifling authorship of fathers. Transferring knowledge about money from father to son is a necessary part of transferring agency to sons and enabling an independent masculinity. The realm of financial literacy seems to be a particularly male one, as West shows when he reflects on his absent father and how he has had to learn about masculinity from other father figures:

> The men I've met have taught me a lot of things. They taught me how to shave, how to go with the grain and not against it. I never had a father to show me that . . . Little things that my mother could never teach me. Things that you can only learn from another guy. I learned how to use money (Duiker 2001: 295).

Tshepo begins to imagine that when he earns his own money he will overcome his antipathy towards his father and sever the bond of dependence to achieve a self-actualised masculinity.

The link between patriarchal masculinity and money can also be seen in how the illusion of the brotherhood is eventually shattered by the black character Cole. Cole says to Tshepo: 'You're only useful as long as you bring in money' (Duiker 2001: 346), seeming to reduce himself and the other workers to mere commodities. Cole continues: 'It's nice that we're all friendly and everything. I mean, I believe in the brotherhood too. But who's pushing all the buttons? Who's got all the power? Who decides who stays or leaves?', to which Tshepo replies: 'Shaun. White people.' Viljoen explains:

> A sense of family is finally regained when [Tshepo] joins the young men working at the brothel and the bond that exists among them, black and white, is likened to a pre-Raphaelite brotherhood, until racism exposes that sentiment as fraudulent, as just another ploy to keep up efficient production and profits (2001: 50-1).

Gagiano adds to this analysis by explaining that the brotherhood 'has its own, racist, frayed edges' (2002: 74), despite seemingly being embracing of Tshepo. Furthermore, the realisation echoes the trend that Pucherova identifies in post-apartheid South African novels, which 'expresses disillusionment with the fashionable middle-class multiculturalism that only disguises thriving racism, xenophobia, and homophobia' (2009: 937). This moment is significant since it exposes how the myth of the brotherhood fits into the model of paternal narratives discussed above, centring on the maintenance of power relations, the control of money and the obedience of sons to father figures, where the father figure, in this case Shaun, understands the functional value of these narratives. Shaun's character, already shadowed by his isolation in the power base of his office, becomes strikingly patriarchal, using the myths to maintain his position of control over his workers. Cole seems to undermine Tshepo's newfound understanding of masculinity and sexuality based in the myth of the brotherhood when he says: 'This whole brotherhood thing is a clever gimmick. Very convenient, because it works. People want to believe in that sort of thing. But make no mistake, when Shaun's done with you, you'll know' (Duiker 2001: 346).

Gagiano notes how the community at Steamy Windows offers Tshepo a false and tenuous sense of family: 'Tshepo seems to accept, unproblematically, a new male gay leadership as both the family and the aristocracy of his ideal future dispensation, with no anxiety about its patriarchal or misogynist overtones – at least in its erasure of female participation (or icons)' (2004: 820). The community at Steamy Windows seems to be built on misogynist myths, idealising the bonds created through a brotherhood of men, which belie the racial and economic divisions that still exist within it.

The aspect of race that Tshepo brings up puts in a new light Sebastian's objectification of Andromeda, the black sex worker who is admired in a bar, and parallels how Tshepo becomes merely a 'black stallion' (Duiker 2001: 204), as Shaun calls him, or 'Exotic Angelo' (333) as his line in the Cape Ads reads, and not the son or brother that he might have felt himself to be. Tshepo has had to take charge of his own economic education, but he is eventually disillusioned about the empowering effect that money as a symbol of masculinity can have for him. Having control over money and the way in which he earns his money still does not empower Tshepo to author his own narrative, since he is situated within the control of Shaun and still has psychic pain connected with his father. He says:

> Money hasn't boosted my self-esteem. I look good and dress fine. It just means I'm wearing a different mask. Underneath I'm still the same, I still hurt. I still think about my father and wonder why he killed my mother. I still wonder why he has left me with so much confusion, so much self-hatred. There is still the same punishing cycle of introspection (Duiker 2001: 320).

All of these examples show how whiteness, masculinity, paternity and power become conflated in economic processes, where patriarchal narratives, such as the myth of the brotherhood, are used to uphold these power relations. The economic realm is a space where fathers and sons, or symbolically those in power and those subjected to control, are in a constant struggle. The novel suggests that transferring economic knowledge and gaining an awareness of the effects of patriarchal narratives are important steps in overcoming this struggle, a point that might speak to the continued economic deprivation of many in the black majority in post-apartheid South Africa. For various characters, and most clearly for Tshepo, this transference of knowledge and power does not happen, and the sons are left dependent on fathers or with ambivalent masculinities because of their relationships with the symbol of money.

## Homosexuality and freedom

By showing how masculinity can transcend associations with violence, the novel offers sexuality as a means to awareness and a way for Tshepo to deal with his violent past through claiming a new form of masculinity for himself. Sebastian explains to Tshepo: 'You don't have to be a gun-toting idiot to celebrate masculinity. Violence is not a solution. The brotherhood renounces it because it's regressing. To be a man you must be fully aware and you can't be that when you're violent' (Duiker 2001: 303). West speaks to this as well, addressing more directly the aspect of violence that often seems to be made essential to masculinity in many texts, and how sexuality can transcend this:

> It is no coincidence that a gun emits fire that maims and kills. Perhaps some people have looked at that thing only with dark eyes. A gun is the ugliest realisation of that thing between my legs. A gun is a man half realised. But that is not how I have learned to communicate, how I have learned to use that thing. There is tenderness between my legs. That thing is not a weapon but a beautiful instrument (Duiker 2001: 325).

West shatters the conflation of penis and gun, which Muchemwa set up earlier in this argument and which Marnus seems to epitomise in *The Smell of Apples*, allowing West to see his sexuality in a positive light. Pucherova explains that Steamy Windows offers a reconceptualisation of violence and sexuality: 'Releasing sperm instead of bullets, gay men substitute aggression with tenderness and creativity. By liberating their bodies, gay men can escape the constrictions of stereotypical patriarchal masculinity and discover their true, idiosyncratic identities' (2009: 937). Exploring and embracing his sexuality becomes a way to associate masculinity with love and 'tenderness' instead of violence for West, and it similarly becomes a pathway for Tshepo to deal with his past and his feelings about his father.

In contrast to the way in which power is maintained through distance, the realm of sexuality brings forth much stronger and more direct reactions from fathers. Homosexuality seems to not only have implications for individuals, but for conceptions of masculinity and fatherhood more generally, requiring intervention when the limits of sexuality are transgressed. Crous holds that 'central to any theoretical discussion on homosexuality from a masculinity studies perspective is the notion that homosexuality is [a] revolt against the symbolic domination . . . of heterosexual masculinity' (2007: 22). Ratele et al. extend this argument, showing how male-female relations are implicated by the discourse surrounding homosexuality:

> A discussion of masculinity, gay behaviour, and females is a discussion about gender and sexuality, not only about heterosexuality versus homosexuality. Primarily it reflects the continued and entrenched binarism of masculine and feminine and the imperative to prescribe all human identity and practice within such an understanding . . . Gay is a confusing mix of a masculine body and alleged feminine performance (2007: 116).

Not only is homosexuality seen as an unsettling fusion between masculinity and femininity on an individual basis, but it also unnerves the masculine ideal of patriarchal control over sexuality and serves to destabilise power relations. Crous argues: 'Male-male sexual relations are a direct challenge to the heteronormativity of the dominant heterosexual culture . . . particularly since it subverts the hegemonic definition of masculinity' (2007: 23). In this way, the masculinity of the father is threatened by the homosexuality of the son, since the father's patriarchal authorship over sexual practice is being contested. The authorship of father figures is shown when Tshepo's father says to him: 'And what is this business that I hear that you go to faggot nightclubs? I didn't bring you up to be a stabane. Are you a faggot?' (Duiker 2001: 190). It is notable that these words are immediately preceded by violence in the form of Tshepo's father slapping him across the face, a reaction to Tshepo saying that his father is 'not really [his] father'. There is also irony in Tshepo's father saying that he did not 'bring [Tshepo] up to be [gay]', since it is shown that he has mostly been an absent father. As this is his only reference to being involved in Tshepo's upbringing, the extent of his fatherhood, almost above all else, is made to be the prevention of homosexuality, or, by extension, the maintenance of patriarchal heterosexist masculinity.

It is important to note that popular conceptions have constructed homosexuality as 'un-African', a notion that Tshepo challenges. In fact, this moment is so radical that it had not previously been articulated in South African literature, as Pucherova asserts: 'Duiker is the first South African novelist to create a black gay protagonist, whose quest for identity eventually brings him to see his homosexuality as an inalienable part of his African identity' (2009: 936). Thus, Tshepo's struggle with his sexuality might be as much a struggle with patriarchal conceptions based on his race as they are reflections of a largely homophobic society, and the novel presents an important narrative during the transition from apartheid when such depictions were not possible. Tshepo says:

> I mean, people always say that black culture is rigid and doesn't accept things like homosexuals and lesbians. You know the argument – it's very unAfrican. It's a lot of crap. In my experiences that kind of thinking comes from urbanised blacks, people who've watered down the real origins of our culture and mixed it with Anglo-Saxon notions of the Bible. It's stupid to even suggest that homosexuality and lesbianism are foreign to black culture (Duiker 2001: 250).

Sebastian and Tshepo each offer different mythologies of sexuality in the novel. Exploring the differences between these two myths is important for father-son relationships since sexuality becomes a place of struggle between Tshepo and his father, and the way in which this sexuality is understood becomes a way of regaining power for the disempowered son. It also allows the son an opportunity to narrate his own understanding in the 'maternal' form, which serves to undermine the power hold of the father, since both myths deal with interpreting homosexuality positively. An extract from Sebastian's myth shows how it glorifies homosexuality and perhaps even demonises heterosexuality, or more precisely demonises the link with women and children, which heterosexuality entails:

> I think gay men are going to play a more prominent role in future . . . Because they don't have wives. They don't have children, well, theoretically. Straight men are tired, burnt out, raising kids but failing to equip them as best they can. They want to jump ship, they want more sex, they're always looking for better sex, look at Clinton. They are dissatisfied. But gay men have always been liberated sexually because they understand each other's needs better than a woman (Duiker 2001: 254).

Tshepo's myth is pseudo-historical, dealing with three primordial sexes – men, women and hermaphrodites – who were cleaved in half and who wish to be reunited. The hermaphrodites became two heterosexual beings, man and woman, while the initial men and women became homosexuals. Insofar as both of these stories about sexuality undermine traditional conceptions of masculinity and form a basis for self-awareness, they can be seen as counter-paternal narratives, or, in the context of Duiker's novel and this book broadly, they demonstrate the types of narratives that mothers are linked with. There are, however, striking differences between the two narratives. Sebastian's narrative again latches onto the idea of the stifling qualities that women and children represent for men, which is echoed by West when he speaks of Steamy Windows: 'Our fathers don't have anywhere left for them, where men can be on their own without women, you know what I mean? This place it's like a club, an exclusive men's club' (Duiker 2001: 244). It is thus clear that while Sebastian tries to narrate a form of masculinity that resists heteronormativity, he is still denigrating women, leading Tshepo to protest to Sebastian: 'Any woman listening to you would think you're a misogynist, all this pro-male rhetoric' (254). This can also be linked to Sebastian's role as the propagator of the myth of the brotherhood, which serves the economic domination of the father figure, Shaun.

Tshepo's myth differs in that it is articulated through the mother-son narrative, since he relates the myth when speaking with his deceased mother. It also clearly shows up the inherent inadequacy of the maternal myths discussed above, namely, the inability of these myths to deal with reality. His myth does not allow him to deal with the overwhelming loathing that he feels for his father and, by extension, the difficulties in his life. He says soon after his myth of sexuality: 'I feel doomed because I cannot love him, Mother. And not being able to love your father is akin to not being able to love yourself' (Duiker 2001: 381), indicating that despite the distance and resentment, the father is still an important figure for Tshepo. Tshepo's myth also demonstrates an escape from reality when he speaks of an early death, something that he predicts for himself but also seems eerily to long for: 'I have contemplated this fate often enough. I'm going to die young.' It becomes clear that his feelings about his own sexuality are not resolved through the 'maternal' narrative, which he uses to deal with them, but that this narrative is still an important step in him 'becoming aware of [him]self' (380) as he explores his sexuality. In this way, the two narratives of sexuality, while both offering positive understandings of homosexuality, still serve different functions in respect to relative father figures. Tshepo's myth is a way of dealing with the disapproval of his father figure with regard to his sexuality, while Sebastian's seems to serve the interests of the exploitative father figure, Shaun.

The way in which these disapprovals become entrenched and internalised for Tshepo can be seen in his thoughts when he is about to have penetrative sex with a client for the first time: 'I think of my father and it is enough to make me wish for death' (Duiker 2001: 314). The act of anal penetration becomes an important one for Tshepo, and he says: 'It all comes down to that: penetration . . . It's also what they persecute us for, that unspeakable thing that men do together, corrupting nature. That final act.' It becomes a rite of passage for Tshepo, a way of moving beyond societal conceptions of hegemonic masculinity, which are voiced in conjunction with violence by his father. Pucherova explains that 'Duiker's focus on black gay desire as a political, ethical, and aesthetic direction for post-apartheid South

Africa is highly controversial . . . Tshepo (alias Angelo) is drawn into a world where gay desire is not merely a pleasure-seeking principle, but an ethical philosophy' (2009: 937). The act of consensual male-male penetration is particularly transgressive of conceptions of hegemonic masculinity since, as Crous points out, 'from a masculinist, phallocratic point of view, the masculine principle is the active and penetrating principle whereas the feminine principle suggests passivity and "being penetrated"' (2007: 23). By linking this moment with thoughts of his father, Tshepo shows how transgressive the act becomes – he is taking the uncomfortable step of moving outside of the limits placed on his masculinity and narrating an alternative understanding of sexuality for himself.

Sexuality offers a medium through which alternative narratives of masculinity can be explored. These alternative and multivocal narratives can be mindful of the stifling nature of paternal narratives, allow for reinterpretation, and offer sons the possibility of narrating their own understandings of themselves through maternal narratives. Crous argues that 'intimate spheres such as gay bars and brothels are seen as the ideal place to pursue one's sense of identity because outside these spaces, in particular in the rural areas, homosexual behaviour is seen as not being part of black culture' (2007: 31–2). Pucherova adds that in the novel, 'gay desire is presented as liberation from aggressive heteronormative masculinity and an opportunity for the redefinition of the entire society' (2009: 937).

## *Oppressive fathers and gender modelling*

The move from narratives of power to plural stories is also shown in the fact that multiple father figures are adopted and incorporated by Tshepo, not only the voice of his own father, in order to negotiate his self-identity.

An aggressive and controlling paternal figure is Zebron, one of the patients at Valkenberg, who was involved in the murder and rape of Tshepo's mother. Zebron works as a henchman for Tshepo's father and thus serves as a stand-in for him within the space of Valkenberg. When Zebron tries to keep Tshepo away from one of his friends in Valkenberg, Tshepo asserts his freedom by saying: 'You're not my fucking father, okay?' (Duiker 2001: 125).

An aggressive father figure is also found in Mr Saunders, Tshepo's neighbour who first threatens his flatmate Chris for stealing milk but later helps Tshepo move when Chris rapes him. Mr Saunders is initially tied to the symbol of the gun, which he shows Tshepo, but later, after being betrayed by Chris, he says of Mr Saunders: 'His eyes are soft, gentle, friendly and almost maternal in a way that I have come not to expect from men' (Duiker 2001: 216). The use of word 'maternal' is important, distancing Mr Saunders from the paternal discourse of violence and coercion represented by his gun and from the horrors Tshepo has suffered at the hands of hypermasculine men in the novel.

All of these different father figures provide models of gender for Tshepo. The familiar themes of paternal narratives – violence and control – seem to apply to all of these relationships. Some of these father figures allow Tshepo the opportunity to see the role of father as one that can be loving, caring and gentle, and give him the opportunity to assert his own agency in these relationships, as in the case of Zebron. Tshepo negotiates his masculinity and his own ideas about fatherhood around these characters as well as around his father, allowing him to become the father figure, which he does in the final parts of the novel by incorporating plural stories of fatherhood and reinterpreting paternal narratives.

For Tshepo, the difficulties in his relationship with his father seem to reflect his difficulties with his own identity and self-awareness, as Gagiano explains:

> In this text it is not the huge, national, brutal apartheid system that is held to blame for the un-anchored quality of lives like Tshepo's and those of his fellow male prostitutes or Valkenberg inmates, but the original familial trauma – almost invariably characterised by the absence, inadequacy or grotesque violence of the father figure (2004: 819).

Tshepo says of his father: 'Hating him has given me strength . . . We understand each other best when there is some hatred between us' (Duiker 2001: 402). When this hatred begins to falter, the aspects of Tshepo's identity and masculinity, which are based on it, also lose 'strength'. Tshepo seems determined to hold on to this hatred and the understanding that this affords him, outraged at his father who 'has the audacity to say that one day [Tshepo] will love him' (404). He realises that he is forced to negotiate some form of a relationship with his father, just like Toloki in *Ways of Dying*, and that his self-concept is implicated in this relationship, shown when he says: 'I cannot divorce myself from him' (379). Tshepo's entire story can be seen as being about how he comes to a point of being able to narrate love for his father. One of Tshepo's later reflections in the form of a dialogue with his mother clarifies this:

> Father is never far behind, the angels of death eagerly clinging to his black cloak. I dreamt he killed his child and ate him. It could have been me. I fear that he would do the same with me if given the chance, but love burns him with its wild fires every time the noose tightens around my neck in my dreams (Duiker 2001: 381).

Tshepo acknowledges that his father still loves him, and that the identity he has built around hatred of his father needs to be negotiated around this idea, saying: 'It is difficult because I cannot say he hates me' (Duiker 2001: 379). However, the violence that he refers to, in being killed and eaten by this father, serves to reflect how he still needs to negotiate this love within the context of oppressive paternal narration. The image of being consumed by his father highlights how overwhelming the paternal narratives become for him, so that he can no longer separate himself from the way that he is narrated. He could thus fear letting go of hatred for his father because it might seem to spell an acceptance of darker elements of his own personality, as well as an acceptance of his own masculinity when he associates masculinity with violence and control. When Tshepo's father asks him, just before his death: 'Would you avenge me?' (400), he is asking Tshepo to participate in and uphold the paternal narrative of violence so that he can cement his influence over Tshepo. Tshepo's father is associated with death, violence, power and control, the worst in what he considers masculine:

> Why is he so evil, this lord of the underworld? I caught a glimpse of him in town going in a fancy car, chauffeured by men with brutal facial scars who look like askaris; men who wouldn't hesitate to shoot, to maim, to kill. When I think of him I become depressed, I feel dark. He is like the night that eats the sun (Duiker 2001: 379).

Tshepo's psychological scars might be partially linked to acknowledging not only that he is consumed within paternal narratives, but also the unbreakable connection that he has with his father, and how his father is a reflection of a part of himself.

His closeness to his father is also shown physically, a pervasive device in novels about fathers: 'There is nowhere to run, I have to confront him. "Your father is here," Themba says. "You guys look alike." It is a painful truth. For a while I wore dreadlocks to disguise the similarities, to erase his face, my face' (Duiker 2001: 144). Tshepo deals with this tension mostly through his reflections spoken to his mother, the maternal narrative that offers reinterpretation. He realises, however, that he is still situated within paternal narratives. He engages with both paternal and maternal narratives in order to negotiate not only his relationship with his father, but also his relationship with himself. He says early in the novel: 'I think of my father. I think about you, Mama. And the whole thing doesn't make sense: you, me and him' (91). This trinity can be seen to encapsulate Tshepo's central tension throughout the novel: having to exist within paternal and maternal narratives and through them to develop a sense of self.

By the end of the novel this trinity might be seen as making sense to Tshepo: he becomes a father figure to orphaned children and incorporates both forms of existence, valuing plural narratives: 'I am a dancer, a painter. My gaze is filled with fecund stories that come from my mother's womb. I must create and delight, that is my mother's way. I must keep moving, that is my father's way' (Duiker 2001: 457). Tshepo realises that he is already positioned within narratives but that he still has the ability to author new and empowering stories for himself. When he says: 'I am Horus, the son of the sun' (456), Tshepo is able to narrate himself within a father-son story and still maintain a positive self-concept. His father is no longer 'the night that eats the sun' (379), but the sun itself.

Gagiano notes how this ending offers Tshepo a sense of hope: 'There is nevertheless a healing sanity in the decision of Tshepo (and the author?) that takes this character out of the weirdness of his Cape Town context as he returns to Johannesburg to play the adult, socially responsible and (particularly significantly) the fatherly role of housemaster to a community of rehabilitated street children' (2004: 820), a similar nurturing paternal role as the one inhabited by Toloki at the end of *Ways of Dying*. Viljoen explains how Tshepo overcomes the strict labels that have been placed on his identity: 'Tshepo however insists on seeing himself not as a psychotic man or a black man or a gay man but rather as a rich amalgam of shifting, intermingling identities' (2001: 51).

These changing subjectivities and the desire to move beyond the strict paternal narratives of race, ethnicity and gender characterise the shift to post-apartheid authorship in South Africa. Characters resist father figures and point to the inconsistencies of narratives; however, identity is unstable and self-narration does not alleviate the material hardships and trauma that these characters must live with. Later novels will see the fathers become even more distant as the transition period ends.

CHAPTER 5

# Fatherhoods in Post-Transitional South African Novels
'The Declining Patriarch'

The end of the Truth and Reconciliation Commission (TRC) process created a further imperative to interrogate the past through literature, especially exploring the ways in which the past bleeds into the present and informs visions of the future. As Shane Graham explains: 'The TRC must be read as merely the opening chapter in the vast, ongoing process of transformation – a transformation of political structures, yes, but also of larger spatial schemas and of narrative frameworks for understanding the past' (2009: 3). By ostensibly exposing the secrets of the past, South African society was seen as writing a new national narrative. Post-transitional literature thus can be viewed as attempting to expose and often confess these secrets as an act of reconciliation, especially for white characters, who were mostly divorced from the TRC process. These narratives are both an attempt to reconcile the self with the changing country, as well as to reconcile a national community, which has been fractured through violence and systemic oppression.

Sarah Nuttall and Carli Coetzee analyse the genre of confessional literature that emerged in this period, explaining that for white writers in life-writing texts, the 'self . . . is in some ways "split." The narrating self in these texts typically aims to effect a distance from an earlier, politically less enlightened or in other ways unacceptable, version of the self' (1998: 6). By confessing the past, there is a necessary distance between the self now, and the self who was complicit in the horrors of apartheid. This can be seen in earlier texts, such as Mark Behr's *The*

*Smell of Apples*, as well as in post-transitional texts, such as Lisa Fugard's *Skinner's Drift*, which is explored in this chapter.

The novels under discussion often make reference to ghosts, as Nedine Moonsamy points out is common in many post-transitional texts. Not only are parental or authority figures ghostlike in the post-transitional moment, but the sons and daughters themselves become spectral in the changing South Africa, no longer feeling connected to their history or to the country. Moonsamy elaborates:

> In contrast to a post-apartheid national imaginary that more typically employed representations of death as a discursive experience of radical alterity, the 'post-transitional' seemingly invites a spectral form of citizenship that introduces us to a liminal reality in which the notion that life and death are divisible entities is compromised. The pervasive use of ghosts in these texts evoke a desire to learn to live with the unspoken atrocities of history, as well as the spectral, phantasmagoric history of the events that have not taken place in the national imaginary. In this regard, they articulate an ethical ideal that voluntarily employs the unfinished economy of melancholia whilst depathologizing it (2014b: 70).

As David Medalie argues, many South African novels from this period seem to demonstrate 'a widespread desire to cauterize history with the end of formal apartheid in April 1994 and to establish and promote the idea of radical discontinuity as a way of shrugging off the past and its shadows' (1997: 512). Medalie also notes that 'South African literature of the post-apartheid period is difficult to categorise. It is both diverse and encumbered with sameness, profound and glib, predictable and unpredictable, linguistically ambitious and linguistically drab' (2012: 4). While Medalie holds that it is difficult to summarise the nature of post-apartheid literature, 'if one looks at the most significant literary texts [after the end of apartheid], what is central to most of them is a preoccupation with the relationship between the apartheid past and the post-apartheid present. They seem unable to engage the present without summoning the past.' He explains this trend in three important post-apartheid texts, Zakes

Mda's *The Heart of Redness* (2000), Marlene van Niekerk's *Agaat* (2004) and J.M. Coetzee's *Disgrace*, each of which deal with the discomfort of facing the injustices of the past in light of a changing country. These trends can be seen in many of the texts discussed in this chapter.

Anette Horn adds to this by showing that post-apartheid literature always carries the traces of apartheid that necessitate the act of looking back and re-narrating apartheid itself; the ghost of apartheid always lingers in the realm of post-apartheid fictions:

> The post-Apartheid novel has the ability to interrogate new ways of looking at the past. The 'post' in post-Apartheid therefore does not indicate a clean break with the past, but rather looks at stories that cut across such boundaries. It demonstrates that the past is not resolved in such gestures as the Truth and Reconciliation Commission [which was] not without its own silences and limitations (2012: 129).

This leads to the trend that Dirk Klopper identifies: characters in several recent novels are often looking back as well as physically *going* back, often to the farm setting: 'Much recent South African narrative fiction deploys the motif of a return to a place associated with the past, specifically a home town, family farm, childhood landscape or ancestral site . . . The homecoming involves a return to apartheid-era South Africa' (2011: 147). In the return to the setting often associated with childhoods in these texts, there is a necessary engagement with the father, which is explored at length in this chapter.

Recent South African novels, constituting what Ronit Frenkel and Craig Mackenzie (2010) label 'post-transitional' literature, show many shifts in the representations of fathers and paternal narratives. The novels are also much more aware of the multiplicity of voices in South Africa, self-referential in their role as being part of the literary landscape and providing a narrative tapestry of a country that has undergone a powerful transition. This is done through referring to other South African novels and their roles in facilitating or reflecting reconciliation, including many novels discussed in earlier chapters of this book. The texts in this period call into question the paternal narratives that earlier novels presented, and look at them in highly critical, post-modernist ways.

Fathers, in these novels, become relics of the past. They are shown to be almost ghostly figures, often dying or associated with death. The dying father means that the children are left without the certainty and authority of familiar paternal narratives. The offspring abandon ideas that the father is often tasked with propagating: race, ethnicity, gender, sexuality, religion, violence, history, tradition and law. All of these need to be re-narrated by the sons and daughters themselves, and, through their discovery of new narratives, the novels offer hope of transcending the stifling paternal narratives associated with the apartheid era.

## Lisa Fugard's *Skinner's Drift*
### *Voicing the father's silences*

Lisa Fugard's *Skinner's Drift* (2005) notably incorporates a multiplicity of narrative voices, destabilising traditional narrative power structures even further. The novel accomplishes this by not only focalising the white protagonist, Eva, and her father Martin, but also including the voices of the black labourers on the farm and how they experience the secrets and tensions that underlie their lives. Lisa Propst, discussing both *Skinner's Drift* and *Playing in the Light*, comments that through this tendency of incorporating previously 'silenced' voices, 'the novels intimate that shared narratives with the power to build new relationships require ceding control over the limits of one's story in a necessarily incomplete responsibility for the voices of others – the stories they have to tell, the experiences they have undergone, and the conditions in which they live' (2014: 198). Mairi Neeves, examining the multiplicity of voices in Fugard's novel, says: 'Fugard draws attention to those silenced by Apartheid, highlighting the oppressive regime under which relationships are determined as much by what remains unsaid as by what is spoken aloud' (2008: 116). Of course, in addition to the black farmworkers, Eva herself is silenced when she is young, and the novel is as much about her voicing her own silences and interrogating her identity in the space of the family farm as it is about addressing the silences of racial violence.

Propst sees both *Skinner's Drift* and *Playing in the Light* as looking to the past in ways that show how complex the present period in South Africa still is. Whereas earlier novels, such as Behr's *The Smell of Apples* and its contemporaries, 'ultimately [relegate] questions of responsibility to the past' (Propst 2014: 197), and many do not address the continuing legacy of apartheid, 'Fugard and Wicomb insist on the importance of excavating traces of the past in order to create new narratives for the future. But they consider how predicating reconciliations on shared accounts of the past can oversimplify the complexities of the present' (198).

The image of the father, while central to the secrets of the novel, is peripheral to its main thrust, namely, the psychic struggles of Eva, who feels culpable through hiding these secrets. *Skinner's Drift* will thus be briefly discussed as it is an early example of the post-transitional text, bearing many of the hallmarks of unstable paternal narratives that become more pronounced in the novels of Behr and Wicomb, which form the main focus of this chapter.

The plot is set in 1997 and interspersed with flashbacks to Eva's childhood on the farm. When Eva returns to South Africa from her new home in New York after a ten-year absence, having 'all but denounced her past and her national identity' (Neeves 2008: 114), she is told that her father is dying. She had cut off contact with him when she left the country, but she still feels a strong emotional connection to him. She cries as her plane is ready to land in Johannesburg: 'She was crying for her father, because of her father. She shook her head in mild disgust at herself. Her mother was dead, worthy of her grief, and yet here she was weeping for that miserable ghost clinging to life in a hospital in Louis Trichardt' (Fugard 2005: 1). Importantly, the father is referred to as a ghost. This relates to the white father's association with the apartheid ideologies that afforded him power, and once this position is threatened by democratic change and political power shifts, the father is rendered ghostly, frail and in many ways powerless.

Eva reflects on the changing of names in South Africa, a contentious issue that has created great division and debate in recent history. She sees it as indicating how the country has changed:

> With the end of apartheid, Jan Smuts International airport had become Johannesburg airport. The Witwatersrand, the area encompassing Johannesburg, Randfontein and a few other towns, and which was named after a cascade of white water

that the early settlers had seen, was now part of Gauteng – Eva had no idea what Gauteng meant. The conservative Transvaal, province of stoic farmers, sofa-sized rugby players and insatiable hunters, had been divided into the Northern Province and Mpumalanga. A new country, and she sensed it the minute she passed through customs (Fugard 2005: 4).

Eva associates these changes with fundamental shifts that rendered South Africa a 'new country', and, indeed, compared to the South Africa she left during apartheid, represented by the masculinist images of sport, hunting and stoicism that she references here, the changes in the country are overwhelming for her.

These social shifts are highlighted when Eva goes to visit her father in hospital. He is being attended to by a black nurse, who confronts him about his assumed racism and says to him:

Your nightmare, hey, Mr van Rensburg, to have me looking after you? You know what my revenge is for all you old white farmers? To do such a good job that I bring you back to health. Maybe I get some *muti* from the *sangoma* and mix it into your jelly and custard and make you younger. Mmm hmm, start a conspiracy, all across the country, turn all the dying old *boere* into young men! . . . So you have many, many years to experience the joy and freedom of our new South Africa (Fugard 2005: 19).

Martin's physical deterioration is linked to his loss of symbolic masculine power as well as his loss of political power in South Africa: 'Martin had once been a boyishly handsome man with intense blue eyes, the lines on his high forehead giving him a slight quizzical expression; now his cheeks were sunken and salted with stubble, and one of the strokes had smeared the left corner of his mouth into a grimace' (Fugard 2005: 20).

The most important image of masculinist power in the novel, informing the tragedies on the farm, is the symbolic power of gun violence. As highlighted throughout this book, the gun can be seen as the phallic symbol of masculine power. Martin's obsession with guns, hunting and violence foreshadow the brutal acts that will frame Eva's life. When she is young, Martin takes Eva to hunt an impala. He asks her to take the gun to shoot it:

> He waited, watching her hands briefly touch the gun and then curl back into fists. She refused. Since she had started at boarding school he'd been coaxing her to take her first animal and she always said, next time, I promise. Now, she shook her head adamantly and said that she didn't want to. He was stunned, and hurt. He reached across the passenger seat and pulled his old silver hip flask out of the glove compartment. A silent bitter toast to his wife. *So you finally claimed our daughter* (Fugard 2005: 34).

The gun and the sport of hunting are associated with the father, and having her hunt with him is a way of bonding with his daughter and incorporating her within his paternal narratives. When she refuses to do what he asks her, she is seen as being 'claimed' by the mother, again contrasting not only the gender constructions in the novel but also hinting at the dichotomy between violent paternal and nurturing maternal narratives. Martin associates Eva with traits he admires, such as being cunning and clever, but also contrasts this with descriptions of 'something soft' and 'emotions', which he sees as negative traits: 'She was cunning and clever but it was always in the service of something soft. That was her problem, he thought, no matter how cunning and clever she was her emotions could get the better of her, and emotions led to mistakes' (Fugard 2005: 35). Ironically, Martin's own mistakes and those of his hunting mates are the cause of the death of his wife as well as the black child whom he kills on the farm.

When she is fifteen, Eva asks a farmworker, Lefu, to ride with her to bury the bodies of the animals Martin kills during his hunts. She reflects that his hunting has become more malicious and violent in nature: 'Martin wasn't hunting any more . . . he was killing. And [Eva] seemed intent on burying every predator that her father shot' (Fugard 2005: 72). Eva had already witnessed that her father killed a black child on the farm, thinking that the child was an animal, and every killing he makes now becomes reframed because of this violence. Eva's defiance and distance from the father is solidified in this moment, yet by not questioning him or exposing what he has done, she is still complicit. Her acts of burying the bodies of animals, just as she had earlier buried the body of the murdered child, expose her desire to hide and maintain the secrets of her father and the damage his violence has caused. This burying of secrets, in light of the post-transitional moment, is symbolic of the silent complicity of many in South Africa in apartheid ideology. By not confronting injustices, the sins of the father never go punished. In light of the TRC process, which had ended a few years before the novel was published, this silencing and burying of the sins of the father become especially relevant, and Eva's fear of the violence of black workers, and that her role in covering up the killing of the child will be exposed, lead her to a highly anxious state at the end of the novel.

Eva becomes more and more distant from her father after discovering the body of the child. She associates herself much more closely with her mother. These tenuous paternal narratives and Martin's inability to successfully maintain his masculine power on the farm are shown through the failing of his voice. Whereas the power of the father figure's voice is often highlighted as indicating his authority, Martin's stutter is negatively referred to throughout the novel, indicating that this is symbolic of his inability to fully reproduce paternal power.

In reaction to Martin's stutter, his wife Lorraine invents a myth about him, showing that she has a strong degree of narrative power within the text in many ways, a fact that is also shown through her diaries, which Eva reads. When Lorraine first meets Martin while they are both studying at university in their youth, she constructs a loving, maternal narrative about him:

> When he walked into the ladies' bar later that night, Lorraine, who was taking a class in Greek and Roman mythology for her bachelor's degree, had already made up a myth about Martin van Rensburg. Every word in the world had been poured into him, but he had fallen out of favour with the Gods and they had stopped up his throat with rocks. She was the one who could free him (Fugard 2005: 101).

While Martin's stutter is shown to be a limit to his power in some ways, he uses violence to counteract any sense of powerlessness during the apartheid-era sections of the narrative. He takes his role as protector of his family seriously. The novel presents the ever-present danger of farm killings, referring to two neighbouring farmers, a father and a son, who were butchered, and constantly referring to the threat of 'terrorists'. Martin is always vigilant, constructing a fence around the farm and being on the lookout for potential threats. Ironically, there is no black violence against the family, despite this initial fear and Eva's intense dread at the end of the novel that the black workers will attack her. Here, Martin fails at his assumed paternal role of protector, but not because of the external threats he anticipates; rather, the danger within the confines of the farm fence are far more threatening than the perceived dangers from outside. Martin proves himself to be this danger when he kills the black child.

The night Martin kills the child on the farm is crucial to Eva's development; it changes her perspective of her father, ostensibly being a catalyst to her leaving the country, as well as making her complicit in maintaining this secret. Eva suspects what her father has done, and eventually she goes to find and bury the child's body. Lefu, the farmworker who joins Eva to bury the animals her father shoots, finds the skull of a child, and shares this story with his grandson Mpho. When Eva returns to the farm as an adult, she finds Mpho's diary in his home. Mpho practises his own narrative power to expose the truth of what Martin did, and refuses to be silenced. Eva reads in the diary:

> Martin van Rensburg Shot an Afrikan Child on the Farm Called Skinner's Drift. This is the storie. My grandfather found the body in the donga near the dam after the rains. He knew it was one of our people because the body had been thrown away. My grandfather had been riding horses with MISS EVA. He beried animals for her near the dam and when he told her about the body she would not look at him. She said she would tell the police he was stealing the horses if he spoke to them. My grandfather carried this storie for many years. When I was thirteen and a man he gave it to me. He told me to remember

the child. He said it is my responsibilitiy. I am now in the army in Walmaanstal. I have not forgotten the child running, while Makakaretsa chases him in the bakkie, pretending he will drive over him, scaring him. Makakaretsa had a machine gun. He shot the animals, the jackals and the lion. The white people think we are animals and they shoot us. They throw our bodies away. They think they are safe. But I am not afraid. This is my land. I speak now. I will tell them what happened. Amandla Awethu. JUSTIS IS MARTIN VAN RENSBURG PAYING FOR WHAT HE DID (Fugard 2005: 222).

The shift in narrative power indicates the confrontation of white privilege and the paternal narratives of Martin, in contrast with the past, in which the black workers would have no power to challenge him or to voice these secrets. Propst argues:

> By juxtaposing the perspectives of Eva and her parents with the viewpoints of Lefu, his daughter Nkele, and his grandson Mpho, and by undermining the final reconciliation between Eva and Lefu, Fugard dramatizes a persistent struggle for control over narrative and shows how the desire for reconciliation can subsume the recognition of ongoing responsibilities (2014: 202).

Neeves elaborates on this by demonstrating that both Eva and Mpho resist the established modes of conduct that their parents had demonstrated for them, showing how the novel can be seen as a renouncing of parental, especially paternal, authorship:

> Eva and Mpho, who are both born at the latter stages of Apartheid, are alike in their refusal to acquiesce to Apartheid's oppressive regime. Both struggle to follow the models established for them by their parents and instead strike out independently, attempting to forge new identities in the new society of post-Apartheid South Africa. However, where Eva chooses to escape from her homeland and ignore the traumas of her past by remaining silent, Mpho is empowered

by democracy and the arrival of the Truth and Reconciliation Commission in the region (2008: 122).

The novel deals with important tropes within recent South African discourse, especially the fear of black violence and the white guilt for enforcing control over black lives during apartheid. By indicating that the danger might not be solely located *outside* for white characters, the novel underscores the shifting of the position of paternal narratives, which would have once set up clear binaries and conflicts in terms of race.

On Eva's last night on the farm before she returns to New York, she is confronted with anxieties about the fear of Mpho attacking her, and she realises that these fears are located in the same space that caused her father to be violent, the danger that is assumed to come from outside:

> Eva's heart swelled with terror. Mpho and his friends climbed the stairs. They raped and tortured her. They cut her into pieces while she was still alive. In the pockets of time when she broke free of these lurid imaginings, she recognized how base and primitive her fears were, that they were the fears that had lurked in all of their bellies, had made her father fence the house, stockpile the guns (Fugard 2005: 228).

Eva recognises that she is falling within the paternal narratives that constructed the danger as residing in the outsider, even though she and her father had done real harm to their farmworkers. The text highlights the ironies and the obstacles to reconciliation inherent in a changing South Africa, and Eva again feels like an outsider to the country of her birth when she is unable to reconcile these tensions. Eventually, she decides to stay in the country for an extra week, showing that she still wishes to be confronted with the place she now sees as different, but which can no longer accommodate her secrets and those of her father. Propst explains:

> Eva's willingness to extend her stay signifies not so much a desire to redefine her relationship to South Africa as a return to

the family network . . . Eva lays claim to her lineage. Her desire for continuity wars with her recognition of how much has to change for South Africa to move past the inequalities of the recent decades (2014: 204).

The backdrop created by this reading of *Skinner's Drift* is useful when investigating two texts that received more national and international attention, and dealt more closely with the image of the ghostly father, *Playing in the Light* and *Kings of the Water*.

## Zoë Wicomb's *Playing in the Light*
### *The father's narrative control*
In Zoë Wicomb's *Playing in the Light* (2006), the conflict of traditional paternal narratives with the changing political landscape of South Africa is demonstrated by the complexities of racial identities. Marion, the owner of a travel agency in Cape Town in the 1990s, was raised to believe that she and her parents are 'white,' but discovers that her parents were actually originally classified as Coloured. Her parents discovered that they could 'pass for white' when they moved to Cape Town from their rural homes in Wuppertal. Marion wrestles with her racial identity by confronting her father, John, who tries to maintain the secrets of their past, and in this way the novel shows up the contradictions and nonsensical nature of racial classifications and laws in South Africa, as well as exposing how, in the words of Sarah Nuttall, 'secrecy – and lies – have been constituent elements of white privilege and power' (2009: 74).

Andrew van der Vlies has characterised Wicomb's novels *David's Story* and *Playing in the Light* as creatively engaging with the past, calling them 'a sensitive and imaginative engagement with the archive, and in a manner that is particularly rewarding to scholars interested in the literary mediation of ideas of history and in narrative encounters with notions of "truth" in post-apartheid South Africa' (2010: 584). The novels thus can be seen as a form of archiving histories of South Africa that might have been omitted or obscured by the 'silences' inherent in apartheid ideology. These silences become uncovered and spoken in post-transitional texts, especially once the myth of the 'rainbow nation' fades and the TRC is critically assessed as insufficient.

Moonsamy adds to this by characterising the past as something spectral, which haunts Marion and other characters: 'Wicomb portrays post-apartheid South Africa as primarily informed by a fundamental unwillingness to attend to its ghosts' (2014b: 73). These ghosts, however, cannot be avoided and expose themselves in ways that call into question identities and ideologies in post-transitional South Africa.

Marion's father, John, lives alone after his wife has died. John's age and the failing of his body are used to highlight the fact that he is struggling to reconcile his racist and racialist ideologies with a changing South Africa. The failing of his body is shown as a failure of his masculine power, and, by extension, the fact that his paternal narratives are unravelling.

At the introduction of his character he is connected with the familiar paternal narrative of religion, and the failing of his body is demonstrated through his inability to urinate:

> Panic rises, for he has been standing for some time over the lavatory bowl. His bladder is letting him down; it is finished and klaar. Ag please almighty God . . . The words tumble out before he can stop them. Then he reprimands himself: it isn't right to speak to God of such things (Wicomb 2008: 8).

There is an immediate connection between this failure of his body, the fact that 'his bladder is letting him down', and a loss of masculinity: 'Womanish tears threaten to spill from his eyes as he shakes the useless old tollie, begging for the dribble to stop' (Wicomb 2008: 8). The failure is located in his penis, a 'useless old tollie', which no longer serves him, and his frustration is followed by 'womanish tears'. Each of these descriptions reinforces how his masculinist power has faded, and he has become a decrepit, ghostly figure after the transition from apartheid.

Marion's physical link to the father is important as it signifies the immediacy of the link to the father's ideology. She reflects on a presumed family heritage that she infers from her physical resemblance to her father, constructing a history that, she will later learn, is a fiction, which allowed them to live a life of privilege during apartheid South Africa:

> The right corner of her mouth lifts ever so slightly, like that of her father and of his father before him, and so on, generations of Campbells, she supposes, going back to the old snowbound days in the Scottish Highlands, passing on the involuntary muscle movement to the men in the family. It is a pity that there are no photographs of her ancestors, something to do with relatives having fallen out with her father, a family feud of sorts, but John assures her that the giveaway lift of the corner of the mouth betrays the deep-down Campbell good humour, with which Marion, although a woman, is as well endowed as any (Wicomb 2008: 26).

There is also the familiar reference to the father's power of creating narratives that support his masculine power through the use of his voice. Once Marion becomes suspicious that John is keeping secrets from her, she reflects on the power he has to weave narratives to deceive her:

> She hears, knows with certainty that the lies are not new. Her father, no, both her parents, have always kept something from her; something they did not want her to know. That is why John has drawn her since childhood into the nonsense of myth, in order to drown his secrets, and her heart hardens against him: she'll ask nothing, not rely on him for anything (Wicomb 2008: 58).

John's deceit leads to a distance between Marion and him, although Marion recognises that she was swayed by her father's influence over her and that her entire life up to that point was framed within the paternal narrative.

She is similarly critical of John when he chastises her for using the racist term 'hotnosmeid' (Wicomb 2008: 58) to refer to their late housekeeper Tokkie, who, in fact, was Marion's maternal grandmother. John is upset that she would use the term to refer to Tokkie, saying to her: 'And you shouldn't be using words like that; she was no hotnosmeid' (59). However, Marion again reacts by explaining that she is merely reiterating the voice of her father: 'Marion laughs harshly.

And where would I have picked up such fine words? From none other than you.' John distances himself from the accusation, locating his racism within his historical context: 'Ag, my child, you'll just have to forgive your old Pappa. That was just how we spoke in the old days; it wasn't our fault.' This exchange highlights how Marion sees John as constructing ideas of race that she has adopted, and she uses the offensive term to call attention to John's hypocrisy in distancing Tokkie from a term he would easily have used for other Coloured people.

John is located within deceit, and his power is gained through the racial fiction that he constructs. Marion contests his power by confronting him with truth and by discovering as much as she can about their past. John suggests that men are the controllers of truth, and that he should have exclusive access to it and not 'burden' his wife Helen with the knowledge of the oath he had to take in swearing that he is white:

> Helen had not known of the oath he had to take. John thought it unmanly to burden her with such details, believed that he should shield her from unnecessary distress. Now he is equally determined to shield Marion. These are not things with which to burden women. He is her father; he is there to protect her. Only, Marion wants to know everything (Wicomb 2008: 154).

John's control of information and truth is something he adopts as his masculinist and paternal duty. He wishes to 'shield' Marion from the implications of his own deceit. Marion later refers to this paternalistic control as reflecting religion:

> He has sealed off the past so that the cold spotlight of the present does not flood its pointlessness, the silence and lack of colour that makes up his whiteness. His mantra of we-did-our-best-for-you is infuriating, typical of a generation who bullied their children and believed that they could mould them in their own images. Like God (Wicomb 2008: 175).

### The father's fiction of whiteness

The image of John's ageing is often shown to highlight how he is out of place in the context of post-apartheid South Africa. In an early scene, he is looking through a window and sees a young woman walking in the street:

> She tosses her bleached yellow hair and snarls, Fuck off dirty old man; mind your own fucking business. So that he retreats hastily, pulls back the curtain and sits far back in his chair, shaking with rage and terror. Yes, this is what it boils down to: the young terrorising the old. No respect, he mutters, and a flash of his former self on the traffic island in Long Street, in his uniform, giving white-gloved directions, comes to his rescue then goes again as he staggers out of his chair (Wicomb 2008: 13).

John tries to hold on to an image of himself in a position of power, when he worked as a traffic officer, in order to counteract the powerlessness he feels in the face of this woman and the assault she represents of a country where he is no longer as univocally powerful as he was under apartheid. He remembers himself as a young traffic officer, controlling traffic in the same way that he was able to dictate the terms of his race, and able to benefit from his manufactured whiteness and the deceit with which he maintained his family's power.

Later in the novel, when Marion finally discovers the truth, John completely retreats into the past as he loses his sense of power in the present. He dresses in his traffic officer uniform again when Marion visits him. The image of him trying to relive the power he felt during his past is comical but also uncanny and pitiable. He is constructed as a 'ghost from the past', someone who no longer fits in with his surroundings:

> Her father stands in the doorway like a ghost from the past. With the help of the doorposts and a newfound courage, he is fiercely erect, all but salutes her. He is dressed from head to toe in his old airforce-blue traffic-cop's uniform. The buttons strain around his expanded belly, but he stands smartly to attention, his braided hat fallen deep over the shrunken head. The gloves, yellow with age, are slack around the withered hands. In this get-up, his skin waxy like a corpse and enveloped

in the mustiness of dust and mothballs, he is an emblem of the phantasmagoric past (Wicomb 2008: 155).

Marion recognises that John is attempting to hold on to his paternal narrative of whiteness and the power that it afforded him in the face of her search for truth. She reflects:

> He has no idea . . . none at all of the terrible injury he has done to her, to his family, to himself. His belief in the might of whiteness surpasses everything else; he does not know that the world around him has changed, that it has lost its pristine, Reckitts Blue whiteness. He is a child, selfish in his drive to escape, selfish in his belief that he has done the right thing (Wicomb 2008: 155).

Moonsamy comments on this moment by focusing on the discomfort it causes Marion: 'In the moment in which he tries to recover the former glory of a job that he only managed to obtain because he had passed as a white citizen, Marion feels something of a ghost that needs to be slain' (2014a: 95). Marion recognises the incongruity of her father's desire to exercise power that only deceit had given him, and how he is divorcing himself from his new reality. Not only does she desire to counteract her father's display, but it also leads to her recognising that she has to confront her own racial identity and the 'performance' that she was a part of as well.

Marion's own relationship with her 'whiteness' is tumultuous throughout the novel. She seems to have simplistic racial ideas and does not recognise her white privilege when she is met by two parking attendants:

> She'll be damned if she's going to tip these skollies for hanging about her car. You can't go anywhere nowadays without a flock of unsavoury people crowding around you, making demands, trying to make you feel guilty for being white and hardworking, earning your living; and of course there's no getting around it: hundreds of rands it costs per month, being blackmailed by

the likes of these every time you park your car. And then the impudence of watching as you get out, watching as you lock the door, willing you to feel uncomfortable about your own belongings (Wicomb 2008: 28).

Marion reflects on this as an annoyance of dealing with men who are not white and seem to make her feel guilty about her own whiteness and wealth. Whiteness affords privilege, something that John was aware of and the reason why he chose to 'play white'. John thinks that his decision to play white is a good one when he thinks about parents being relocated because of their race: 'He, John Campbell, would never be bullied like that by the law; and as for his child, his little mermaid, she would hold the world in the palm of her pretty hand' (Wicomb 2008: 114). The power afforded by the category of whiteness represents John's paternal narrative power; he is able to renegotiate his position because of the colour of his skin and align himself with a narrative that gives him greater power as he is able to 'play white'. Marion, consequently, takes her privileges as a white person for granted, and the novel constructs an uncomfortable reflection of how fictional race and racialism are in South Africa; the categories of race are deconstructed. When Marion learns of her past, she finally begins to reflect on her white privilege and is critical of it, but her father is never able to do this.

John holds on to his racism as it was vital in giving him the power that he held during apartheid, and which remained after the end of apartheid. When Marion offers to bring a gardener to his house, he says: 'They kill you in your own garden . . . These kaffirs of the New South Africa kill you just like that, just for the fun of it' (Wicomb 2008: 13). John shows that he cannot move past his own racist thinking and the narratives associated with it.

John is despondent about the state of democratic South Africa, often demonstrating his racism and his own role in maintaining paternal narratives of apartheid, as well as his connection to the masculine symbols of the military and violence. When Marion receives a call that the security alarm at her office has been activated, John reflects on his role as father and of the changing country:

> Thus moved by his own helplessness, his inability to protect his darling child, he lets on after all: This country is going to the dogs, he says, wringing his hands. To think how hard we fought, took up arms for a decent life, for a country of which we can be proud (Wicomb 2008: 14).

Marion is confused by her father's statement, and the depths of John's racism is revealed to her:

> Marion stares at him in amazement. Is he losing his marbles? But Pappa, she says, you've never supported the liberation movement. What on earth are you talking about? He pushes back the frail shoulders and, once more the reservist soldier fighting for his country, tugs at the imaginary uniform. Sis man, he says with indignation, I'm not talking about that lot, about terrorists. Remember Sharpeville, remember the kaffirs here on our own doorstep in Langa? Well, I was one of those who volunteered as a reservist to defend South Africa against the blarry Communists. Oh, your mother was proud of me alright; she always liked a uniform. But all in vain, hey. Look what's happened: kaffirs and hotnots too lazy to work, just greedily grabbing at things that belong to others, to decent people (Wicomb 2008: 14).

John demonstrates his link to the apartheid past through how he uncritically fights to defend the system that would have oppressed him and his family if he had not been able to 'play white'. He is unable to reconcile himself with the national narrative after the end of apartheid, still employing ideas of liberation fighters as nothing more than 'Communists' and 'terrorists', and employing racist language to attempt to assert his power.

### *The deconstruction of race*

The character who is most responsible for Marion's reflections on race and racial dynamics in South Africa is Brenda. Brenda is a Coloured employee in Marion's travel agency, who often clashes with her white colleague, nicknamed Boetie. When Boetie reads a story about a killing in the newspaper, he says: 'So this is what democracy has brought us, hey, he sighs. Just chaos and violence, that's what we can thank the new government for' (Wicomb 2008: 36). Brenda responds by trying to make Boetie understand the history of racial division and white privilege in South Africa, telling him: 'And you don't think you should take any responsibility for it?' In response to this, Boetie becomes enraged, trying to construct a narrative of South Africa that supports his own power, as well as his innocence in the problems of the country:

> Boetie leaps out of his chair, flinging aside the *Argus* as if it had uttered the offensive words. Me, *me*? He splutters. Are you out of your mind? This is your lot, killing each other and causing mayhem; nothing to do with us. Really? You don't think that years of oppression and destitution and perversion of human beings, thanks to the policies that you voted in, have anything to do with you? Boetie wags his finger. Now listen here: first of all, I never voted for apartheid . . . No? No, of course not, Brenda interrupts. It's impossible to find a person in this country who voted for the Nationalist Party. God knows how that phantom called apartheid came into being all by itself (Wicomb 2008: 36).

This exchange is important as it highlights how whiteness has been divorced from privilege in popular conceptions of South Africa during the transition, with white characters denying their complicity in the apartheid system. Brenda serves to disrupt this simplistic narrative, reminding other characters about how their narratives of innocence are incompatible with the reality of apartheid. Stéphane Robolin says that the novel is set at a time when 'Cape Town's residents are in the midst of uneasily recalibrating the terms of their cosmopolitan lives and redefining their relationships – political, personal, and ethical – to one another, while struggling with and against desires for continuity' (2011: 349). Brenda highlights how race has divided people in South Africa to have such vastly different experiences that even agreement on a common narrative of history becomes extremely challenging, or in her thinking, impossible: 'Brenda is angry with herself for rising to the bait. She does not usually speak out: there is no point in talking about these things. It is not possible for people from the different worlds of this country to talk to each other' (Wicomb 2008: 38). Conversation and understanding, in Brenda's view, are limited because of the racial divisions of the past and how these bleed into and inform the social landscape of South Africa today.

As someone who would have been disadvantaged because of the colour of her skin, Brenda is able to offer a perspective that characters like Boetie and even Marion, early in the novel, would not have wanted to hear. Indeed, Brenda offers a counter-narrative to the simplistic, racialised narratives that Boetie and Marion use to explain the problems in South Africa.

Later, after Brenda accompanies Marion on a visit to Wuppertal to find out more about Tokkie, Marion learns that Tokkie was in fact her grandmother. Brenda says to her:

> So it turns out you're coloured, from a play-white family, Brenda says. So what? Haven't you heard how many white people, or rather Afrikaners of the more-indigenous-than-thou brigade, are claiming mixed blood these days? It's not such a tragedy being black, you know, at least you're authentic. And just think of the other benefits: you need no longer speak in hushed tones – you're free to be noisy, free to eat a peach, a juicy ripe one, and free of the burdens of nation and tradition (Wicomb 2008: 102).

Brenda, with the help of the maternal narrative introduced by Tokkie, shows that Marion has attained a sense of freedom from the strict racial identity she held before. She is no longer confined to act in a way that she might have been expected to because of her race. Brenda also points to the fact that many people are re-narrating their pasts to undo the simplistic racial identities that they might feel no longer afford them the same power as during apartheid. Race becomes an unstable concept, and racial identity becomes something that more and more people are willing to 'play' with. Even though the reasoning of those adopting new racial histories might not be innocent, Brenda shows that there is a sense of freedom when this paternal narrative of race becomes undone.

When Marion tells Geoff, who she is dating, about what she has discovered on her trip, he responds by again sharing a non-racialist, idealistic and naive ideology about why it should not matter to Marion:

> He says that it doesn't matter, that he along with the entire country has got beyond all that old stuff about race, and that she too should put it behind her. They've just had the first democratic elections. It's the New South Africa, almost a new century, a new groove, so what is she fretting about? (Wicomb 2008: 105)

Geoff tries to discount the actions of her parents and Marion's confusion by claiming that race does not matter in the 'New South Africa', but she is not convinced, as she begins to reflect on the meaning of her whiteness. Her father acts as a mirror of white privilege and the myths around race that she so strongly subscribed to before she discovered that her own racial identity is not what she thought. She gives consideration to the complexities of race in an interesting extended passage:

> It may be true that being white, black or coloured means nothing, but it is also true that things are no longer the same; there must be a difference between what things are and what they mean. These categories have slimmed down, may no longer be tagged with identity cards, but once they were pot-bellied with meaning. The difference – that is what Marion cannot get her head around. How can things be the same, and yet be different? Is the emptiness about being drained of the old, about making room for the new? Perhaps it's a question of time, the arrival of a moment when you cross a boundary and say: Once I was white, now I am coloured. If everything from now on will be different (which is also to say the same), will the past be different too? (Wicomb 2008: 106)

Marion engages in a deconstruction of her own racial identity, wondering if this absence of meaning is at odds with the great amount of meaning that her race once held and the obvious meaning that it still holds, not only for herself, but for South Africa as a whole. While Geoff tries to get her to look past the question of race, and tries to tell her that race has no more meaning, she wonders how this affects her identity. She tries to understand herself as someone defined by the past but now without definition because the category of race is one so strongly avoided in everyday South African discussions of identity. She says to Geoff:

> My parents were the play-whites; *they* crossed over. I was white, now I will have to cross over; but if those places are no longer the same, have lost their meaning, there can be no question of returning to a place where my parents once were. Perhaps I can now keep crossing to and fro, to different places, perhaps that is what the new is all about – an era of unremitting crossings (Wicomb 2008: 106–7).

Geoff wonders in response to this assertion: 'Is she theorising the rainbow nation?' (Wicomb 2008: 107). Marion's theory, however, is far from this ideal, which Geoff wants to believe in, and she is instead theorising identity politics that is based in nothingness or the avoidance of history.

Marion visits the library after confronting John to find out more about 'play-whites'. She discovers that whiteness is an extremely slippery concept. She reflects on her parents during this investigation:

> Marion takes the wedding photograph out of her handbag to look again at the country-shy couple who betrayed their families, who obliterated their histories, who stripped themselves of colour to be play-whites. According to the National Library, they did not exist. Did they think of themselves as dissidents, daring to play in the light? Or as people who could mess up the system, who could not be looked up in libraries, who had escaped the documentation of identity? She thinks not. They thought only of their own advancement (Wicomb 2008: 122).

The decision was based on seeking the privilege of whiteness, an incredibly tenuous concept that Marion is now told to ignore in the

New South Africa. While her parents were confined within the strict boundaries of race, one of the foundations of the patriarchal apartheid system, they managed to disrupt this system, something deemed to be impossible. Their existence exposes the unstable nature of paternal narratives and patriarchal systems of oppression. While paternal narratives try to locate subjects simplistically within hierarchies, this is often not achievable. For Marion, this disruption is extreme, with the concepts being rendered absurd and meaningless.

John and Helen are focalised in sections where they also reflect on whiteness:

> Vigilance is everything; to achieve whiteness is to keep on your toes. Which, John reasons, indicates that they cannot achieve it after all; being white in the world is surely about being at ease, since the world belongs to you. But they, it would seem, cannot progress beyond vigilance, in other words, beyond being play-white (Wicomb 2008: 152).

True whiteness in the apartheid system is seen as a position of carefree power, not the struggle that John and Helen constantly face. They reason that they can never truly be white, but will constantly be engaged in deception. Later they also reflect that 'they must raise the child without the burden of history' (Wicomb 2008: 152), indicating that being defined as something other than white is located within history, while whiteness is ahistorical, something transcendent that allows for history to not affect those who are white. This might indicate why Boetie is able to ignore his own complicity in apartheid and explain away his privilege.

### *The image of the mermaid*
The tenuous relationship of reality and fiction, history and ahistory, black and white are captured in the image of the mermaid, a meeting of two worlds. John hints at this by referring to Marion affectionately as a mermaid: 'Ever since she can remember, her father has been fixated on mermaids . . . Marientjie was his very own meermin, with her long light-coloured hair that waved like the sea' (Wicomb 2008: 46). John sees the dual worlds captured within Marion, who is a

product of his fiction and a living symbol of the power that the fiction gives him access to. Minesh Dass notes that the image of the mermaid is evocative in many ways, indicating a sense of homelessness in Marion:

> The mermaid is hybrid, both human and fish ... In myth mermaids called hauntingly (much like sirens) to homesick sailors, offering an alluring comfort which drew the sailors from their ships (arguably liminal vessels themselves, designed to move between destinations) to their doom. The idea of race is like the mermaid's song, I would suggest: as an escape from it or as an acceptance of its validity, its purity, which can then be mixed to create the impure hybrid, race beckons us with the promise of a mythic home (2011: 142).

Helen helps with the childhood games of turning Marion into a mermaid, but resents the duality suggested by the image and uses it as a way to chastise John. Helen seems more committed to whiteness than John is in these moments, even though he symbolises the power associated with whiteness in the novel after Helen dies. Marion remembers how her mother binds her legs into a tail to turn her into a mermaid:

> Her mother snorted, even as she helped to wind the cloth into a bound tail. It's Campbell's nonsense that prevents him from getting on in life. No good being half woman and half fish, half this and half that; you have to be fully one thing or another, otherwise you're lost. Mermaids are the silly inventions of men who don't want to face up to reality, to their responsibilities, the fantasy of losers who need an excuse. I've been led astray by a mermaid, Helen mimicked in a plaintive voice, casting an accusing look at John. And see, she said, now you're all bound up, you won't be able to move (Wicomb 2008: 47).

Helen seems to favour choosing whiteness and completely distancing the family from any association with their past, even telling John to avoid seeing his sister and parents. This resentment is shown in her anger towards the image of the mermaid. Within this novel, the familiar maternal narratives are not associated with the dead or ethereal mother herself, as in many others, because the mother is steadfast in her association with narratives of power and race; however, maternal narratives are instead located in Helen's mother Tokkie, the figure who becomes a reminder of the suppressed past.

Later in the novel, Marion reflects on the mermaid again when she thinks of Tokkie. Marion reads an article in the newspaper about a woman who was tortured while in prison as part of the resistance movement, and begins to think dreamily of Tokkie. Tokkie becomes a spectre that haunts Marion in the novel, as Horn, in her reading of the novel, explains: 'Marion Campbell's life is disrupted by the spectre of an unfamiliar yet uncannily familiar face on the ocean [near to] her apartment in Blouberg, an upmarket suburb where mainly wealthy white Afrikaners live, ironically with a direct view of Robben Island, where political prisoners were kept' (2012: 130). This demonstrates Marion's position between the past and present, and how she can never escape the secrets of her past in the same way that Robben Island haunts the periphery of Blouberg. Tokkie becomes a ghost to Marion, a figure that Horn places as important within post-apartheid South Africa: 'The ghost is inextricably linked to ideology and the imagination. The ideology of Apartheid that was predicated on the racial superiority of Afrikaner whites becomes spectral when the repressed Other haunts the imagination of those on the right side of the racial divide' (127). In a scene that is a mixture of the fear of the secrets of her past as well as signifying her connection with her maternal grandmother, whom she had been told was their housekeeper, Marion associates Tokkie with the ocean:

> From her balcony, she stares in horror at an enlarged face floating on the water, a disfigured face on the undulating waves, swollen with water. A smell of orange, the zest as freshly peeled orange skin, wafts up from the shore, mingling with brine. It is not until she goes back indoors that recognition beats like a wave against the picture window: Tokkie, it is Tokkie's face on the water (Wicomb 2008: 55).

Tokkie is not shown to be a mermaid in the image, but is shown to be out of place in the water, seeming to have drowned with a face 'swollen with water'. This image of horror represents that Tokkie was unable to exist in two worlds as Marion did. Meg Samuelson suggests that in the novel, the sea operates as 'an archive of stories suppressed and drowned out by official narratives and a textual space able to articulate unspeakable loss' (2013: 15).

### *The role of literature in reconciling the past and present*
Marion's reaction to these conflicts is similar to the reconciliatory method undertaken in Behr's *Kings of the Water*, where literature offers a bridge into imagining difference and working towards reconciliation within the changing South Africa. Marion starts to immerse herself in narrative when she takes a trip overseas, similar to Rosa's ability to gain a sense of identity in *Burger's Daughter* once she is able to leave the country. The allusions to earlier works of South African fiction seems to be intentional on Wicomb's part, as she references many prominent South African novels, including Gordimer's and Coetzee's novels, to show Marion's growth as a character.

Marion has lived her entire life under the paternal narrative of racialism and the power of whiteness, and she now seeks to escape this narrative. Brenda is the one who offers her literature as a way for Marion to learn to connect with others more, a maternal narrative approach of openness and multiplicity: 'Brenda harangues her about reading. Her failure to understand human relations can apparently be traced to the fact that she doesn't read good novels or poetry' (Wicomb 2008: 162). Brenda continues: 'To live vicariously through other people's words, in other people's worlds, is better than not living at all' (163), insinuating that Marion's existence is a sort of liminal one, linking to her earlier concerns about not having a definitive identity. She also identifies with the character Magda in Coetzee's *In the Heart of the Country*, whose identity is shown to be characterised by an absence, and Brenda seems to imply that she can fill that absence through literature. During her time in Garnethill, Scotland, Marion begins reading Coetzee's novel again:

> Now she has started again, slowly, drawn into the crazed thoughts of Magda, a hole crying to be whole. Marion tosses the phrase in her mind, but she does not identify with Magda; that father is not her father. So Garnethill, she thinks, is also a place where she learns to read, and who knows, perhaps this time Magda's stones will crack open to reveal meaning in pearly, red pomegranate seeds (Wicomb 2008: 202).

The association with Magda again places Marion as the rebellious daughter trying to break free from the narrative dominance of her father and of the apartheid state. Dass explains how literature and distance allows Marion the possibility of renegotiating her identity:

> Marion, in this literally foreign land, is able to discover in the stories of her country new versions of herself. It is as if the foreignness, the state of being necessarily unhomed, allows a certain sense of identity to become possible. This sense of self, or more properly selves, is achieved through fiction and narrative (2011: 145).

Marion's growth is obvious when she returns from her trip to Scotland. She begins to see that the paternal narratives of race and nationality are limiting, and instead challenges John's prejudices when she sees him again. She had met a man named Dougie, who gives her a gift of a tie with the Campbell family crest:

> The Scots, [John] pronounces, are a stingy people who won't part with a cent. Marion explains patiently that that is nonsense, that one should be wary of so-called national characteristics, that it takes only one Dougie, who parted voluntarily with a great deal of money for the tartan tie, to prove that John is talking rubbish. To which he nods sagely: yes, he has been catching himself out lately, thinking rubbish thoughts (Wicomb 2008: 211).

John has also been affected by Marion's confrontation of the ideas of race and identity, and this moment signals that he begins to shift into more inclusive views as well.

Marion is greeted by a surprise party on her return from Europe, and John's 'Coloured' sister Elsie attends as well, indicating a reconciliation for John with the past. The final scenes reflect the major themes of the novel: the fluidity of identity and how race is not the fixed identifier that apartheid ideologies would have wanted to portray it as. John shows that he has changed as well because of Marion's questions and her journey, portraying one of the few fathers in South African fiction who is actually influenced to reassess his paternal narratives due to his child. *Playing in the Light* is thus much more hopeful for stagnant paternal narratives to shift in post-transitional South Africa than other texts, such as *Kings of the Water*:

> He sings tunelessly: Afrikaners is plesierig dit kan julle glo / Hulle hou van partytjies en dan maak hulle so – conducting with his stick and winking conspiratorially at Geoff. Ag no sis, Boetie John, don't go spoiling the party with Boere nonsense, Elsie says, bearing a tray, and he laughs uproariously, tapping her behind with his stick. Man in this New South Africa we can play at anything, mix 'n match, talk and sing any way we like. Because of freedom, he explains (Wicomb 2008: 213).

John embraces the idea that identity is a lot more fluid than simply being assigned or even choosing a race, and he is finally given the freedom to play with his identity in any way he chooses, no longer strictly confined by the expectations of whiteness.

## Mark Behr's *Kings of the Water*
### The heritage of power

With his third novel, *Kings of the Water* (2009), Mark Behr explains that he wanted to write a '*plaasroman* for the 21st century' that 'grapples with what is unique about South Africa while simultaneously insisting that we are radically and inextricably linked to the outside world, that our uniqueness is nothing special . . . that we, in South Africa, are in fact, at last, quite ordinary' (Behr 2010). This appeal to the global 'ordinary' country signifies that the 'spectacular' nature of the country during apartheid and even the transition has finally come to an end, and that human stories about 'ordinary' occurrences have become possible.

The story is set in September 2001, once the TRC process had been completed, and the country seems radically different to the returning expatriate character Michiel. The account of Michiel can thus be seen much more as a global novel, one that deals with a character who can see South Africa both as an insider and an outsider, and who can engage with its political reality critically while rejecting both the narratives of apartheid ideology as well as the simplistic narrative of a 'New South Africa'.

Once again, as with many other novels, these issues of national narratives are focused through the father figure, who in this novel comes to represent apartheid systems of white economic and social oppression of the black majority through the microcosm of the farm. As Jeanne-Marie Jackson notes: '*Kings of the Water* explicitly tackles the so-called New South Africa and its place in the world. And yet, it does so almost entirely through confinement to a remote farm steeped in fraught apartheid history, where the family patriarch, though withered, still reigns' (2013: 179). By returning to the family farm after the death of his mother Beth, Michiel represents the almost otherworldly and isolated nature of this location in the eyes of an expatriate character. Jackson notes that 'Behr, who like his main character lives mostly in the USA, seems to embody the next frontier for South African studies now that the transition model has run its course' (175). Jackson elaborates on how the novel can be seen as 'global': 'Its protagonist, Michiel Steyn, lives with his half-Jewish, half-Arab partner Kamil in a trendy San Francisco neighborhood full of transplants. Michiel works as a language instructor for international students – he's planning a trip to China – and recounts his social awakening as a young émigré in London and Australia.' Jackson places this novel in a trend of post-colonial writing where transnational fluidity is symbolic of a connected and post-modern world, and where stifling paternal narratives are resisted: 'The construct of nationhood gets left in the twentieth century; networks thicken and expand; cosmopolitanism becomes not the achievement of a worldly elite but the everyday reality of hyper-connectivity; fiction rushes to keep pace' (176). However, the chief concerns of the novel are negotiated in the farm setting, again showing this site's narrative resonance in South African literature, as Jackson notes: 'It is through maintenance of the farm's confines that Behr depicts national and personal change' (187).

Wamuwi Mbao frames his engagement with the novel through the ethics of mourning, questioning who is allowed to mourn whom in post-transitional South Africa: 'What foreclosures occur in South African society that may limit or prevent the grieving of certain losses?' (2013: 81). Behr's novel can be seen as symbolically mourning the assumptions of a hegemonic privileged white Afrikaner identity, which was becoming increasingly interrogated and problematised after the end of apartheid: 'In the aftermath of the first democratic elections of 1994, the oppressed and the forgotten came under scrutiny, as the country sought ways to deal with its unresolved past.' Michiel's interrogation of his past and of the identity politics that he sees as entrenched in life at the family farm, Paradys, are mirrored with the moment of mourning his mother. Mbao explains that confronting the past after apartheid often involved destabilising assumed identities of power:

> Of particular concern was the way in which white South African nationalism was arranged around a central narrative that defined how men behaved, how they defined themselves, and how they acted in society. The ideal male figure in this society was a willing proponent in the masculinist hegemony. Propped up by the pillars of sports, religion, and military participation, South Africa's white patriarchal order was openly hostile to those who went against its dictates. The mythmaking which sustained the Apartheid order was at the expense of those minorities which did not fall within the heteronormative scheme. It instilled a model of hyper-aggressive masculinity steeped in history and culture and implicated in various forms of interpersonal and institutional violence. This model, importantly, was the scaffolding underpinning the daily routines and rituals of white South African males: at school, where sporting prowess and obedience to rigid authority were promoted; in the home, where obedience to the father and not showing weakness were of paramount importance; and finally in the military, where the collective state-sanctioned violence was regarded as a de rigeur assertion of masculinity (2013: 81).

All three of Behr's novels can be seen as confronting the way in which white Afrikaner masculinity and patriarchal apartheid ideology intersect, with his second novel, *Embrace* (2000) exploring a teenager named Karl de Man, who wrestles with his sexuality and with the expectations of his cultural background. Mbao points out that in *Kings of the Water*, 'Michiel Steyn's surname is a homonymic evocation of the unjustness at the heart of White relations to the farm' (2013: 87). Within transitional and post-transitional South Africa, when the dominance of white patriarchy is (ostensibly) unseated, Michiel confronts this 'stain' but can distance himself from it much more than characters in Behr's other texts can.

The connective image of physical resemblance is used to highlight the biological as well as the narrative link to the parents. Michiel returns to his family farm to attend his mother's funeral, and reflects on what led him to leave South Africa for San Francisco. Interestingly, for Michiel, the first mention of family resemblance actually refers to his mother, subverting the traditional construction of father-son relationships as paramount, and signalling a shift in paternal narratives and a greater distance from the father. His partner Kamil says to him when his mother visits them in San Francisco: 'You have her nose' (Behr 2009: 6). There is also a link to the mother shown in the fact that Michiel is interested in language and literature, and his mother is often connected with works of literature. Michiel reflects: 'She was the retired high-school English teacher . . . He (the apple had not fallen far from the tree), with an MA in English Literature from Berkeley, the director of International House, a transnational company that teaches English as a Second Language' (5). This common interest in literature also places an emphasis on the idea of maternal narratives, which are achievable through progressive literature, giving power to many different voices, shifting perspectives and allowing for stifling paternal narratives to be renegotiated.

However, the novel also shows that Michiel has a physical resemblance to the father, signalling that he is subject to the narrative power of his father. Their housekeeper Alida says when she first sees Michiel: 'Kleinbaas! It's like looking at Oubaas when he was a young man!' (Behr 2009: 18). However, both Michiel and his father resist this association, suggesting their psychic distance and their ideological differences. In an exchange between Michiel and his father, this becomes clear: '"You're going bald," Oubaas says. "I've heard it's a gene from the mother's side, Pa. Grandpa Ford never had much hair." "Your Mother's child, in bone and marrow"' (22). The physical link to the mother is highlighted again to show that the father does not connect with the son, and, by extension, the father's ideology will not be passed on to the son.

Kamil, however, deflates this physical connection by showing that it is purely indicative of biology and does not point to any deeper bond. He says this in reference to Michiel's tumultuous relationship with his mother and his struggle to forgive. Kamil says: 'Parents don't redeem themselves. Rarely to their children, anyway. It is a relationship of blood, not choice' (Behr 2009: 9). This indicates that Michiel has a choice to break free from the struggles of his relationships with his parents, despite the physical link he has with them. This is an important moment since it sets up Michiel's distancing from his father, who does not ask for forgiveness and does not seek to truly reconcile their relationship.

Michiel is unable to break through the barriers between him and his father. This is powerfully demonstrated when his father asks Michiel to give him a bath. Michiel sees this as a moment of possible redemption, where his father is softening towards him and might be ready to reconcile. However, his father goes on to blame Michiel for the death of his mother, saying: 'What I'm ready for is to join Ounooi. Heartbreak killed her, you know. You have a way with women, don't you?' (Behr 2009: 27). Michiel, who is still washing his father's body, understands the implications of this statement by his father, namely that his mother was heartbroken that Michiel is gay. He reflects:

> He looks up; what Michiel reads in the blue eyes is contempt. Clearly the insistence that his son – *this* son – be the one to bath him is not some grand gesture of reconciliation. No, this is born from a disdain still simmering all these years later. This is not a mother's funeral; it is to be a father's final showdown with a son. For this he has been lured to the farm (Behr 2009: 27–8).

Michiel hardens towards his father again at this point, realising the immutable fissure between the two of them. This disconnect is symbolic of the larger disjuncture between the ideology that his father represents, namely, traditional patriarchal masculinity and what Michiel represents to him as a gay man who abandoned his military duty and his role as father and left South Africa.

Jackson notes that this bath scene 'reinforces Paradys' robustness vis-á-vis a similar scene of caretaking in San Francisco' (2013: 184), where Michiel lovingly baths Kamil when he is extremely ill. These contrasting bath scenes demonstrate again Michiel's distance from his father and South Africa, and how he has forged a new identity outside of the country, finding love overseas. Jackson elaborates on this by explaining that a moment that seems to signify bonding, and a joke about Michiel washing his father's penis, again turns sour and shows how his father tries to assert his authority: 'In the space of just five lines, Behr moves from the relief of laughter over a crude joke shared between father and son to Oubaas' reinvigorated tenacity and patriarchal authority. The rapid shifts in his demeanor and the tonal recalibration they demand of Michiel accentuate Paradys' uniquely confrontational capacity' (185). Michiel responds negatively to this provocation and resolves to maintain his emotional distance from his father in the same way that he recognises how inconsistent his father's ideology is with his own transnational sensibilities.

## *The father's fading power*

The fading of the father's ideological power is located in his body again. When once his father was powerful and exercised this power over Michiel and his brothers through his physical presence, now his body and his power are fading, as Mbao notes: 'The father's crumbling corporeality subverts his authority, that authority being located in his status as masculine patriarch' (2013: 97). Michiel reflects: 'Already he senses how light the old man is. What have time and disease left undone to the behemoth before which they quivered until deep into their teens?' (Behr 2009: 29). Mbao, however, also refers to an interesting physical intertwining of father and son during the bath scene when Michiel cannot separate his father's smell from his own:

'He is increasingly aware of his own proximity to the aged patriarch, noting his father's inescapable "stale smell" and wondering if it is possible that his own odour (the result of not having washed while in transit) is co-mingling with his father's' (Mbao 2013: 96). Thus, despite the fading of the father, there are implications that the son has not fully escaped his influence.

The power of the father's voice is also shown when Michiel refers ironically to the power that silence has had in their relationship. The voice of the father seems to become internal for Michiel, inspiring an 'unyielding vigilance' to fulfil the requirements that his father has of him. However, the words were not directly spoken to Michiel except when he is commanded to leave the farm:

> You and I have never had much to say to each other might be the most truthful response. Silence has always reigned between us. As a boy I tried constantly to read you to know what you thought of me and wanted of me. I twisted myself in knots to please you; embraced an unyielding vigilance I'm still trying to unlearn. You spoke more to me – at me – as you sent me packing than in all the years before (Behr 2009: 32).

Mbao notes that despite the father's physical deterioration, his gaze and voice, and the power they afford, are still shown to be unchanged: 'Crucially, it is the gaze of the father that remains rooted: the eyes that have looked on in condemnation and the voice that had pronounced [Michiel's] banishment have not altered' (2013: 95). These factors emphasise his patriarchal authority.

Words and language play an important role in demonstrating the changes in their relationship. Michiel wills himself not to use the affectionate word 'Oubaas' to refer to his father: 'He cups his hands around his mouth and calls down the hallway: "Pa!" He won't, he resolved way back, ever again speak the word *Oubaas*' (Behr 2009: 15). The title would place him at a position of inferiority to his father, as he sees it as a word of respect. He refers to how the housekeeper Alida uses the titles 'Kleinbaas' and 'Oubaas' to refer to Michiel and his father respectively: 'The absence of personal pronouns. Similar to the way Afrikaans kids never addressed their parents or other white adults without the honorific' (20). The titles indicate a sense of respect and fondness, and Alida, because of her race and position, is forever relegated to the position of a child who needs to employ these honorifics in order to communicate with white people. Michiel resolves never to position himself as his father's subordinate again.

There is no intimacy between Michiel and his father when he returns, but the novel suggests that there never was. Michiel had struggled to overcome the distance between them, and seems resolved to no longer try to do so. The lack of intimacy can be seen when Alida turns the wheelchair away from Michiel as he first sees his father, and he reflects: 'Turning the wheelchair, solves the problem of whether Michiel will shake his father's hand. Or hug him. A kiss would have been unthinkable' (Behr 2009: 20). The lack of physical closeness indicates the fundamental chasm in their relationship.

When Michiel's father challenges him about his decision to leave when he had conceived a child with Karien, whom he had dated when he was younger, Michiel is also shown to be a failed father figure to this unborn child. Karien eventually loses the child after a failed attempt to terminate her pregnancy, but she refuses to talk to him again. Michiel's father says to him upon his return to the farm: 'How could you leave her when she was pregnant? . . . That was not how I raised my sons' (Behr 2009: 34). Michiel reflects on this: 'If we were the way you raised us, Michiel could say, there would be nowhere on earth for us to live.' Michiel implies that his father's ideology would be out of place in a democratic South Africa and with his new status as a 'global citizen'. The changes in the country are at odds with the traditionalist paternal narrative, which the father sought to pass on to his sons.

Jackson elaborates that the novel suggests a shift from Behr's *The Smell of Apples*, where ideology is now able to be resisted by the son: 'The claustrophobia of a place and ideology which Behr's earlier, child narrator cannot escape is replaced in *Kings of the Water* with a protagonist who *did* escape, and who has ostensibly found happiness and self-acceptance in his new, San Franciscan existence' (Jackson 2013: 179). This escape, however, does not negate the entanglements that Michiel has with his past and with South Africa, and, indeed, Jackson notes: 'The narrative structure in which he is embedded tells a different story, in which the dynamism of "going back" to the farm offsets the relative thinness of the worldly identity that succeeded it.'

## The mother's role in reconciliation

Despite Michiel's continuing distance from his father, he does, however, find closeness with his mother again before she dies. His mother seems to seek to reconnect with Michiel and even visits him in San Francisco to repair their relationship. His mother says to him when her visit ends: 'I have loved you, child of my heart, through everything' (Behr 2009: 9). She later says: 'A mother understands. And I know you do too. Love takes a thousand and one shapes' (10). Through her acceptance of Michiel being gay, she is able to find closeness with him again and express her love. Importantly, this is only able to happen outside of South Africa. The country is still associated with the father, and the mother's love only finds expression outside of these confines. The father's homophobic ideology and his association with tradition and patriarchy leave the country forever hostile to Michiel, even when he tries to reconnect with him.

This is evident in how he sees South Africa once he returns for his mother's funeral, questioning the simplistic construction of a 'New South Africa', while still seemingly being optimistic about the changes he notices. As Moonsamy highlights, Michiel is 'invested in a historical reading of sameness and is thus exasperated by his South African friends and family who are seemingly "duped" by narratives of historical progress and transformation' (2014a: 88). Jackson notes that Beth is the only other character shown to occupy the national and international space, signifying that she serves as a bridge for Michiel's return. However, 'this live connection is literally severed for it to even begin: it is her death that serves as the catalyst for Michiel's return to Paradys. In other words, the only bridge between these places other than the protagonist is quite literally a ghost' (Jackson 2013: 183). This could further cement Michiel's disconnect with the country as he does not have the comforting, accepting presence of his mother outside of the memory of her.

Michiel's mother is associated with positive changes in South Africa since the dawn of democracy, as she explains to him:

The changes: the township now has electricity and running water; there is renewal and a buzz of energy in the education system; the New South Africa where *things are positive, growth as far as the eye can see. The country looks like one enormous building site.* She'd just read and admired *Long Walk to Freedom* (Behr 2009: 8).

Importantly, literature gives her access to alternative narratives, and her interest in literature implies her association with maternal narratives, which favour change and the sharing of power.

Despite the transformative power of the maternal influence, Michiel no longer sees himself as part of South Africa, not the version his father belongs to nor the one his mother embraced. Alida's daughter, Lerato, was educated and became a successful businessperson, and Michiel sees this as indicative of the changes that are possible in a democratic South Africa. Jackson highlights the fact that Lerato's position is also complex in relation to the race, gender and class relationships on the farm:

Behr speculates about how this powerful black woman might relate to the many workers who still reside on the farm. Her relation to them thus forms a kind of third zone between apartheid South Africa and its modern 'global' successor, complicating the transitional linearity that might seem to hold from the outside (Jackson 2013: 181).

Michiel reflects on his and Lerato's tumultuous positions within the country:

I have returned, Michiel thinks, as little more than a voyeur. No longer a participant but in a brief walk-on part as a spectator, a member of the chorus. *South Africa's Miracle* he sees and hears in the media, the phrase of both earnest and self-congratulatory dinner-party conversations. A miracle, he knows too, fraught with a thousand and one challenges obscured by Lerato and her bright children driving in a new Swedish car past the path she once took barefoot to school (Behr 2009: 50).

Michiel's mother was responsible for making sure that Lerato was educated, again showing her commitment to sharing power and to working towards the ideals of reconciliation. However, Jackson notes that 'Little Alida [Lerato] remains xenophobically allied with Michiel's father despite her prominent standing in the New South Africa' (2013: 181) by sharing negative comments about a visit to China, echoing a tone of racism that the novel associates with Michiel's father. This indicates that Lerato is still inexorably linked to paternal narratives, both personally in her relationship with the patriarch as well as politically and narratively as she still sees herself as an outsider: 'The fact that Little-Alida at first resumes her place outside the farm's main house despite her powerful job reads most readily as an illustration of the *plaasroman*'s incompatibility with a new, internationalized social hierarchy of which she sits at the top' (186).

At his mother's funeral, Michiel learns that Beth has been involved in many community projects, including attempting to reopen a community swimming pool. The pastor who conducts her funeral service says:

> [She] believed that the younger our children play together and learn to swim together, the sooner the town will heal . . . Beth put her shoulder to the wheel in surprising ways: she raised funds for the children's shelter, she joined the Women's League to lobby the state for seSotho-language books in the Langenhoven Library. And even after she retired, she and Karien Burger founded the Women's Literacy Program. For most, it was the first time our people sat at the same table (Behr 2009: 93).

The desire for children of different races to swim together indicates the potentially transformative role that water has in the text, and the children playing together with their mothers at the end of the novel mirrors Beth's vision. It is also significant that literature and reading, in the form of the library, is seen as a way of bringing about reconciliation and togetherness, highlighting the power that narratives can have in broadening understanding.

Michiel again feels closeness with his mother when he hears that his mother 'wanted to know what she and others could do to promote dialogue about what was happening with HIV and AIDS' (Behr 2009: 93). In response to hearing this, he feels pride and love for his mother: 'Michiel's heart swells. Ounooi, my hero. Beloved, through everything.' Because Kamil is HIV-positive, Michiel sees this as a way of his mother championing Michiel.

Tanja Gruber notes that this moment is significant as it demonstrates how apartheid required 'compulsory silences' enforced through patriarchal systems, such as Michiel and his brother Peet's silence about being gay or Karien's silence about her failed abortion. Ounooi's ability to work towards 'dialogue' here signals that she is resisting the silences implicit in paternal narratives, offering a voice to an issue that largely affects the voiceless and powerless in society:

> It could also not have happened before the change of the regime that Ounooi promoted the dialogue about HIV and Aids in the community. Michiel learns only after his return to the farm, how important the topic had become to his mother and how much she had done for the community by addressing its problems. She and the mayor had realized that 'silence is killing our people' . . . Of course, this is not only true for the community, but, in fact, rather for Ounooi herself who has not only lost Peet, but in a way also Michiel as consequence of the compulsory silencing (Gruber 2014: 48).

## *Exile and whiteness*

Despite the positive advances that his mother was a part of, Michiel is struck by the superficiality of the discussions about the end of apartheid and change in South Africa, reflecting: 'So far, the words white and black have not been uttered' (Behr 2009: 93). The issue of racial inequality is not addressed in an outright manner, and Michiel becomes frustrated that the changes in South Africa are so idealised.

Michiel wonders about how white people can so casually speak of change and ignore their own complicity in apartheid. He also sees himself as an outsider to the country because of having left: 'Have histories been revised? This, he thinks, is at long last the new being born, dragging its afterbirth along with it, scratching its head to figure out a way to imbibe the past or otherwise see itself perish. And he has chosen to remain apart from it. *Exile*' (Behr 2009: 94). He wonders about the meaning of this word and whether it can really be applied to his situation because of his race and the reasons why he left South Africa: 'He thinks of the word as belonging in the realm of politics and coercion . . . It has never been appropriated for himself, for whatever he is it does not make him the blood kin of exile . . . He left here with a white skin, a thousand and one choices, change to spare and only personal scores he wasn't sure he wanted settled.' Michiel is conscious of his privilege as a white person in the national and international arena. His earlier criticism of the idealised discussions about change in his community shows that many others do not acknowledge the racial inequalities that still exist.

Michiel again reflects on white privilege when he sees his father, brother and nephew all leaving the funeral service together in Benjamin's expensive car. His assessment highlights the generational inheritance of wealth and the heritage of white privilege in South Africa: 'Oubaas is leaving with Benjamin and Thomas. The boy wheels the chair to the slick silver Mercedes-Benz. There, Michiel thinks, go the last three generations that will have it like this' (Behr 2009: 118). Michiel seems to think in this moment that there will be an end to white privilege with the changes in South Africa, and that the matter-of-fact transference of wealth and privilege will be curtailed somehow.

After the funeral, the entire family gathers for a meal at Michiel's father's farm, and because of a hailstorm, the farmworkers and Lerato are unable to leave the main house, so they gather for dinner as well. Michiel reflects on this unusual gathering by thinking of his mother, a conversational maternal narrative associating the mother with the possibility for this gathering: 'Unbelievable, I know: Ounooi, are you here, rather than on the other side of your orchard, to witness this? Face to face, side by side, yesterday today and tomorrow. They bow their heads for Dirk to say grace as the rain at last starts coming down on the roof' (Behr 2009: 127). Despite Michiel's apparent cynicism, he is shown to be hopeful and to be swayed by the image of reconciliation that this dinner represents.

However, Michiel still recognises that economic inequality is a major source of racial tension in the country. In a discussion of farm killings in South Africa, and a brutal murder of a white family in the community, he reflects: 'It goes without saying that the intruders had no jobs, no homes, no investment in not executing their deed. No motivation to adhere to morality or laws designed over three and a half centuries for the express purpose of keeping them out and in their place' (Behr 2009: 157). Michiel acknowledges the collapse of the laws, which would constitute a paternal narrative of maintaining racial segregation and the exploitation of black people in South Africa. This has very negative consequences, as violence ensues due to the lack of material resources for these black perpetrators, as Michiel imagines them. The violence is shown to be a result of structural inequalities, and serves as a revolt against inequities rooted in laws of the past, with the legacy of these laws still existing in South Africa today, a moment reminiscent of Alan Paton's early constructions in *Cry, the Beloved Country*.

## Violence and masculinity

In Behr's novel, violence is often linked to masculinity. Daniella Coetzee elaborates on how conflict and violence are constructed as masculine endeavours that serve patriarchal structures: 'The notion of "combat" plays . . . a central role in the construction of concepts of "manhood" and in justifications of the superiority of maleness in the social order' (2001: 303). Violence in the novel is gendered through the father, represented through his conflict with his sons, especially Michiel, and his demand for Michiel to complete his military service. Gruber argues that 'aggressive and suppressive patriarchal structures which rule life on the farm in *Kings of the Water* can also be seen as a microcosm representing the suppressive macrocosm of the apartheid regime in South Africa' (2014: 39). When Michiel refers to his time in the military to his psychologist Glassman, Glassman responds: '*basics and boot camp* – euphemisms for young men trained not to feel so they can kill without thinking and live on, without feeling' (Behr 2009: 24).

Michiel reflects on violence and rage as located in his father during the pivotal scene when he is giving his father a bath:

> He meets his father's eyes, sensing that something between them has altered. For ever, or only here, while the declining patriarch is drifting at his son's mercy? With Glassman he

has speculated whether the old man suffered from a kind of bi-polar disorder. Could the outbursts at his boys and at farm workers be given a neurological rather than a psychodynamic diagnosis? (Behr 2009: 30)

Michiel refers to his father as the 'declining patriarch', indicating that he is in the process of losing his power and control. This is, again, linked to a decline in his body, but importantly in this scene, Michiel is starting to re-narrate his father and understand him in new ways, particularly through the lens of mental illness. He has discussed his father with Glassman, and seems to gain a form of narrative power himself when trying to understand his father, which might allow him to feel less intimidated by the 'declining patriarch'. Michiel later reflects on how his violence was only directed at other men, particularly his three children:

But how to account for the selectivity of his rage? Never, in Michiel's memory, was the physical or verbal violence directed at Ounooi or at Alida. Oubaas could clobber a worker or any of his sons, shout or growl at incompetence but be as friendly as summer dawn the instant Ounooi or Alida came near. Or Karien; all those weekends and holidays here (Behr 2009: 30).

Michiel then sees his father within the lens of patriarchal, masculinist power, explaining to Glassman: "'My dad suffers from more than biochemical imbalance or misfiring neurons. Whatever it is is mixed in with the delusions of raw white South African male power. You have to have grown up there to know what I mean." And Glassman laughed out loud and said: "Michiel, I'm from Texas"' (Behr 2009: 31). The reference to 'white South African male power' indicates the privileged position of these men and how they are represented as using violence as a means to maintain their power, similar to patriarchal structural violence to maintain the apartheid system. Glassman's response is important as it universalises the idea of masculinist power and its link to rage or violence.

Michiel's own complicity in the reproduction of paternal narratives, and how he is almost unconsciously framed within these narratives, is shown when he decides as a young man to become an officer in the army and to go to war. Glassman asks him:

> Why did you choose to become an officer and go to war in a foreign country? Why not a pen-pusher or drive a truck? Michiel, some sessions later: There was no decision, no choice that I remember making consciously; it was as easy as breathing. Michiel, another year later: I was too embarrassed not to go. Too ashamed not to be an officer. Glassman: Shame masquerading as pride? Michiel: I didn't see it like that at the time (Behr 2009: 40).

Michiel eventually rebels against this by running away from the army and simultaneously abandoning a pregnant Karien. He denies his position as potential father and escapes the narration of his own father, who demands that he stay and complete his army service. When a friend of his in San Francisco questions why he left the army, portraying it as a highly sexualised space, Michiel responds: 'I felt ridiculous . . . like an imposter in the army' (Behr 2009: 181). Michiel explains that he felt 'relentlessly ashamed of being part of it and at the same time so apart from it: a fraud, an interloper in the conspiracies of violence. Nothing sexy about that.' He sees himself as distant from the violence that constitutes idealised masculinity, even though he does not seem critical of the ideology underpinning these masculinist displays.

This idea of failed masculinity haunts Michiel, and he is confronted with it in very striking ways when he returns to South Africa to face his father. During the bathing scene, Michiel's father says to him that he only invited Michiel to the funeral because of Beth: '"I asked you here because she loved you! Perversions and all . . ." "Is there no mercy in you?" "Mercy! You sound like a woman, for Christ's sake. If you must be this thing you are, can't you at least pretend to have balls?"' (Behr 2009: 35). By shaming Michiel and simultaneously linking him to being 'like a woman' and not 'hav[ing] balls', his father demonstrates Michiel's deviation from the idealised masculinity that he espouses.

### Benjamin as paternal successor

Michiel's brother Benjamin seems to be the paragon of masculinity, perfectly encapsulating the paternal narratives that his father values highly. As Gruber phrases it: 'Benjamin symbolizes the ideal patriarchal successor' (2014: 38). Michiel links Benjamin to many symbols of masculine power, from business acumen to sport and even the military. He watches his brother who has 'his eyes cast up, allowing Michiel to notice the chin still chiseled despite some weight, the sun-tanned skin and the gait still throbbing with the stuff that makes a rugby captain, and an army officer who throughout life never breaks rank; whose gentle balding merely cowls his supreme confidence' (Behr 2009: 65). Michiel reflects how this pleases his father:

> The middle brother's character radiated everything Oubaas wished for. That was Benjamin's luck, which more often than not the other two were grateful for: that Benjamin accepted himself as the ready repository of their father's every ambition meant that at least some of what may have been demanded of them frequently was not (Behr 2009: 76).

Because of Benjamin's hypermasculinity, and his easy adoption of the ideals of masculinity, Michiel and his brother Peet were spared at least some level of scrutiny and scorn. Benjamin shows the capacity for leadership and control, and these are again linked to images of violence, which Michiel earlier distanced himself from. Michiel reflects how Benjamin seemed ideally suited to work on the farm: 'Benjamin rattled off inventories of sheds and storerooms, assessed the annual harvests from individual trees without glancing at a logbook as efficiently as he could slit a sheep's throat' (Behr 2009: 76). Indeed, the traditional Oedipal conflict is most clearly demonstrated between Benjamin and his father through violence. The battle of wills that often encapsulates father-son relationships in literature can be seen through Benjamin and his father. Gruber explains that 'socially accepted aggressiveness as part of hegemonic masculinity is visible in the novel in the clashes between "the old Oubaas" and the potential new Oubaas Benjamin' (2014: 39). The conflict is a way of strengthening the bond of respect between father and son and ensuring that the son is capable of perpetuating the paternal narrative. Michiel says:

> [Benjamin] confronted his father in ways Peet had no impulse to do and Michiel was too timid for . . . No argument on Paradys reached the pitch of those between Oubaas and the Chosen. Cut from the same cloth, they were like bulls aware of each other's strength, the older knowing only time kept the younger from bringing him down. One either killed the other or abided by – or got off on – the violent camaraderie (Behr 2009: 77).

The 'violent camaraderie' demonstrates how this conflict is a form of bonding for father and son, because, unlike Michiel, Benjamin does not threaten the paternal narratives that the father promulgates. As Mbao explains of the fight that seems to secure Oubaas's respect for Benjamin, violence is a way for the bond between father and son to be solidified through the masculinist symbol of violence, as Michiel looks on at his brother whispering something into his father's ear after their fight: 'Michiel's distance is inscribed explicitly in this scene, as is his brother's proximity to their father' (Mbao 2013: 108). Benjamin is an idealised masculine male in the view of his father and of his society, and thus he is easily accepted and favoured by the father. It is evident here that 'the father requires an adversarial intimacy with his sons, for the simple reason that without this contestation, his power is untested and becomes unfulfilled. Oubaas's fear of Michiel comes down to a desire to test the limits of his patriarchal strength' (109).

Michiel seems resentful of his brother's adherence to idealised masculinity, and recognises that because he is unable to easily perpetuate this form of masculinity, he will never be close to his father. He explains to Karien, reflecting on the scene where he baths his father: 'For a while he seemed to want a kind of reconciliation with me. Then he got angry. That life hasn't succeeded in toughening me up seems to piss him off' (Behr 2009: 149).

## *Gay men as outsiders*

Glassman suggests that Michiel might have found a way to reconnect with the masculine expectations of his father if he had become a father himself. He asks Michiel about Karien's attempted abortion and her eventual miscarriage:

> Glassman: No sense of disappointment? Michiel: Why would there be? Glassman: Is there no part of you that wishes you'd fathered a child of your own? Michiel: Not under those circumstances. Glassman: Contemporary culture places a premium on man's worth as a procreator. If she had the baby . . . regardless of or even because of your being gay, would that not in a way have compensated . . . (Behr 2009: 152).

Being a father himself, according to Glassman, might have allowed Michiel a way to regain some of the masculine power that his father demanded from him. As Gruber explains, homosexuality 'violates the procreative function of sexuality and therefore the possibility for strong, (white) male successors' (2014: 51), and Glassman seems to offer the possibility that becoming a father would negate this element of being gay. However, Glassman highlights, as Michiel frequently does, that being gay is an impenetrable barrier between Michiel and his father, one that is never transcended in the novel. Even though Michiel had the opportunity to be a father and perhaps transcend this, there is the suggestion that this might not have been enough to bridge the gap between him and his father.

The fissure created by Michiel's sexuality is shown in another scene related to water, where Michiel suggests that the titular 'king' of the water is effectively his father. The morning before Michiel initially leaves South Africa and escapes his army service, he is found by his father:

> He was naked on the dam wall, legs dangling in, weighing options as thoughts of Karien – *I can't bear the thought of you near me again* – bumped against despair and the impulse to escape. This is where Oubaas found him. He stood on the sawed-off eucalyptus stump, looking down on his son's head of short army hair. Michiel dropped his hands to his crotch, vulnerable below the man who owned the dam, the orchard, the farm. The world. He looked up; his father looked away.

> Michiel tried to broach the idea of going overseas (Behr 2009: 58).

The moments of Michiel leaving South Africa and his return are both marked by nakedness and water. Michiel's nakedness here indicates his vulnerability, and his father positioned above him shows his relative power over Michiel, a part of what Michiel needs to escape from. Gruber explains that this scene shows that 'in Michiel's view his father is not only the highest authority of the Afrikaner farm household, but appears almost as a god-like figure who possesses everyone and everything – even the world' (2014: 38). The distance between them, even in this intimate scene, is apparent, and it is echoed again when Michiel is bathing his father. At the time Michiel leaves South Africa, his father again refers to his masculinity and him not 'be[ing] a man' when he says: 'I will not acknowledge this thing and what you are. Be a man, for once. Go back for your national service and face yourself. After that we can talk' (Behr 2009: 58). When Michiel refuses, Gruber explains that 'the consequence of this . . . is of course the expulsion from the farm – the heteronormative space, or, in other words, Michiel's fall from Paradys. Oubaas leaves him no other option' (2014: 44).

Michiel finds out after Peet's death that Peet was also gay and was HIV-positive, signalling the connection between the two brothers as well as explaining why their father could not connect with either. Gruber notes:

> Peet could not live with the pressure and the shame he would have had to face when confessing his homosexuality and his illness. Growing up in a stereotypical male world consisting of violence, a lack of emotion and the rejection of everything that deviates from the patriarchal norm, he saw no escape other than committing suicide (2014: 47).

Gruber highlights that 'two out of three sons had challenged the hegemonic Afrikaner masculinity and consequently had to pay a high price for it' (2014: 48).

While the father is often linked to the nation in paternal narratives, there seems to be an interesting contrast with regards to sexuality. Michiel's initial abhorrence for South Africa can be linked to his disdain for his father and the fact that as a gay man he did not feel like he was accepted by father or country. Gruber further clarifies that 'Behr shows how homosexuality can shatter the idealized image of a hegemonic masculinity as well as patriarchal structures. The novel also outlines how homophobia, in turn, serves as a means to reinforce heteronormative masculinity as an ideal in a patriarchal society' (2014: 36).

When he leaves South Africa for London, Michiel is swayed by a woman involved in the African National Congress (ANC), and he attends a meeting where liberation politics is discussed. He seems to be persuaded by the discussion and even feels a sense of connection with South Africa again because of it. However, the question of gay and lesbian rights is brought up at one of the meetings that Michiel attends, and the same woman who gave him a book on liberation politics responds in homophobic terms:

> Gay men and lesbians are jumping on the back of the democratic movement and exploiting the struggle for their own ends. I don't see them homeless or hungry or suffering. Where does this business come from? It's very fashionable over here in the West. It will disappear along with colonialism and racism. We haven't heard of this problem in Africa until recently. In a liberated South Africa people will be normal. Tell me, are lesbians and gays normal? If everyone was like that the human race would die out (Behr 2009: 132).

Michiel leaves the meeting after this, feeling a distance not only from apartheid South Africa, represented by his father, but also from the liberation movement since neither will accept him for being gay. He reflects: 'Let them stew in their hateful white and black fat, together. May that country burn with all of you in it. He never returned to anything hinting at South Africa' (Behr 2009: 132).

Later, after the first democratic elections, he hears from his neighbours in San Francisco who have visited South Africa that LGBT rights have become a part of the democratic agenda:

South Africa's new constitution prohibits the death penalty and, astonishingly, contains a clause protecting people from discrimination on the basis of sexual orientation. He relives the incident at the Commonwealth Institute. Was that not only the other day? How could Africa's oldest liberation movement so rapidly have changed its mind? So much for democracy: let courageous elites change policies behind closed doors and drag the great unwashed kicking and screaming into the new millennium (Behr 2009: 180).

Michiel maintains the sense of distance from South Africa and does not feel that the change in policy allows for him to swiftly change his attitude to the country that had once rejected him.

Despite his broad rejection of traditional masculinity and the symbols associated with it, Michiel, however, does practise one of the symbols of masculinist power through his sexual freedom. He cheats on his partner Kamil, and tells him: 'Men like fooling around a bit, Kamil, for god's sake' (Behr 2009: 81). Kamil connects Michiel's infidelity to his father, asking Michiel: 'Did your old man have affairs? Michiel: Thank god for small mercies, not as far as I know. Kamil: Then where did you get it from?' (114). Kamil implies that Michiel's sexual infidelity is part of a paternal legacy, and later Michiel explicitly connects his sexual appetite to masculinity. Glassman says to him, linking sex to many symbols of masculine power like violence and sport:

> That may be where both football and war can be read as erotic: you can touch as long as you violate. Michiel: Instead of fucking? Glassman: Even fucking may be a defense against intimacy. You know that. Michiel: What if it is just part of a healthy, normal masculinity to give and receive sexual pleasure widely, like animals? (Behr 2009: 182)

Michiel sees himself as enacting masculinity by having sex with many partners and being unfaithful to his partner Kamil. Importantly, this is not linked to real intimacy, but rather is seen as a way of escaping intimacy with Kamil by seeking out sex with other men. In the same conversation, Michiel again connects this form of what he sees as masculinity to the father: 'Michiel: In some ways I still feel ashamed of that, in myself. Glassman: Of wanting to be loved, wanting to give love? Michiel: As though I am a lesser male. Glassman: Tell me more about this normal masculine. Michiel: Just being a regular guy. Glassman: Who is this regular guy? . . . He looks back at Glassman and sees Oubaas at the dam wall' (Behr 2009: 182). It is important that he thinks of the father in this moment, as the father represents Michiel's shame at his feelings of not being masculine. By seeking out sex with many men as a way of avoiding intimacy, Michiel imagines that he is mirroring his father's masculinity.

Because Kamil represents everything outside of the expectations of Michiel's father, genuine intimacy with him will constitute the ultimate betrayal of paternal narratives for Michiel, as Mbao elaborates: 'Kamil is everything Michiel's early conception of masculinity and concern with concealment is against: he is camp, self-assured, and a member of outspoken activist groups. He has none of Michiel's anxieties, and he moves through the novel being and saying the things that Michiel is reluctant to be and say' (2013: 119).

However, sex can also be seen as a way of transgressing the paternal narratives around race. Because Michiel prefers sex with black men, he constructs it as a form of differing from his father even further. Glassman asks him:

> And why is it that you could go to bed with the Indian lieutenant then and not with the white lieutenant a few weeks earlier at the camp in the desert. I even imagine a blind eye turned more frequently to such things in a war zone. You: You're trying to get me to say it was because he was black, or not white. You want me to say it was because of the extra thrill or that the risk to me was smaller because as a man of color his word didn't stand a chance against mine, even with my lower rank (Behr 2009: 112).

Michiel recognises his white privilege in this moment, that he faced a smaller risk for having sex with a person who is not white, as this creates a power differential. Michiel later makes it explicit that the sex is seen as a way of defying the father:

> Glassman: Your country of birth is finally shedding its racist government and you're in my office, staying away from compulsive casual sex with black men. Is this mere coincidence? Michiel: Why must you always explain who I sleep with in terms of where I come from? Why link it to shame and guilt or to defiance of the goddamn father? (Behr 2009: 138)

Michiel's actions are contextualised again in relation to his father and country. Through defying his father's racism and heterosexism by sleeping with black men, Michiel can actually be seen as enacting a type of Oedipal resistance against the father in the same way that Benjamin does through violence. In this sense, it could explain Michiel's feeling that having affairs allows him to be masculine.

## Challenging the father and creating new narratives

The reference to race is important, and Michiel's father is shown to hold racist ideas, which Michiel resists. His racism also puts him at odds with the changes in South Africa, again signalling the precarious position of the father in a changing country. Michiel's father exposes his racism when he says to Michiel:

> You won't find a white face [in nearby towns]. Nothing has seen a coat of paint in years. They slaughter goats and cattle right in the town center – even in churchyards – for whatever sacrifice or witchcraft their gods demand. Every main street now has some sort or other *boy* name. Everything's gone to the dogs (Behr 2009: 62).

Earlier in the novel, when Michiel and his brothers are children and their mother is driving them to school, his brother Benjamin does not want to sit on the spot where Lerato sat in the car because he says he will smell when he gets to school, saying: 'I'm not sitting where that *kaffir girl* sat. I don't want to smell of kaffir when we get to school' (Behr 2009: 48). His mother reprimands him, and Benjamin responds by exposing the racism of the father as well as demonstrating how he is encapsulated within the paternal narrative: 'Oubaas says kaffir when you're not around, Ounooi!' She takes a very strict stance against this and demands that Benjamin walk to school instead of driving in the car with them. Her resistance to his racist outburst demonstrates how she will become a figure for reconciliation in the novel, and how she is able to also heal her relationship with Michiel when his father is unable to do so.

The various symbols of masculine power present throughout the novel are undermined in favour of more inclusive, multivocal narratives. These shifts demonstrate the undoing of the power of the paternal narratives and move towards narratives that favour democracy and reconciliation, alterations that reflect changes nationally. The paternal narratives seem to be replaced or reimagined by younger generations of South Africans.

These multivocal narratives are shown by referencing older texts, a trend also seen in Wicomb's *Playing in the Light*. There are various references to literature throughout the novel, what Christopher Hope has referred to as Behr's 'weakness for reading lists of favourite South African writers' (2010), and literature is shown to have a reconciliatory function. Michiel demonstrates the emergence of narratives early in the novel when he quotes a line from a novel by André Brink and reflects: 'Had the book once been banned?' (Behr 2009: 2). This demonstrates that narratives that were once suppressed are being exposed.

Behr reveals in his interview with Van der Vlies why the novel is so concerned with literary allusion, and shows how his novel is framed around the idea that narratives have a powerful impact on the subject:

> We live in a time where consciousness and knowledge is formed by unquantifiable exposure to narrative and to narrative behind narrative and the narratives behind those. We no longer have an easy time knowing why we know and say things the way we do. Epistemology is now, more than ever, a fascinating subject: where does our knowledge come from; how do we know what we think we do when language and stories come over us in such volume? The inclusion of a list of allusions (which is not exhaustive) at the end of *Kings of the Water* was my idea. It was not demanded or expected by my publishers. I put it in for three reasons: to call attention to literature as a constituent part of epistemology; to acknowledge and celebrate that much

of what Michiel thinks and what the narrator and I as the manipulator of the narrator know or say comes from others' work; and, finally, I included the bibliography as prophylactic against those who may have wished to reduce public review of the book to a drama about plagiarism (Van der Vlies 2011: 19).

Karien also explains how narrative power is being diversified nationally and how stories of black writers are being shared. She says to Michiel:

And a world is opening up here through the pens of old writers like Mphahlele, Modisane and Kuzwayo, who wrote in English. And voices she has just now been discovering: Njabulo Ndebele, Zoë Wicomb, Damon Galgut, Zakes Mda, Marlene van Niekerk and Mandla Langa. Oh, and Yvonne Vera from Zim. She and Dirk – they read to each other in bed – are almost through a novel called *The Quiet Violence of Dreams* by a young writer called K. Sello Duiker. From among these, one will arise to take over from the great Gordimer and the even greater Coetzee (Behr 2009: 189).

Literature, as demonstrated in these moments, has the power to give a voice to silences and to resist power structures. Coetzee and Gordimer, whose works are prominent in the South African literary landscape during apartheid and today, are now in the company of many black voices. Mbao adds that this demonstrates an awareness that the novel itself is a part of a literary community:

The novel declares its membership of a community beyond itself. It signs to further places of escape from the limiting and limited positions of the discursive economy within which it is situated . . . it signals to that which remains, that experience of community which forms around this text and the works with which it converses (2013: 90).

Karien shows this again as Michiel is leaving by giving him a CD with recent arrangements of traditional Afrikaans folk music: 'From a carrier bag she produces a CD and two slender books. The CD is of

Afrikaans folk music, rearranged by a new wave of young musicians. She wants him to hear how the fetters of language and music are being undone. Listen to the drive, she says' (Behr 2009: 225). She demonstrates that narratives that might have been seen as oppressive or stifling are being reimagined and re-engaged with in ways that show change and vitality. The novel, thus, offers a hopeful image of the transitioning South Africa, even though Michiel can never truly feel at home in the country and even though he is highly critical of the simplistic narratives of reconciliation and change.

Michiel is eventually able to gain a sense of narrative power for himself. He practises this by telling the story of the pied piper to his niece Bianca, and she tells him that he is wrong about them having peppermint tarts 'in the olden days' (Behr 2009: 184), to which he responds: 'Would you indulge me? May I be allowed narrative control?' He discovers his own sense of control over the stories, which might be as deep-seated and familiar as the story of the pied piper.

When the piper in his story leads the children out of town after not being paid for clearing the rats, Bianca assumes that he leads them 'back to the river, where they all drown' (Behr 2009: 185), but Michiel responds that this is not how his narrative goes: 'No, he says. No one drowns because of what grown-ups who always think they know better did or didn't do.' This shifting of the narrative, where the sins of the father are not visited on their children, ends the novel on a note of hope for the democratic South Africa. Michiel, as the symbolic son and father figure in the novel, is able to alter the narrative as he chooses, and is not bound by the choices and will of his own father.

### Zukiswa Wanner's *Men of the South*

Zukisa Wanner's *Men of the South* (2010) represents urban black fatherhoods that defy conventions and gender expectations. It offers an insight into how ideas about fatherhood are shifting in South Africa and how gender expectations are being confronted to unsettle established paternal narratives.

The novel explores three black male characters, whose narratives are connected by a woman named Slindile. The first character focalised is Mfundo, a musician living in Johannesburg who is a stay-at-home father, while his wife, Slindile, is the breadwinner of the family.

Slindile resents him for not working and their relationship crumbles as a result. The second central character is Mzilikazi, a gay father of two who, after coming out to his wife, gets a divorce and moves to Cape Town. He is good friends with Mfundo and Slindile. Finally, Tinaye is a Zimbabwean man who is seeking citizenship in South Africa. He dates a woman named Grace and wants to marry her even though he does not love her, but he meets Slindile after she divorces Mfundo and they fall in love. He decides to leave Grace for Slindile, but Grace informs him that she is pregnant, and he stays with her.

Investigating these three fathers indicates the rising critical stance towards masculinities, where men become similarly viewed in terms of their gendered identities as women traditionally were. This displaces the assumed 'naturalness' of being male, and could destabilise the power of masculinist narratives.

The representation here is not predominantly of a dying or ghostly father, but young, urban, black fathers who defy gender expectations and experience their fatherhood as a dynamic, conflicted part of their lives. There is also the commitment from Mfundo and Mzilikazi to be loving, attentive fathers to their children, overcoming the distance between fathers and their children, which has often defined literary representations of fatherhood in South Africa. The novel shows that fatherhood is not one thing to all men, but fathers are diverse in South Africa and experience their roles as fathers very differently.

Early in the novel, Mfundo does show the archaic view of traditional patriarchal fatherhood when he refers to his brother Sindiso, explaining how Sindiso tells his parents that he does not want to attend school anymore because he has found a better way to make money. He says: 'Papa, I am not asking, I am telling you' (Wanner 2010: 13). Mfundo reflects: 'My father was the law in our house. No one had ever answered him the way Sindiso had,' demonstrating a dominant father similar to many earlier representations. This reflection by Mfundo, set within apartheid, demonstrates a father who practises his power within his home and who is challenged by his rebellious son.

Sindiso also shows his disruption of paternal narratives when he questions his father's assertion that education will allow him to gain more power in society. When his mother tells him that he needs an education, Sindiso says: 'What education, Ma? Bantu education that teaches us to be slaves to white people?' (Wanner 2010: 14). Later, he frames this criticism by referring to his father being subservient to white men and white interests: 'Papa, you had an education and look at you now. Is that rich? "Ja, meneer. Nee, meneer. Yes, sir. No, sir."' Sindiso's early rebellion in the novel demonstrates the fact that traditional paternal narratives were already failing in South Africa during apartheid, indicating how these narratives will shift later in the text once apartheid ends.

Mfundo also specifies how he essentially loses his father to politics, showing that paternal narratives, such as apartheid or even liberation politics, would often lead to the father being removed from his role as father:

> Papa was a supporter of the ANC-aligned United Democratic Front, a Charterist like the rest of the neighbourhood. And it was this support that would leave our house fatherless. The tighter [P.W.] Botha's noose became around anti-apartheid activists, the more active my father became in the movement, and one day, when I was thirteen, my father disappeared – no one knew where to, but a certain notorious Special Branch man (black, not white) was suspected of knowing what had happened. The Special Branch man never did get to testify at the TRC because he had managed at the right moment to align himself with the ANC and was now considered one of them. Carry a few bags, wash a few feet and claim you have found God, and you are absolved of all murders. Bloody benevolent comrades. Politics is kak, man (Wanner 2010: 16-17).

Mfundo is critical of politics and the hypocrisy he observes, even in the ruling party, which is at the forefront of the liberation struggle. He is rendered fatherless by the paternal narrative of politics, and he never receives justice for his father's disappearance and assumed death. The reflection highlights the tensions surrounding the TRC process, which was essentially a device that sought to expose a more inclusive, perhaps even maternal narrative of the various stories of South Africa's violent history, but in the end also served political ends and created new versions of silences.

Mfundo reflects that he has to assume the role of 'man of the house' (Wanner 2010: 17) when his brother and father are absent. He uses this moment to consider masculinity and the expectations he faces because of the position he is in. What Mfundo exposes is the immense pressure he is under to define a slippery concept, namely, masculinity. The expectations seem to be reminiscent of the oppressive fatherhoods shown in many of the texts in this book. However, Mfundo wants to break free from these roles and be a different sort of father figure:

> It was a difficult role, too, since in my neighbourhood it was never defined what it was that men did, exactly. There were two types of them, you see. There were the happy-go-lucky men in the neighbourhood who would send me to buy them some loose skyfs at the nearest spaza shop as they sat drinking at all hours of the day. Then there were the salt-of-the-earth type of men like my father and Mzi's father, who looked after their families and came home on time. But these men were dictatorial. Their wives feared them, their children feared them. I never wanted to use either of the two groups as a role model. What examples of men do I see? I once asked Mzilikazi. How am I to turn into a better man if these are the only men I am encountering? (Wanner 2010: 17)

Mfundo highlights the fact that masculinities outside of these narrow margins are very rare. He does not have any examples of fathers who do not merely repeat these common patterns, either being the extremely oppressive men who rely on their power to control their wives and children, or escaping their circumstances by drinking.

Mfundo discovers that Slindile is pregnant, and he begins to reflect on the position of fathers in light of the women's liberation movement, which allowed for women to have much more control over their reproductive choices than before. He sees this as placing men in an uncomfortable position, where they are not given the same choice to decide whether or not they want to be fathers:

> I overheard [Slindile] telling Buhle that she had decided that she was now ready to have a child. I started laughing, thinking how interesting life was for men now that women had control of their own sexuality. They could decide when they wanted to have a child without consulting you, but gods forbid a man failed to take care of that child when the child came. One would have to contend with the full wrath of womankind and the maintenance court (Wanner 2010: 36).

Mfundo's conflict becomes apparent here, wrestling with the expectations placed on him by his gender and the feeling of obligation to fulfil his fatherly duties.

Mfundo eventually loses his job because of a violent outburst with a famous musician who takes an interest in Slindile, and he becomes a stay-at-home father. He feels pressure because of his choice to stay at home with his daughter, with Slindile being the breadwinner of their household. In his own estimation, he is a good father, finally able to break free from the types of fatherhoods he was exposed to as a child, which he vowed not to repeat, but he feels judged because of this choice:

> Was not the most important thing that I fed my little girl her first meal, I saw her off to bed at night, and made some quality time to play her the trumpet or watch *Teletubbies* with her? It was important to me that I taught Nomazizi to crawl, watched her when she took her first step and heard her when she first said 'Dada'. Why then was society in general and South African society in particular crueller to me because I was a man who chose to stay at home? (Wanner 2010: 55)

Mfundo faces the pressure of society because he is not enacting the patriarchal norm, he is not able to demonstrate public power in the way men are expected to, and he is not the provider for his family in terms of financial resources. These aspects serve to feminise him, and Slindile judges him harshly. He responds to her with violence, and eventually their relationship ends. The novel seems to suggest that this transgressive form of fatherhood is still at odds with the largely strict patriarchal social setting in modern, urban South Africa. Mfundo is not able to be the type of father he wants to be because through this version of fatherhood he seems to offend expectations of masculinity.

The second section of the novel deals with Mzilikazi. He is gay and immediately discusses his sexuality by referring to his own father. When he imagines telling women who flirt with him that he is gay, he reflects: 'But I cannot say that, of course. It would definitely be the death of my relationship with my father' (Wanner 2010: 85). Being gay is an affront to the father, as it signals a fracture in the paternal narrative, which requires heterosexuality in order for patriarchal power relations to be maintained. If Mzilikazi's father were to find out that he is gay, it would irreparably damage their relationship.

His father was a mineworker but eventually receives an education and becomes a teacher. He starts a new family in Johannesburg and does not return to Mzilikazi and his family in the rural village. When Mzilikazi's mother dies, the three children go to live with their father in the city. His father's own absence and abandonment of his family is glossed over, whereas Mzilikazi's sexuality is much more severe and would spell the 'death of [his] relationship with [his] father' (Wanner 2010: 85), indicating again how important heterosexuality is in maintaining paternal relations.

Mzilikazi also considers his sexuality an impediment to his own role as father and husband. He wonders: 'Why had I failed to be content to be a father to the twins and a husband to Siyanda?' (Wanner 2010: 112). The affront of gay identities and same-sex sexual experiences to the paternal narratives, as seen earlier in novels like *The Quiet Violence of Dreams* and *Kings of the Water*, functions both in the relationship of the gay individual and his father, as well as his position as a father himself. Mzilikazi seems to suggest that he becomes frustrated with his role as father because of being gay, echoing the masculinist ideal of distance from the family, as shown by characters at Steamy Windows in Duiker's novel. However, Mzilikazi, just like Tshepo in the earlier text, eventually reconciles these tensions and is still an attentive father to his two children, finding a new sense of meaning and self-acceptance in his role as father figure.

Mzilikazi remembers his father's disdain towards same-sex marriage particularly: 'I remember watching the news with [my father] the one time. A clip about same-sex marriages having finally been permitted in South Africa by the Constitutional Court came on, and a look of disgust came over his face' (Wanner 2010: 122). Same-sex marriage, legalised in 2006 in South Africa, indicates the fundamental shifts from the strict paternal narratives that dominated South African fatherhoods and families until recently. The law, the domain of the father figure, begins to recognise a multiplicity of realities that run counter to established patriarchal conceptions, and this is met with resistance by fathers like Mzilikazi's. He reflects on the appeals to authenticity that are captured in paternal narratives, such as religion, culture and ethnicity, in the face of same-sex marriage and how it is seen as 'unAfrican':

> Deep down I thought of the hypocrisy of my father, talking of what is not African when he could not find it in him to embrace other Africans unless they were South Africans. Or talking of Christianity, at that, when he himself had not been to church since I was in Standard 5 (Wanner 2010: 123).

The paternal narratives are thus shown to be hypocritical and used by the fathers who wish to maintain hierarchies of power, rather than being independent convictions.

When Mzilikazi moves to Cape Town, he experiences a new sense of freedom, finally away from his father. He escapes the influence of the paternal narrative and begins to narrate his own life:

> Now I could be the person I always wanted to be, but downplayed because of my and society's skewed expectations of what an African man should be like. In this city, without my father and all those relatives from emakhaya, I could now become an individual and not a person who conforms to the expectations of society no matter how unreasonable those expectations are (Wanner 2010: 127).

Mzilikazi begins to date a man named Thulani in Cape Town. He learns that his father has died, but he does not want Thulani to accompany him to the funeral as he is still afraid of confronting his family with his sexuality. However, he does feel a sense of release at the funeral from the control that his father has had over his life.[1] There is also a sense of gratitude for what his father has meant to him:

> We have just buried my father. I loved him, insofar as everyone is supposed to love his or her father; but more than that, I feared him. When I dropped some earth into his grave just after my mother had done the same, it felt as though I dropped some of the fear. And I cried, because for all his fearsomeness, I may never have achieved in life what I achieved without my father pushing me as he did (Wanner 2010: 148-9).

After his father is buried, Mzilikazi begins to wrestle with how his sexuality conflicts with ideas of masculinity, tradition and culture. He begins to construct a new narrative of how his father might see him in death, even allowing for the possibility that his father might understand the fact that he is gay. This more maternal form of narrative of imagining acceptance, ironically, yet provocatively, employed with the once-oppressive father figure in this novel, allows for Mzilikazi to reconcile his feelings for his father to some degree. He is given the masculine role of protector of his family in his father's absence, with the familiar symbols of masculine power in the form of weapons, but he recognises that his sexuality unsettles these rituals:

> Soon, my uncles will gather together and call me for umcimbi. As the eldest son in the family, I shall be given my father's traditional weapons (spear, shield and kierie) to remind me that I am now the head of the family and must protect all within the household. I wonder how these snuff-taking, mqombothi-drinking uncles of mine would react if they were to know

---

1. An interesting shift here is that the father is no longer dying but has already died, again similar to the end of Duiker's novel, placing his influence in the past tense and giving his son a chance to redefine his life without the paternal influence. This is not seen in the texts with white characters, as the legacy of the sins of the father seemingly haunts them, even though they can distance themselves from the aged father due to his loss of power.

that the man of the house is gay? Would they still give me the weapons? Would my father turn in his grave if, looking from above, or wherever it is that dead people go to, he got to know that his eldest son is not Zulu enough in *his* sense of the word? Or would he perhaps start having a good debate with some long-dead Zulu warrior on the untruths of how homosexuality is human and has nothing to do with Africanness or Zuluness? (Wanner 2010: 150)

Mzilikazi is able to imagine his father finding acceptance for him being gay, even when he engages in masculinist and patriarchal rituals. He presents a conflicted, dynamic version of masculine expression, incorporating both the traditions and expectations of his father as well as his own gay identity. The paternal narratives here are reimagined by the son, demonstrating shifts in narrative power.

The final character focalised in the novel is Tinaye, a Zimbabwean man working in Johannesburg. He meets and falls in love with Slindile while he is still dating a receptionist named Grace. Grace tells Tinaye that she is pregnant, and he talks to his own father about the choice he has to make between the two women. His father responds with an appeal to the importance of biological fatherhood within his cultural framework, pressuring Tinaye into marrying Grace: 'How will you explain that you have married a woman with someone else's child while leaving the mother of your own child? In our culture we don't do that' (Wanner 2010: 206).

Tinaye is swayed by this reasoning, falling into the expectations of 'tak[ing] responsibility and do[ing] the right thing' (Wanner 2010: 206) in reaction to being a father. However, he laments the fact that he could not marry Slindile out of love, and he feels trapped by fathering a child with Grace: 'Grace would never be the great wife that Sli could have been to me, would never match the wonderful company.'

Having a child is seen as a hardship for Tinaye, and he is kept in his position as father due to the pressure he faces from Grace. He reflects on similar concerns to those raised by Mfundo earlier in the novel, about women's choice in whether or not to carry their pregnancies to term and men's lack of choice in deciding whether or not to be fathers:

Grace would not let me go if she knew about Slindile. She would remind me all the days of my child's life. She was that type. And when the child was born, she would take me to the Maintenance Court and get her family to come and see me so I could pay damages, forgetting that she was the one who chose to have the baby and my life was the one damaged by the unplanned baby (Wanner 2010: 206).

Tinaye is resentful of his role as father, feeling trapped by his situation.

The three protagonists demonstrate the very diverse forms of fatherhood being represented in current South African fiction. None of the fathers are completely vilified or completely idealised in their positions. They are shown to relate to their roles as fathers in complex ways, often feeling torn between traditional expectations and their own desires. The novel demonstrates that conceptions of fatherhood are shifting drastically in the South African literary landscape; a novel with this stance on masculinities and fatherhoods could not conceivably have been produced or published at any of the earlier periods discussed in this book. Masculinities are also being re-evaluated in the light of unemployment, sexuality and even love. The fathers represented here defy the traditional family structures in earlier texts, and demonstrate a greater critical engagement with what it means to be a father in contemporary South Africa.

The power of narrative in shaping ideas and in refiguring realities is also highlighted, showing the necessity of recognising and empowering diverse narratives. The four novels discussed in this chapter show major shifts in how narratives about fathers are addressed. Fathers who favour traditional paternal narratives are relegated to ghostly figures, or, in the final text, to death. Truths that unsettle the father's power are being exposed. Young fathers are shown to transcend and be flexible around the expectations placed on them by their gender. Importantly, maternal narratives are also being included in an effort to imaginatively engage with the realities of South Africa currently.

These shifting paternal narratives offer the possibility for fatherhood to be reimagined in a broader and more inclusive framework. Fatherhoods are being interrogated in literature, and the fathers are not simply being seen as the paragons of narrative power within their surroundings, but narrative power has shifted to sons and daughters. These changes indicate an interrogation of history and of national identities, both of which the father represents. When the father's power is confronted and challenged, possibilities for a multiplicity of voices are generated.

CHAPTER 6

# Conclusion

Paternal narratives are a pervasive and important element of South African literature, intersecting in dynamic ways with the changing social climate of the country. The way that fathers are represented in literature and the way that these fathers engage with dominant social myths and ideologies serve to demonstrate shifts in constructions of patriarchal power structures. The symbolic father, arbiter of knowledge and meaning and creator of narratives that inform hierarchies of power, is treated differently depending on the historical period, and recently he becomes unseated from his assumed role and distanced from the symbols of masculinist power that he traditionally made use of in order to cement his position. These shifts in stories about fathers, stories that fathers create and perpetuate, or stories and ideologies in service of patriarchal power, collectively referred to as 'paternal narratives', provide insights into how characters understand and grapple with structures of power, on a personal and national level. As Lesego Rampolokeng puts it in the opening paragraph of his account of brutal South African fatherhood, entitled *Whiteheart: Prologue to Hysteria*, where he describes a father abusing his wife and children, 'it is personal, it was national' (2005: 1).

The father, in many ways, comes to represent the nation, especially through links to the apartheid state, which is most clearly aligned with rigid patriarchal power, and secondarily through links to the liberation movement, where fathers were given the authority to define a new vision of the nation. When the apartheid state dismantles, both the liberation father figure and the oppressive patriarch begin to fade. In post-apartheid and post-transitional narratives, fathers become ghostly and their positions of power are more actively resisted by sons and daughters. They often become cruel and violent forces to be escaped from. Their world views are questioned by their sons and daughters, and sometimes the narrative power is given to offspring, who can now even influence fathers. The paternal narratives become deconstructed, and new, previously silenced, multivocal narratives are given power. Sons and daughters can narrate their own lives, transcending the constraints of traditional paternal narratives.

The first text investigated, Alan Paton's pre-apartheid *Cry, the Beloved Country*, still showed the father as moral authority, linked completely to ideologies that supported his power, namely, religion, ethnic separatism and the law. Those who transgressed these constructs in the text were shown to suffer the consequences of straying from the dominion of the ideal father, represented primarily by Stephen Kumalo, whose son Absolom is put to death for his crimes and betraying the law and religious teachings of his father. James and Arthur Jarvis act as dual father figures, with James being able to bring about practical change in the lives of the residents of the rural village Ndotsheni, and Arthur able to be an ideological leader who nonetheless exhibits ideas of white superiority and an underlying belief in the boundaries of race and ethnicity. Arthur functions as a sacrificial lamb to demonstrate the brokenness of the exploitative and racially oppressive state. His father James is able to act as the white authority that Arthur had envisioned, leading Ndotsheni into renewal. The death of the son here is able to give the father new purpose, and Arthur stands as a father himself who can act as a moral leader to others. Thus, the novel presents a reinforcement of patriarchal authority; paternal narratives, while shown to be conflicted, are still presented as authoritative. Imaginative and multivocal maternal narratives are only briefly hinted at for their role in creating better understanding, although women and mothers are never given voice and authority in the novel.

Nadine Gordimer's *Burgher's Daughter* and J.M. Coetzee's *In the Heart of the Country* were selected for inclusion in this book for their publication in the 1970s, after the Soweto uprising, and for their depiction of daughter characters who resist very different versions of paternal authority. In both cases, father figures die (perhaps an imagined death in *In the Heart of the Country*), yet their presences are never absent from the texts. The fathers seem to narrate the lives of daughters almost completely, where in Coetzee's text Magda sees herself as being nothing without the authorship of her father, and Gordimer's Rosa is similarly defined by her father's name and legacy to the point where she struggles to reconcile herself with her own identity. In both cases, the daughters resist this paternal control, trying to forge their own narratives. However, both daughters fail, with Magda descending further into meaninglessness and confusion at the end of the novel, and Rosa seeming to repeat the narrative of her parents by becoming a political prisoner.

Representations of daughters are important here, as they indicate distance from the masculinist ability to narrate, and they unsettle paternal narratives: women are not able to perpetuate structures of power in the way men are. Both Rosa and Magda lament the fact that they are not the sons that their fathers might have wanted, with Conrad seeming to take on this role for Lionel Burger and thus being given narrative power himself, and with Magda's narrative leading to a sense of nihilism in the end. These daughters offer new possibilities for interpreting paternal narratives during the high-apartheid period, and demonstrate a resistance to paternalistic influences that seemed to be failing the nation; the liberation leaders were being imprisoned and killed, and the apartheid state was spiralling out of control and would descend into the states of emergency in the 1980s. The novels offer a resistance to paternal narratives, but it is a resistance that still seemed unresolved and almost futile.

Once the apartheid regime had fallen and the transition had begun, more critical images of fathers were introduced into South African literature. The cruel and oppressive father is tied to the horrors of apartheid, and distance from him and his death indicates that his influence is relegated to the past. Mark Behr's *The Smell of Apples* shows a paedophile father who also served to uphold apartheid, and features the many secrets and silences that maintained the apartheid state. By Marnus fighting in the border war, he demonstrates how paternal narratives were uncritically reproduced by sons, who served to uphold the oppressive systems espoused by their fathers. The death of the son in this novel, instead of the usual death of the father, highlights how paternal power is perpetuated.

Zakes Mda's *Ways of Dying* shows a father who is cruel and demeaning to his son, using violence and verbal abuse to control

Toloki. The novel is set during the transition, and Toloki distances himself from his father in order to nurture his own creative power and those of the children in the township where he ends up living. Toloki is an example of the resistance of strict paternal narratives and the shift to new versions of fatherhoods, which are depicted in democratic South Africa. Tshepo in K. Sello Duiker's *The Quiet Violence of Dreams* continues this tradition, with a father who has killed Tshepo's mother and removed her nurturing presence, and many other examples of violent and distant father figures. Tshepo wrestles with his own psychological scars, constantly haunted by his past and what his father had done, and only once his father dies is he able to become a positive father figure to orphaned children in Johannesburg. These novels demonstrate a hopeful vision of the transition, where the cruelty or absence of the father is located in apartheid South Africa, and the stifling nature of paternal narratives is able to be overcome during the transition period.

Post-transitional texts become more deconstructionist in nature, re-evaluating the concepts underlying paternal narratives and rendering them absurd or destabilised, such as Zoë Wicomb's engagement with race in *Playing in the Light* and Behr's assessment of idealised masculinities and sexuality in *Kings of the Water*. These novels are set closer to the present and are concerned with unearthing the secrets and silences of the past and giving voices to those who were once rendered voiceless. Many expatriate characters are depicted, indicating a distance of especially white South African characters from the changes in the country. The fading father is linked to the apartheid past, now relegated to abstraction, yet still powerfully remembered and excavated for meaning in the post-apartheid present.

In *Skinner's Drift*, Lisa Fugard's Eva focuses on the secret of her father having killed a black child on their family farm, and how this secret affects her, as well as the black farmworkers in the context of the Truth and Reconciliation Commission. Exposing this truth is anxiety-inducing for Eva and she realises her own complicity in maintaining the secrets of her father.

Wicomb's novel presents the complexity of race in post-apartheid South Africa and how apartheid classifications had a profound influence on lives, but were also arbitrary categories, which were transgressed, such as how the protagonist Marion's parents were 'play-whites' when they were initially classified as Coloured. Marion's father is shown to still be deeply rooted in the power that his 'whiteness' afforded him, just as Marion was before she learned of her past. This novel offers a rare instance where the reflections of the daughter are able to influence the thinking of the father, who begins to question his ideas of race and identity by the end of the novel.

Behr's *Kings of the Water* challenges the heterosexist and masculinist ideologies underpinning apartheid society by demonstrating how the gay protagonist Michiel transgressed the expectations of his strict father in many ways. Michiel does not unquestioningly perpetuate the paternal narratives in the way that Marnus does in Behr's *The Smell of Apples*, and he abandons his military service as well as his role as potential father. The novel presents a transnational text, which allows for Michiel to negotiate his identity both within and outside of South Africa, and, by extension, both in relation to and in defiance of the influence of his father. The father, as in Wicomb and Fugard's novels, is a ghostly and dying figure, out of place in the democratic South Africa, and the sons and daughters can create new meanings when his influence fades.

The final novel investigated, Zukiswa Wanner's *Men of the South*, presents dynamic new forms of fatherhoods. There are still glimpses of the older oppressive fathers and masculinist assumptions, such as Mzilikazi's homophobic father, who dies in the text, and how the roles of men are still often enforced in strict and uncompromising ways. However, many of these fathers are able to create new forms of fatherhoods not displayed in South African literature before: a stay-at-home father who enjoys this role; a gay father who is open about his sexuality; a father out of convenience who uses his relationship in a quest to gain citizenship. The archaic and stagnant position of fathers in literature has become more diverse, and men and fathers begin to question the roles they have been afforded within society.

It could be argued that South Africa is moving beyond the post-transitional malaise, no longer looking to the past and blaming the father figure for apartheid or idealising him as the liberation leader, but, instead, as demonstrated through the emergence of many black literary voices writing about contemporary urban realities, focusing on a tumultuous and uncertain present. Rather than trying to negotiate identities through destabilising categories associated with paternal narratives, the social outlook is increasingly forward-looking.

This new historical movement can be seen by the rising discontent shown through massive student protests beginning in late 2015 against, among other concerns, rising student fees (where notably many female students were leaders in co-ordinating the protests). The paternal authority figure, whether in government or in the leadership of universities, is rejected by a new cohort of young people seeking to define their own power and authority. This could signify the realisation that the promises of a democratic country are not being delivered on for the majority of impoverished, mostly black South Africans, and locating horrors, struggles and corruption firmly in the apartheid past no longer has the power it once held.

The father is destabilised as a character in literature; his position as paragon of power and leadership, or representative of the apartheid past, is increasingly questioned. How representations of fatherhoods continue to evolve as South African history moves into the next phase after the post-transitional moment will have to be the work of a future study.

# Select Bibliography

Abrahams, P. 1946. *Mine Boy*. Cape Town: Heinemann.
Ahn, J. and M. Filipenko. 2007. 'Narrative, Imaginary Play, Art, and Self: Intersecting Worlds'. *Early Childhood Education Journal* 34(4): 279-89.
Alexander, P.F. 1994. *Alan Paton: A Biography*. Oxford: Oxford University Press.
Althusser, L. 2005 [1969]. *For Marx*. Translated by Ben Brewster. London: Verso.
Anchor, R. 1987. 'Narrativity and the Transformation of Historical Consciousness'. *Clio* 16(2): 121-37.
Attwell, D. 1993. *J.M. Coetzee: South Africa and the Politics of Writing*. Berkeley: University of California Press.
Barnard, R. 2000. '*The Smell of Apples*, *Moby-Dick*, and Apartheid Ideology'. *Modern Fiction Studies* 46(1): 207-26.
———. 2004. 'On Laughter, the Grotesque, and the South African Transition: Zakes Mda's *Ways of Dying*'. *Novel* 37(3): 277-302.
Barthes, R. 2001. 'The Death of the Author'. *Contributions in Philosophy* 83: 3-8.
Baskerville, S. 2002. 'The Politics of Fatherhood'. *Political Science & Politics* 35(4): 695-9.
Behr, M. 1997a. 'Living in the Fault Lines'. *Security Dialogue* 28(1): 115-22.
———. 1997b [1995]. *The Smell of Apples*. New York: Macmillan.
———. 2000. *Embrace*. Dublin: Ireland Books.
———. 2009. *Kings of the Water*. London: Abacus.
———. 2010. 'Interview by Jennifer Crocker'. *Crocker's Shelf*. 14 November, http://crockers-shelf.blogspot.com/2010/11/kings-of-water-review-and-intervew-with.html.
Berger, P.L. and T. Luckmann. 1991. *The Social Construction of Reality: A Treatise in the Sociology of Knowledge*. London: Penguin.
Black, M. 1992. 'Alan Paton and the Rule of Law'. *African Affairs* 91(362): 53-72.
Blackburn, D. 1903. *A Burgher Quixote*. London: W. Blackwood.
Bordo, S. 2003. *Unbearable Weight: Feminism, Western Culture, and the Body*. Berkeley: University of California Press.
Boyers, R. 1984. 'Public and Private: On *Burger's Daughter*'. *Salmagundi* 62: 62-92.

Breytenbach, B. 1994 [1985]. *The True Confessions of an Albino Terrorist*. Oxford: Mariner Books.

Briganti, C. 1994. 'A Bored Spinster with a Locked Diary: The Politics of Hysteria in *In the Heart of the Country*'. *Research in African Literatures* 25(4): 33-49.

Brink, A. 2008 [1978]. *Rumours of Rain*. London: Random House.

———. 2011 [1979]. *A Dry White Season*. London: Random House.

Brown, A.D. 2006. 'A Narrative Approach to Collective Identities'. *Journal of Management Studies* 43(4): 731-53.

Bruner, J. 1991. 'The Narrative Construction of Reality'. *Critical Inquiry* 18(1) 1-21.

Butler, J. 1988. 'Performative Acts and Gender Constitution: An Essay in Phenomenology and Feminist Theory'. *Theatre Journal* 40(4): 519-31.

Cabrera, N.J., C.S. Tamis-LeMonda, R.H. Bradley, S. Hofferth and M.E. Lamb. 2000. 'Fatherhood in the Twenty-First Century'. *Child Development* 71(1): 127-36.

Callan, E. 1982. *Alan Paton*. New York: Twayne Publishers.

Canepari-Labib, M. 2000. 'Language and Identity in the Narrative of J.M. Coetzee'. *English in Africa* 27(1): 105-30.

Chapman, M. 2003. 'African Literature, African Literatures: Cultural Practice or Art Practice?' *Research in African Literatures* 34(1): 1-10.

Chodorow, N. 2012. *Individualizing Gender and Sexuality: Theory and Practice*. New York: Routledge.

Clegg, S.R. 1993. 'Narrative, Power and Social Theory'. In *Narrative and Social Control: Critical Perspectives*, edited by D.K. Mumby, pp. 15-45. Newbury Park, London: Sage.

Clingman, S. 1986. *The Novels of Nadine Gordimer: History from the Inside*. Johannesburg: Ravan Press.

Clowes, L., K. Ratele and T. Shefer. 2013. 'Who Needs a Father? South African Men Reflect on Being Fathered'. *Journal of Gender Studies* 22(3): 255-67.

Coetzee, D. 2001. 'South African Education and the Ideology of Patriarchy'. *South African Journal of Education* 21(4): 300-4.

Coetzee, J.M. 1986. 'Farm Novel and "Plaasroman" in South Africa'. *English in Africa* 13(2): 1-19.

———. 1992. 'Man's Fate in the Novels of Alex La Guma'. *Studies in Black Literature* 4(4): 16-23.

———. 2000 [1999]. *Disgrace*. London: Penguin.

———. 2004 [1977]. *In the Heart of the Country*. New York: Penguin Random House.

———. 2015 [1983]. *Life & Times of Michael K*. New York: Penguin Random House.

Collins, P.H. 1986. 'It's All in the Family: Intersections of Gender, Race, and Nation'. *Hypatia* 13(3): 62-82.

Conway, J.K. 1989. *The Road from Coorain*. New York: Vintage.

Cooke, J. 1985. *The Novels of Nadine Gordimer: Private Lives, Public Landscapes*. Baton Rouge: Louisiana State University Press.

Cooper, B. 1996. 'Review: *Ways of Dying* by Zakes Mda'. *World Literature Today* 70(1): 228-9.

Cope, J. 1970. 'A Turning Point in South African English Writing'. *Crux* 4(4): 10-20.

Cornwell, G., D. Klopper and C. MacKenzie. 2010. *The Columbia Guide to South African Literature in English since 1945*. New York: Columbia University Press.

Cronin, J.F. 1967. 'Writer versus Situation: Three South African Novelists'. *Studies: An Irish Quarterly Review* 56(221): 73-84.

Crous, M. 2007. 'On Men and Masculinity in Phaswane Mpe's *Welcome to Our Hillbrow* and K. Sello Duiker's *The Quiet Violence of Dreams*'. *Journal of Literary Studies* 23(1): 16-40.

Dangor, A. 2001. *Bitter Fruit*. Cape Town: Kwela.

Dass, M. 2011. 'A "Place in Which to Cry": The Place for Race and a Home for Shame in Zoë Wicomb's *Playing in the Light*'. *Current Writing: Text and Reception in Southern Africa* 23(2): 137-46.

De Beauvoir, S. 1974. *The Second Sex*. Translated by H.M. Parshley. New York: Vintage.

Derrida, J. 1976. *Of Grammatology*. Translated by G.C. Spivak. Baltimore: Johns Hopkins University Press.

Devarenne, N. 2009. 'Nationalism and the Farm Novel in South Africa, 1883-2004'. *Journal of Southern African Studies* 35(3): 627-42.

Dhlomo, R.R.R. 1928. *An African Tragedy*. Alice: Lovedale Press.

Dimitriu, I.S. 2000. *Art of Conscience: Re-reading Nadine Gordimer*. Timisoara: Hestia.

Donaldson, L.E. 1988. 'The Miranda Complex: Colonialism and the Question of Feminist Reading'. *Diacritics* 18(3): 65-77.

Dovey, T. 1988. *The Novels of J.M. Coetzee: Lacanian Allegories*. Johannesburg: Ad Donker.

Driver, D. 1988. '"Woman" as Sign in the South African Colonial Enterprise'. *Journal of Literary Studies* 4(1): 3-20.

Duiker, K.S. 2001. *The Quiet Violence of Dreams*. Cape Town: Kwela.

Durrant, S. 2005. 'The Invention of Mourning in Post-Apartheid Literature'. *Third World Quarterly* 26(3): 441-50.

Farred, G. 2000. 'Mourning the Postapartheid State Already? The Poetics of Loss in Zakes Mda's *Ways of Dying*'. *Modern Fiction Studies* 46(1): 183-206.

Fisher, W.R. 1984. 'Narration as a Human Communication Paradigm: The Case of Public Moral Argument'. *Communications Monographs* 51(1): 1-22.
Foley, A. 1998. '"Considered as a Social Record": A Reassessment of *Cry, the Beloved Country*'. *English in Africa* 25(2): 63-92.
Freeman, M. 2015. *Rewriting the Self: History, Memory, Narrative*. London: Routledge.
Frenkel, R. and C. MacKenzie. 2010. 'Conceptualizing "Post-Transitional" South African Literature in English'. *English Studies in Africa* 53(1): 1-10.
Fugard, A. 2009 [1982]. *'Master Harold'... and the Boys*. New York: Vintage.
Fugard, L. 2005. *Skinner's Drift*. London: Simon and Schuster.
Gagiano, A. 2002. 'Shades of Bakhtin'. *Scrutiny* 27(1): 71-5.
———. 2004. 'Adapting the National Imaginary: Shifting Identities in Three Post-1994 South African Novels'. *Journal of South African Studies* 30(4): 811-24.
Gardner, S. 1982. 'Still Waiting for the Great Feminist Novel: Nadine Gordimer's *Burger's Daughter*'. *Hecate* 8(1): 61-76.
———. 1990. '"A Story for This Place and Time": An Interview with Nadine Gordimer about *Burger's Daughter*'. In *Conversations with Nadine Gordimer*, edited by N.T. Bazin and M.D. Seymour, pp. 161-75. Jackson: University Press of Mississippi.
Gevisser, M. 1995. 'Review: *The Smell of Apples*'. *Mail & Guardian*, 26 May - 1 June.
Gilbert, S.M. 1985. 'Life's Empty Pack: Notes toward a Literary Daughteronomy'. *Critical Inquiry* 11(3): 355-84.
Gordimer, N. 1982 [1981]. *July's People*. London: Penguin.
———. 2000 [1979]. *Burger's Daughter*. London: Bloomsbury.
———. 2003. 'What the Book Is About'. In *Nadine Gordimer's* Burger's Daughter *A Casebook*, edited by J. Newman, pp. 149-66. New York: Oxford University Press.
Gordimer, N. and S. Sontag. 1985. 'Nadine Gordimer and Susan Sontag: In Conversation'. *Listener*, 23 May.
Goyal, Y. 2011. 'The Pull of the Ancestors: Slavery, Apartheid, and Memory in Zakes Mda's *Ways of Dying* and *Cion*'. *Research in African Literatures* 42(2): 147-69.
Gqola, P.D. 2009. '"The Difficult Task of Normalizing Freedom": Spectacular Masculinities, Ndebele's Literary/Cultural Commentary and Post-Apartheid Life'. *English in Africa* 36(1): 61-76.
Graham, L.V. 2012. *State of Peril: Race and Rape in South African Literature*. Oxford: Oxford University Press.
Graham, S. 2009. *South African Literature after the Truth Commission: Mapping Loss*. London: Palgrave Macmillan.

Gramsci, A. 2006 [1994]. 'Hegemony, Intellectuals and the State'. In *Cultural Theory and Popular Culture: A Reader*, edited by J. Storey, pp. 85-91. New York: Pearson Longman.

Green, M. 2008. 'Translating the Nation: From Plaatje to Mpe'. *Journal of Southern African Studies* 34(2): 325-42.

Grosz, E. 2002 [1990]. *Jacques Lacan: A Feminist Introduction*. London: Routledge.

Gruber, T. 2014. 'The Patriarchal Trap: Deconstructing the "Real Man" in Contemporary Anglo-African Literature'. Master's thesis, University of Vienna.

Gumede, W.M. 2007. *Thabo Mbeki and the Battle for the Soul of the ANC*. London: Zed Books.

Haggard, H.R. 2007 [1885]. *King Solomon's Mines*. London: Penguin.

Hanne, M. 1996. *The Power of the Story: Fiction and Political Change*. New York: Berghahn Books.

Hatty, S.E. 2000. *Masculinities, Violence and Culture*. London: Sage.

Herman, L. and B. Vervaeck. 2005. *Handbook of Narrative Analysis*. Nebraska: University of Nebraska Press.

Heyns, M. 2000. 'The Whole Country's Truth: Confession and Narrative in Recent White South African Writing'. *Modern Fiction Studies* 46(1): 42-66.

Hogan, P.C. 1992. 'Paternalism, Ideology, and Ideological Critique: Teaching *Cry, the Beloved Country*'. *College Literature* 19/20(3/1): 206-10.

hooks, b. 1992. *Black Looks: Race and Representation*. Toronto: Between the Lines.

Hope, C. 2010. 'Review of *Kings of the Water*, by Mark Behr'. *The Guardian*, 23 January.

Horn, A. 2012. 'The Specter of Tokkie - Facing the Past, Inventing the Future: Zoë Wicomb's *Playing in the Light*'. *Kritika Kultura* 18: 127-33.

Hussey, M. 2003. 'Husbands, Sons, and Fathers'. In *Masculinities: Interdisciplinary Readings*, edited by M. Hussey, pp. 162-3. New Jersey: Prentice Hall.

Jackson, J. 2013. 'You Are Where You Aren't: Mark Behr and the Not-Quite-Global Novel'. *Safundi* 14(2): 175-90.

Jacobs, R. 2006. *My Father's Orchid*. Cape Town: Umuzi.

Jameson, F. 1981. *The Political Unconscious: Narrative as a Socially Symbolic Act*. London: Methuen.

Kirkegaard, A.M.O. 2007. 'It Couldn't Be Anything Innocent: Negotiating Gender in Patriarchal-Racial Spaces'. In *Manning the Nation: Father Figures in Zimbabwean Literature and Society*, edited by K. Muchemwa and R. Muponde, pp. 115-26. Harare: Weaver Press.

Klopper, D. 2011. 'The Place of Nostalgia in Zoë Wicomb's *Playing in the Light*'. *Current Writing: Text and Reception in Southern Africa* 23(2): 147-56.

Krog, A. 2007 [1998]. *Country of My Skull: Guilt, Sorrow, and the Limits of Forgiveness in the New South Africa*. New York: Broadway Books.

Lacan, J. 1977. *Écrits: A Selection*. Translated by Alan Sheridan. London: Tavistock.
La Guma, A. 1967. *The Stone Country*. Cape Town: Heinemann.
Langa, M. 2000. *The Memory of Stones*. Cape Town: New Africa Books.
Larson, C.R. 1973. 'Alan Paton's *Cry, the Beloved Country* after Twenty-Five Years'. *Africa Today* 20(4): 53–7.
Lesejane, D. 2006. 'Fatherhood from an African Cultural Perspective'. In *Baba: Men and Fatherhood in South Africa*, edited by L. Richter and R. Morrell, pp. 173–82. Cape Town: HSRC Press.
Lindegger, G. 2006. 'The Father in the Mind'. In *Baba: Men and Fatherhood in South Africa*, edited by L. Richter and R. Morrell, pp. 121–31. Cape Town: HSRC Press.
Liscio, L. 1987. '*Burger's Daughter*: Lighting a Torch in the Heart of Darkness'. *Modern Fiction Studies* 33(2): 245–61.
Lorber, J. 1994. *Paradoxes of Gender*. New Haven: Yale University Press.
Macaskill, B. 1994. 'Charting J.M. Coetzee's Middle Voice'. *Contemporary Literature* 35(3): 441–75.
MacIntyre, A. 1981. *After Virtue*. Notre Dame, IN: University of Notre Dame Press.
Mafeje, A. 1971. 'The Ideology of "Tribalism"'. *Journal of Modern African Studies* 9(2): 253–61.
Maggard, S.W. 1983. 'Cultural Hegemony: The News Media and Appalachia'. *Appalachian Journal* 11(1/2): 67–83.
Marcus, F.H. 1962. '*Cry, the Beloved Country* and *Strange Fruit*: Exploring Man's Inhumanity to Man'. *The English Journal* 51(9): 609–16.
Matshoba, M. 1979. *Call Me Not a Man*. Johannesburg: Ravan Press.
Mbao, W. 2013. 'Unavowable Communities: Mapping Representational Excess in South African Literary Culture, 2001–2011'. PhD thesis, Stellenbosch University.
McDonald, P.D. 2009. *The Literature Police: Apartheid Censorship and Its Cultural Consequences*. Oxford: Oxford University Press.
McMurtry, M. 1998. 'Perverted Rites of Passage'. *Agenda* 14(37): 101–3.
Mda, Z. 1995. *Ways of Dying*. Cape Town: Oxford University Press.
———. 1997. 'Acceptance Speech for the Oliver Schreiner Prize'. *English Academy Review* 14: 279–81.
———. 2003 [2000]. *The Heart of Redness*. London: Picador.
Medalie, D. 1997. 'Old Scars, Old Bones, and Old Secrets: Three Recent South African Novels'. *Journal of Southern African Studies* 23(3): 507–14.
———. 2000. '"Such Wanton Innocence": Representing South African Boyhoods'. *Current Writing: Text and Reception in Southern Africa* 12(1): 41–61.
———. 2012. '"To Retrace Your Steps": The Power of the Past in Post-Apartheid Literature'. *English Studies in Africa* 55(1): 3–15.

Meretoja, H. 2014. *The Narrative Turn in Fiction and Theory: The Crisis and Return of Storytelling from Robbe-Grillet to Tournier*. London: Palgrave Macmillan.
Mervis, M. 1998. 'Fiction for Development: Zakes Mda's *Ways of Dying*'. *Current Writing: Text and Reception in Southern Africa* 10(1): 39-56.
Moonsamy, N. 2014a. 'Nostalgia *Contretemps*: A Theory of Contemporary South African Literature'. PhD thesis, University of the Witwatersrand.
———. 2014b. 'Spectral Citizenry: Reflections of the "Post-Transitional" in Contemporary South African Literature'. *English Studies in Africa* 57(2): 69-78.
Morrell, R. 2005. 'Youth, Fathers and Masculinity in South Africa Today'. *Agenda* 30(8): 84-7.
———. 2007. 'Do You Want to Be a Father? School-Going Youth in Durban Schools at the Turn of the 21st Century'. In *From Boys to Men: Social Constructions of Masculinity in Contemporary Society*, edited by T. Shefer, K. Ratele, A. Strebel, N. Shabalala and R. Buikema, pp. 75-93. Cape Town: UCT Press.
Mossman, R. 1990. 'South African Literature: A Global Lesson in One Country'. *The English Journal* 79(8): 41-3.
Mpe, P. 2001. *Welcome to Our Hillbrow*. Pietermaritzburg: University of Natal Press.
Mphahlele, E. 1962. *The African Image*. London: Faber & Faber.
Muchemwa, Z.K. 2007. '"Why Don't You Tell the Children a Story?" Father Figures in Three Zimbabwean Short Stories'. In *Manning the Nation: Father Figures in Zimbabwean Literature and Society*, edited by K. Muchemwa and R. Muponde, pp. 1-16. Harare: Weaver Press.
Muponde, R. 2007. 'Killing Fathers'. In *Manning the Nation: Father Figures in Zimbabwean Literature and Society*, edited by K. Muchemwa and R. Muponde, pp. 17-30. Harare: Weaver Press.
Myambo, M.T. 2010. 'The Limits of Rainbow Nation Multiculturalism in the New South Africa: Spatial Configuration in Zakes Mda's *Ways of Dying* and Jonathan Morgan's *Finding Mr. Madini*'. *Research in African Literatures* 41(2): 93-120.
Ndebele, N. 1996. *Death of a Son*. Johannesburg: Viva Books.
Neeves, M.E. 2008. 'Apartheid Haunts: Postcolonial Trauma in Lisa Fugard's *Skinner's Drift*'. *Studies in the Novel* 40(1/2): 108-26.
Nelson, A.A. 2002. *Political Bodies: Gender, History, and the Struggle for Narrative Power in Recent Chilean Literature*. Lewisburg, PA: Bucknell University Press.
Nelson-Born, K.A. 1996. 'Trace of a Woman: Narrative Voice and Decentered Power in the Fiction of Toni Morrison, Margaret Atwood, and Louise Erdrich'. *Lit: Literature Interpretation Theory* 7(1): 1-12.
Newman, J. 1985. 'Prospero's Complex: Race and Sex in Nadine Gordimer's *Burger's Daughter*'. *Journal of Commonwealth Literature* 20(1): 81-99.

Nochlin, L. 1978. 'Lost and Found: Once More the Fallen Woman'. *The Art Bulletin* 60(1): 139-53.
Nuttall, S. 2009. *Entanglement: Literary and Cultural Reflections on Post-Apartheid*. Johannesburg: Wits University Press.
Nuttall, S. and C. Coetzee. 1998. *Negotiating the Past: The Making of Memory in South Africa*. Oxford: Oxford University Press.
Oliver, K. 1997. 'Fatherhood and the Promise of Ethics'. *Diacritics* 27(1): 45-57.
Ouzgane, L. and R. Morrell. 2005. *African Masculinities: Men in Africa from the Late Nineteenth Century to the Present*. Cape Town: Palgrave Macmillan.
Paton, A. 1945. 'Who Is Really to Blame for the Crime Wave in South Africa?' *The Forum* VIII(37): 7-8.
———. 1961. 'A Deep Experience'. *Contrast* 1(4): 20-4.
———. 1965. 'The Long View: John Harris'. *Contact* 8(4): 1-3.
———. 1974. *Apartheid and the Archbishop: The Life and Times of Geoffrey Clayton, Archbishop of Cape Town*. Cape Town: Jonathan Cape.
———. 1980. *Towards the Mountain: An Autobiography*. New York: Scribner.
———. 1988. *Journey Continued: An Autobiography*. Oxford: Oxford University Press.
———. 1989 [1987]. *Save the Beloved Country*. New York: Scribner.
———. 2002 [1981]. *Ah, but Your Land Is Beautiful*. London: Random House.
———. 2003 [1948]. *Cry, the Beloved Country*. New York: Simon and Schuster.
———. 2011 [1953]. *Too Late the Phalarope*. New York: Simon and Schuster.
Plaatje, S.T. 2013 [1930]. *Mhudi*. London: Waveland Press.
Prinsloo, J. 2006. 'Where Have All the Fathers Gone? Media(ted) Representations of Fatherhood'. In *Baba: Men and Fatherhood in South Africa*, edited by L. Richter and R. Morrell, pp. 132-46. Cape Town: HSRC Press.
Propst, L. 2014. 'Redefining Shared Narrative in Lisa Fugard's *Skinner's Drift* and Zoë Wicomb's *Playing in the Light*'. *Studies in the Novel* 46(2): 197-214.
Pucherova, D. 2009. 'Re-imagining the Other: The Politics of Friendship in Three Twenty-First Century South African Novels'. *Journal of Southern African Studies* 35(4): 929-43.
Ramphele, M. and L. Richter. 2006. 'Migrancy, Family Dissolution and Fatherhood'. In *Baba: Men and Fatherhood in South Africa*, edited by L. Richter and R. Morrell, pp. 73-81. Cape Town: HSRC Press.
Rampolokeng, L. 2005. *Whiteheart: Prologue to Hysteria*. Pietermaritzburg: University of KwaZulu-Natal Press.
Ratele, K., E. Fouten, T. Shefer, A. Strebel, N. Shabalaba and R. Buikema. 2007. '"Moffies, Jock and Cool Guys": Boys' Accounts of Masculinity and Their Resistance in Context'. In *From Boys to Men: Social Constructions of Masculinity*

*in Contemporary Society*, edited by T. Shefer, K. Ratele, A. Strebel, N. Shabalala and R. Buikema, pp. 112-27. Cape Town: UCT Press.

Resch, R.P. 1992. *Althusser and the Renewal of Marxist Social Theory*. Berkeley: University of California Press.

Richardson, B. 2000. 'Recent Concepts of Narrative and the Narratives of Narrative Theory'. *Style* 34(2): 168-75.

Richter, L. 2006. 'The Importance of Fathering for Children'. In *Baba: Men and Fatherhood in South Africa*, edited by L. Richter and R. Morrell, pp. 53-69. Cape Town: HSRC Press.

Richter, L. and R. Morrell (eds). 2006. *Baba: Men and Fatherhood in South Africa*. Cape Town: HSRC Press.

Richter, L. and W. Smith. 2006. 'Children's Views of Fathers'. In *Baba: Men and Fatherhood in South Africa*, edited by L. Richter and R. Morrell, pp. 155-72. Cape Town: HSRC Press.

Rive, R. 2006 [1986]. *'Buckingham Palace', District Six*. London: Cornelsen.

Roberts, S. 1992. 'Cinderella's Mothers: J.M. Coetzee's *In the Heart of the Country*'. *English in Africa* 19(1): 21-33.

Robolin, S. 2011. 'Properties of Whiteness: (Post) Apartheid Geographies in Zoë Wicomb's *Playing in the Light*'. *Safundi* 12(3/4): 349-71.

Samuels, A. 2003. *The Plural Psyche: Personality, Morality and the Father*. London: Routledge.

Samuelson, M. 2002. 'The Rainbow Womb: Rape and Race in South African Fiction of the Transition'. *Kunapipi* 24(1/2): 88-100.

———. 2008. 'Walking through the Door and Inhabiting the House: South African Literary Culture and Criticism after the Transition'. *English Studies in Africa* 51(1): 130-7.

———. 2013. 'Sea Changes, Dark Tides and Littoral States: Oceans and Coastlines in Post-Apartheid Narratives', *Alternation* Special Edition 6: 9-28.

Sanders, M. 2002. 'Remembering Apartheid'. *Diacritics* 32(3/4): 60-80.

Sartre, J-P. 1964 [1938]. *Nausea*. Translated by L. Alexander. London: New Directions.

Schaub, M. 2000. 'Queen of the Air or Constitutional Monarch? Idealism, Irony, and Narrative Power in *Miss Marjoribanks*'. *Nineteenth-Century Literature* 55(2): 195-225.

Schreiner, O. 2003 [1883]. *The Story of an African Farm*. London: Broadview Press.

Scott, J. 1997. 'Voice and Trajectory: An Interview with J.M. Coetzee'. *Salmagundi* 114/115: 82-102.

Segal, L. 1990. *Slow Motion: Changing Masculinities, Changing Men*. New Brunswick, NJ: Rutgers University Press.

Sepamla, S.S. 1984 [1981]. *A Ride on the Whirlwind*. London: Heinemann.

Serote, M.W. 1983 [1981]. *To Every Birth Its Blood*. London: Heinemann.
Shefer, T. and K. Ruiters. 1998. 'The Masculine Construct in Heterosex'. *Agenda* 37: 39-45.
Slovo, G. 2003 [2000]. *Red Dust*. New York: W.W. Norton & Company.
Spivak, G.C. 1994. 'Can the Subaltern Speak?' In *Colonial Discourse and Post-Colonial Theory: A Reader*, edited by P. Williams and L. Chrisman, pp. 66-111. New York: Columbia University Press.
Stevens, A. 2004. *Archetype Revisited: An Updated Natural History of the Self*. London: Routledge.
Stobie, C. 2008. 'Fissures in Apartheid's "Eden": Representations of Bisexuality in *The Smell of Apples* by Mark Behr'. *Research in African Literatures* 39(1): 70-86.
Suttner, R. 2007. 'Masculinities in the ANC-Led Liberation Movement'. In *From Boys to Men: Social Constructions of Masculinity in Contemporary Society*, edited by T. Shefer, K. Ratele, A. Strebel, N. Shabalala and R. Buikema, pp. 195-224. Cape Town: UCT Press.
Tambling, J. 1990. *Confession: Sexuality, Sin, the Subject*. Manchester: Manchester University Press.
Ten Kortenaar, N. 2008. '*Somewhere in the Double Rainbow*: Representations of Bisexuality in Post-Apartheid Novels, Cheryl Stobie: Book Review'. *English in Africa* 35(1): 187-9.
Tiffin, H. 1987. 'Post-Colonial Literatures and Counter-Discourse'. *Kunapipi* 9(3): 17-34.
Toomey, M. 1992. 'The Price of Masculinity Based on Violence'. *Education Digest* 58(4): 44-6.
Van der Vlies, A. 2010. 'The Archive, the Spectral, and Narrative Responsibility in Zoë Wicomb's *Playing in the Light*'. *Journal of Southern African Studies* 36(3): 583-98.
———. 2011. 'An Interview with Mark Behr'. *Safundi* 12(1): 1-26.
Van Niekerk, M. 2010 [2004]. *Agaat*. Translated by Michiel Heyns. Portland OR: Tin House Books.
Varga, C.A. 1997. 'Sexual Decision-Making and Negotiation in the Midst of Aids: Youth in KwaZulu-Natal, South Africa'. *Health Transition Review* 7(3): 45-67.
Veeser, H.A. 1989. 'Introduction'. In *The New Historicism*, edited by H.A. Veeser, pp. ix-xvi. New York: Routledge.
Velleman, J.D. 2003. 'Narrative Explanation'. *Philosophical Review* 112(1): 1-25.
Viljoen, S. 2001. 'Non-Racialism Remains a Fiction: Richard Rive's "*Buckingham Palace*", *District Six* and K. Sello Duiker's *The Quiet Violence of Dreams*'. *English Academy Review* 18(1): 46-53.
Walby, S. 1990. *Theorizing Patriarchy*. Oxford: Blackwell.

Wanner, Z. 2010. *Men of the South*. Cape Town: Kwela.
Watson, S. 1982. '*Cry, the Beloved Country* and the Failure of Liberal Vision'. *English in Africa* 9(1): 29-44.
———. 1986. 'Colonialism and the Novels of J.M. Coetzee'. *Research in African Literatures* 17(3): 370-92.
Wenzel, M. 2003. 'Appropriating Space and Transcending Boundaries in *The Africa House* by Christina Lamb and *Ways of Dying* by Zakes Mda'. *Journal of Literary Studies* 19(3/4): 316-30.
Werner, A. 1926. 'The Swahili Saga of Liongo Fumo'. *Bulletin of the School of Oriental and African Studies* 4(2): 247-55.
Wicomb, Z. 2001 [2000]. *David's Story*. New York: The New Press.
———. 2008 [2006]. *Playing in the Light*. New York: The New Press.
Williams, J.G. 1949. 'Review of *Cry, the Beloved Country*'. *African Affairs* 48(190): 78-9.
Wilson, F. 2006. 'On Being a Father and Poor in Southern Africa Today'. In *Baba: Men and Fatherhood in South Africa*, edited by L. Richter and R. Morrell, pp. 26-37. Cape Town: HSRC Press.
Wittenberg, H. 2008. 'The Taint of the Censor: J.M. Coetzee and the Making of *In the Heart of the Country*'. *English in Africa* 35(2): 133-50.

# Index

Abraham (biblical figure) 24
Adam (biblical figure) 23-4
African National Congress (ANC) 92, 95, 155, 188
*An African Tragedy* (R.R.R. Dhlomo, 1928) 40 n.1
Afrikaners *see* literature, South African, and Afrikaner identity and nationalism
*Agaat* (Marlene van Niekerk, 2004) 220
*Ah, but Your Land Is Beautiful* (Alan Paton, 1981) 47
Ali, Silas (character in *Bitter Fruit*) 37
Alida (character in *Kings of the Water*) 249, 252, 253, 260
Althusser, Louis 13-14, 20
Altman, Phyllis 96
Andromeda (character in *The Quiet Violence of Dreams*) 207
Angelo *see* Tshepo
apartheid 47, 92
Arne (character in *The Quiet Violence of Dreams*) 194, 195-6, 201, 205
Ask (Nordic mythic figure) 24

Baasie *see* Vulindlela, Zwelinzima
Barthes, Roland 2
Behr, Mark 157-8, 270-1
Bianca (character in *Kings of the Water*) 272
*Bitter Fruit* (Achmat Dangor, 2001) 33, 37, 154

Black Consciousness *see* literature, South African, and Black Consciousness
Bloom, Harry 96
Blouberg (Cape Town) 243
Boetie (character in *Playing in the Light*) 236-7, 238, 241
Bordo, Susan 2
Botha, Naas 201
Botha, P.W. 165
Brenda (character in *Playing in the Light*) 236, 237-8, 244
'Buckingham Palace', *District Six* (Richard Rive, 1986) 91
Buhle (character in *Men of the South*) 276
Burger, Cathy (character in *Burger's Daughter*) 126-7, 133, 138, 140, 141
Burger, Katya (character in *Burger's Daughter*) 143, 144, 148
Burger, Lionel (character in *Burger's Daughter*) 19, 35, 121, 122, 123-4, 125-6, 127, 128-32, 133, 135, 136, 137-8, 139-43, 144, 145-6, 148-9, 285
Burger, Rosa (character in *Burger's Daughter*) 29, 94, 121, 122, 123, 124, 125, 126, 127-9, 130, 131, 132-3, 134, 135-6, 137, 138, 139, 140-1, 143, 144-9, 204, 244, 285

Burger, Tony (character in *Burger's Daughter*) 124, 144
*Burger's Daughter* (Nadine Gordimer, 1979) 121–49
 and Afrikaner identity and nationalism 140–2, 143–4
 banning of 92
 and Black Consciousness 95, 146–7
 and childhood 123
 and Communist Party 121, 148
 family resemblance 160
 farm setting 41
 and justice 35, 139
 maternal narratives in 123, 133–4, 142, 147, 148
 paternal narrative in 19, 35, 91, 95, 122, 124, 125–6, 127, 132–3, 134–5, 136–7, 139–40, 142, 145 148, 284, 285
 and prison 129–30, 131–2, 136, 138, 143, 146, 148–9, 285
 and religion 138–40
 and violence 204
 and white liberals 121
 *see also* Burger, Cathy; Burger, Katya; Burger, Lionel; Burger, Rosa; Burger, Tony; Chabalier, Bernard; Conrad; De Witt, Noel; Flora; Kgosane, Marisa; Theo; Vermeulen, Brandt; Vulindlela, Zwelinzima
*A Burgher Quixote* (Douglas Blackburn, 1903) 40 n.1

*Call Me Not a Man* (Mtutuzeli Matshoba, 1979) 42
Campbell, Helen (character in *Playing in the Light*) 26, 232, 236, 240, 241, 242–3
Campbell, John (character in *Playing in the Light*) 229, 230, 231, 232–4, 235–6, 239, 240, 241–2, 245, 246, 287
Campbell, Marion (character in *Playing in the Light*) 26, 29, 38, 229, 230–2, 233, 234–5, 236, 238. 239–42, 243, 244–5, 246, 287
capitalism *see* literature, South African, and capitalism
censorship 16, 17 n.2, 92–3, 120
Chabalier, Bernard (character in *Burger's Daughter*) 145
chiefs 68–9, 73
childhood *see* literature, South African, and childhood
Chile 17
Chris (character in *The Quiet Violence of Dreams*) 153, 198–9, 214
Coetzee, J.M. 41, 91, 95–6, 271
Cole (character in *The Quiet Violence of Dreams*) 206
Collins, Patricia Hill 2, 16–17
Coloured community *see* literature, South African, and Coloured community
Conrad (character in *Burger's Daughter*) 123, 124, 127, 128, 132, 134, 135, 137, 138, 143, 144, 148, 285
*Country of My Skull* (Antjie Krog, 1998) 152
*Cry, the Beloved Country* (Alan Paton, 1948) 42–5, 47–90
 and capitalism 69–70, 72–3, 78, 80
 and childhood 54, 56, 58, 62, 75, 84–5
 farm setting 42–3, 55, 64, 88
 and justice 56, 86–7, 284
 maternal narratives in 34, 47, 72, 80–4, 85, 86, 88, 284
 and migrant labour system 42, 43, 49, 60, 61–2, 63, 70, 77–8

paternal narratives in 3–5, 22–4, 26, 29–30, 32–3, 34, 35–9, 40, 43, 48–51, 53–60, 61–4, 67, 70–1, 72, 76, 78–9, 80, 84–5, 88, 89, 90, 136–7, 284
and race 43–4, 57, 80
and religion 48, 50, 58, 64–8, 80, 86, 87, 284
and traditional culture 68–9, 70, 71, 73, 75, 78, 80
and violence and crime 51–2, 54, 74–6, 86
*see also* Harrison; High Place; Jarvis, Arthur; Jarvis, James; Jarvis, Margaret; Johannes; Kumalo, Absolom; Kumalo, Gertrude; Kumalo, John; Kumalo, Stephen; Letsisi, Napoleon; Lithebe, Mrs; Msimangu; Ndotsheni; Vincent, Father

*David's Story* (Zoë Wicomb, 2000) 152, 154, 229
De Man, Karl (character in *Embrace*) 249
De Witt, Noel (character in *Burger's Daughter*) 145
*Death of a Son* (Njabulo Ndebele, 1996) 36, 154
deconstruction 2, 286
Democritus (Greek philosopher) 25
Derrida, Jacques 2
Dirk (character in *Kings of the Water*) 271
*Disgrace* (J.M. Coetzee, 1999) 29 n.3, 37, 152, 154, 220
Doreen (character in *The Smell of Apples*) 163, 164
Dougie (character in *Playing in the Light*) 245

*Drum* writers 94–5
*A Dry White Season* (André Brink, 1979) 91

Elsie (character in *Playing in the Light*) 246
*Embrace* (Mark Behr, 2000) 249
Erasmus, Ilse (character in *The Smell of Apples*) 167, 168, 169
Erasmus, Johan (character in *The Smell of Apples*) 154, 155–7, 158–61, 162, 163, 165, 166, 167–8, 169, 170, 171, 172
Erasmus, Leonore (character in *The Smell of Apples*) 160, 163, 167–8, 169
Erasmus, Marnus (character in *The Smell of Apples*) 37, 155, 156, 157, 158, 159–64, 165, 166, 167, 168, 169, 170–1, 202–3, 208, 285, 287
exile *see* literature, South African, and exile

farms *see* literature, South African, farm settings
father figures 3, 21–2, 24, 25–6, 68–9, 152, 288
fatherhood and fatherlessness 24–7, 28–9, 30–2, 33, 34, 283, *see also* literature, South African, paternal narratives
Fatherhood Foundation of South Africa 30
feminist theory 2, 28, 29
Fischer, Abram (Bram) 122
Flora (character in *Burger's Daughter*) 133, 134
Foucault, Michel 11
Founding Fathers (USA) 24

Freud, Sigmund 25
Frikkie (character in *The Smell of Apples*) 157, 161, 163, 170, 172
Fugard, Athol 92

Galgut, Damon 271
Galileo Galilei 25
gender 27-8, 209, *see also* literature, South African, and gender
Geoff (character in *Playing in the Light*) 239, 240
Glassman (character in *Kings of the Water*) 259-60, 261, 263-4, 267, 268, 269
Gloria (character in *The Smell of Apples*) 163
Gordimer, Nadine 41, 91, 93-4, 96, 271
Grace (character in *Men of the South*) 273, 280, 281
Gramsci, Antonio 15
Group Areas Act (1950) 92

Hally (character in '*Master Harold*' ... *and the Boys*) 35
Harrison (character in *Cry, the Beloved Country*) 82
Head, Bessie 95
*Heart of Redness* (Zakes Mda, 2000) 220
hegemony 15-16, 18
Hendrik (character in *In the Heart of the Country*) 111, 112, 114, 115, 116, 117, 118
High Place (farm in *Cry, the Beloved Country*) 43, 55, 60
Hofmeyr, Jan Hendrik 48
homosexuality 31, 38, 209-10, 264, *see also* literature, South African, and homosexuality
hooks, bell 16-17

Horus (Egyptian mythic figure) 24

ideologies 13-15, 16
Immorality Act (1957) 47, 92
*In the Heart of the Country* (J.M. Coetzee, 1977) 95-120
  and childhood 113-14, 115
  farm setting 41, 96, 100
  maternal narrative in 104, 105-6, 110, 114, 196
  paternal narrative in 35, 91, 95, 97-8, 100, 101, 102-5, 106-8, 110, 111-12, 114-15, 116, 117, 120, 284-5
  and race 35-6, 92
  and servants 105-6, 113-14, 117, 119
  structure of 97, 98-9
  and violence 35-6, 112-13, 119
  *see also* Hendrik; Klein-Anna; Magda
Isaac (biblical figure) 24

Jacobson, Dan 96
Jarvis, Arthur (character in *Cry, the Beloved Country*) 39, 43, 46, 49, 51, 52, 53, 54, 55-7, 59, 60, 62, 66, 70-1, 76, 80, 81, 82, 84, 87, 88, 89-90, 284
Jarvis, James (character in *Cry, the Beloved Country*) 39, 43, 45, 49, 50, 52, 53, 55, 56, 59-60, 64, 66, 69, 76, 81, 82, 84, 85, 86, 87, 89, 90, 284
Jarvis, Margaret (character in *Cry, the Beloved Country*) 81-2
Jesus 24, 57, 137
Jim Comes to Jo'burg (trope) 42
Johannes (character in *Cry, the Beloved Country*) 75-6, 85
Johannesburg 60, 62, 72, 73, 75

*Journey Continued* (Alan Paton, 1988) 47
*July's People* (Nadine Gordimer, 1981) 41, 91, 92, 123
Jung, Carl 134
justice 81, *see also* literature, South African, and justice
Jwara (character in *Ways of Dying*) 172, 174, 176-80, 182-3, 184, 185, 186, 190-1

Kamil (character in *Kings of the Water*) 247, 249, 250, 251, 257, 267, 268
Karien (character in *Kings of the Water*) 253, 257, 260, 261, 263, 264, 271-2
Karla (character in *The Smell of Apples*) 167-8
Kgosane, Marisa (character in *Burger's Daughter*) 127-8
*King Solomon's Mines* (H. Rider Haggard, 1885) 40 n.1
*Kings of the Water* (Mark Behr, 2009) 246-72
  and exile 38, 257-8, 265, 271-2
  farm setting 41, 247, 254, 256, 258-9, 262, 265
  and homosexuality 4, 38, 250-1, 254, 261, 263-4, 265-7, 277, 286, 287
  maternal narrative in 249, 250, 254-5
  and mourning 248
  and Oedipal complex 262-3, 269
  paternal narrative in 246, 247, 248-9, 250, 251-2, 253, 257, 259-61, 262-4, 265-6, 267-9, 270, 286, 287
  and race 256, 268-70
  silenced voices in 257, 286
  and violence 258-60, 261, 262
  *see also* Alida; Bianca; Dirk; Glassman; Kamil; Karien; Lerato; Steyn, Benjamin; Steyn, Beth; Steyn, Michiel; Steyn, Oubaas; Steyn, Peet; Steyn, Thomas
Klein-Anna (character in *In the Heart of the Country*) 101, 102, 105, 106, 112, 114, 115, 116, 117, 118
Kumalo, Absolom (character in *Cry, the Beloved Country*) 48-50, 51-2, 54, 57-9, 60, 61, 62-3, 65, 66, 74-6, 77, 82, 84, 85, 87, 90, 284
Kumalo, Gertrude (character in *Cry, the Beloved Country*) 26, 55, 60-1, 63, 64, 65, 77, 84
Kumalo, John (character in *Cry, the Beloved Country*) 49, 66-7, 68, 69-70, 73, 77-9, 80, 84, 85, 86, 87
Kumalo, Stephen (character in *Cry, the Beloved Country*) 39, 45, 48-50, 53, 54, 55, 57-9, 60, 61-3, 64-5, 66, 67-9, 71, 75, 76, 77, 79, 82, 84, 85-6, 87, 88, 89, 90, 284
Kuzwayo, Ellen 271

Lacan, Jacques 21, 99
Langa, Mandla 271
Lefu (character in *Skinner's Drift*) 225, 226-7
Lerato (character in *Kings of the Water*) 255, 256, 258, 269
Letsisi, Napoleon (character in *Cry, the Beloved Country*) 88-9
*Life & Times of Michael K* (J.M. Coetzee, 1983) 91
Lincoln, Abraham 57
Liongo, Fumo 23
literature, African 5

literature, South African 5, 94–5
  and Afrikaner identity and nationalism 41, 140–2, 143–4, 165–6, 171, 172
  apartheid 151, 171, 283–5
  and Black Consciousness 95, 146–7
  and capitalism 69–70, 72–3, 78, 80
  and censorship 92–3, 120
  and childhood 54, 56, 58, 62, 75, 84–5, 113–14, 115, 123, 188, 189–90, 197, 199, 204, 217
  and Coloured community 163, 166, 168, 169, 229, 231–2, 238, 246
  confessional aspects 218–19
  and exile 38, 257–8, 265, 271–2
  family resemblances 160, 249
  farm settings 41–3, 55, 64, 88, 91, 96, 100, 220, 221, 222, 223, 226, 247, 254, 256, 258–9, 262, 265
  and fatherhood *see* literature, South African, paternal narratives in
  and gender 184, 187
  and homosexuality 4, 38, 163, 197, 199, 207, 208–11, 212–13, 249, 250–1, 254, 261, 263–4, 265–7, 277–80, 286, 287
  and justice 35, 56, 86–7, 139, 284
  and liberation movement 274
  magical realism 175
  and masculinity *see* literature, South African, paternal narratives in
  maternal narratives in 34, 47, 72, 80–4, 85, 86, 88, 104, 105–6, 110, 114, 123, 133–4, 142, 147, 148, 185–6, 188–9, 190, 194–5, 196–7, 210, 211, 212, 213, 214, 216, 243, 244, 249, 250, 254–5, 279, 281, 284
  and mermaids 242–3
  and migrant labour system 42, 43, 49, 60, 61–2, 63, 70, 77–8
  and mourning 172–3, 174, 175, 181, 191, 248
  and non-racialism 191–2
  and Oedipal complex 202, 262–3, 269
  paternal narratives in 3–5, 19, 22–4, 26, 29–30, 32–3, 34, 35–9, 40, 43, 48–51, 53–60, 61–4, 67, 70–1, 72, 76, 78–9, 80, 84–5, 88, 89, 90, 91, 93, 95, 97–8, 100, 101, 102–5, 106–8, 110, 111–12, 114–15, 116, 117, 120, 122, 124, 125–6, 127, 132–3, 134–5, 136–7, 139–40, 142, 145, 148, 151, 154, 155–7, 158–63, 164–6, 167–8, 169–70, 171, 172, 174, 176, 177–81, 182, 183–5, 187–8, 189, 194, 195–6, 197, 199–202, 203–11, 212–17, 220–1, 222, 223–4, 225–6, 227, 228, 230, 231, 232–4, 235, 238, 241, 244, 245, 246, 247, 248–9, 250, 251–2, 253, 257, 259–61, 262–4, 265–6, 267–9, 270, 272, 273–4, 275–7, 278, 279–82, 283–6, 287–8
  post-apartheid 150–1, 152, 155, 174–5, 179, 184, 192–3, 219–20, 244, 271–2, 285–6
  post-transitional 218–19, 283–4, 286–8
  prison settings 91, 129–30, 131–2, 136, 138, 143, 146, 148–9, 285
  and race 26, 35–6, 38, 43–4, 57, 80, 92, 235–41, 246, 256, 268–70, 286–7
  and rape *see* literature, South African, and violence and crime
  and religion 48, 50, 58, 64–8, 80, 86, 87, 138–40, 163–4, 171, 230, 284

and the sea 243-4
and servants 105-6, 113-14, 117, 119
silenced voices in 221, 222, 227-8, 229-30, 231, 238, 244, 257, 270, 271, 282, 286
and sport 158-9, 201-2, 223
and traditional culture 68-9, 70, 71, 73, 75, 78, 80
and the TRC 152, 229, 274-5
and violence and crime 35-6, 38, 51-2, 54, 74-6, 86, 112-13, 119, 153-4, 157, 161, 163, 169, 170, 172-3, 180, 181, 183, 184-5, 187, 188, 198, 199, 204, 208, 209, 214, 215-16, 223-5, 226-7, 228, 231, 235, 237, 258-60, 261, 262, 286
and war 156, 160, 162-3, 169, 170-1
and white liberals 121
Lithebe, Mrs (character in *Cry, the Beloved Country*) 26, 84
Lurie, David (character in *Disgrace*) 37
Lurie, Lucy (character in *Disgrace*) 29 n.3, 37
Lyndall (character in *The Story of an African Farm*) 100

Maes, Zane 30
Magda (character in *In the Heart of the Country*) 29, 36, 96-8, 99, 100, 101-19, 122, 136, 244-5, 284-5
Malan, D.F. 48
Mandela, Nelson 24, 122, 152
masculinity 22, 23, 25-6, 27, 29, 30-1, 32, 33-4, 153, *see also* literature, South African, paternal narratives in
'Master Harold'... *and the Boys* (Athol Fugard, 1982) 35
Matshoba, Mtutuzeli 96

Mda, Zakes 179, 271
*The Memory of Stones* (Mandla Langa, 2000) 152
*Men of the South* (Zukiswa Wanner, 2010) 272-81
and homosexuality 38, 277-80
and liberation movement 274
paternal narratives in 4, 34, 38, 272, 273-4, 275-7, 278, 279-81, 287
and TRC 274-5
*see also* Buhle; Grace; Mfundo; Mzilikazi; Nomazizi; Sindiso; Siyanda; Slindile; Thulani; Tinaye
mermaids *see* literature, South African, and mermaids
Mfundo (character in *Men of the South*) 272, 273, 274, 275-7, 280
*Mhudi* (Sol Plaatje, 1930) 40 n.1
migrant labour *see* literature, South African, and migrant labour system
*Mine Boy* (Peter Abrahams, 1946) 40, 42
Mmabatho (character in *The Quiet Violence of Dreams*) 191, 192, 194-5, 196, 197-8, 201, 205
Modisane, Bloke 271
mourning rites 172-3, 175, 181, *see also* literature, South African, and mourning
Mphahlele, Es'kia 271
Mpho (character in *Skinner's Drift*) 226-8
Msimangu (character in *Cry, the Beloved Country*) 63, 71, 72, 74, 75, 79-80, 85, 86
*My Father's Orchid* (Rayda Jacobs, 2006) 36, 154
Mzilikazi (character in *Men of the South*) 38, 273, 275, 277-80

Napu (character in *Ways of Dying*) 181, 183, 184-5, 186, 187
narratives 6-13, 14, 15, 16, 17-19, 22, 270-1, *see also* literature, South African, maternal narratives in; literature, South African, paternal narratives in; literature, South African, silenced voices in
Nasuib (character in *The Quiet Violence of Dreams*) 200
Ndebele, Njabulo 271
Ndotsheni (village in *Cry, the Beloved Country*) 42, 43, 62-3, 64, 66, 68, 73, 77, 84, 85, 87, 88-9, 90, 284
Nefolovhodwe (character in *Ways of Dying*) 181-2, 190
New Historicism 1-2, 3
Nkosi, Lewis 95
Nomazizi (character in *Men of the South*) 276
Noria (character in *Ways of Dying*) 174, 176-7, 178, 180, 182, 183, 184, 185-7, 188, 189, 190, 191

Oedipus 23, 25, *see also* literature, South African, and Oedipal complex
Osiris (Egyptian mythic figure) 24

Pan-Africanist Congress (PAC) 92, 95
Paradys (farm in *Kings of the Water*) 248, 265
Paton, Alan 39, 44, 45-7, 50, 52-3, 74 n.4, 81, 96
Paton, James 45-6
patriarchy 3, 4, 17, 20-2, 23, 26, 28, 153, *see also* father figures; literature, South African, paternal narratives in
Peter (character in *The Quiet Violence of Dreams*) 205

place names 222-3
Player, Gary 160
*Playing in the Light* (Zoë Wicomb, 2006) 229-46
and Coloured community 229, 231-2, 238, 246
maternal narrative in 243, 244
and mermaids 242-3
paternal narrative in 230, 231, 232-4, 235, 238, 241, 244, 245, 246, 286, 287
and race 26, 38, 235-41, 246, 286-7
and religion 230
and the sea 243-4
silenced voices in 221, 229-30, 231, 238, 244, 270, 286
and violence 235, 237
*see also* Boetie; Brenda; Campbell, Helen; Campbell, John; Campbell, Marion; Dougie; Elsie; Geoff; Tokkie
post-structuralism 2, 3
power 11, 12, 16, 19
prisons *see* literature, South African, prison settings
Prohibition of Mixed Marriages Act (1949) 92
Pythagoras (Greek philosopher) 25

*The Quiet Violence of Dreams* (K. Sello Duiker, 2001) 191-217
and childhood 197, 199, 204, 217
and homosexuality 197, 199, 207, 208-11, 212-13, 277
maternal narrative in 194-5, 196-7, 210, 211, 212, 213, 214, 216
and non-racialism 191-2
and Oedipal complex 202
paternal narrative in 4, 33, 155, 167, 194, 195-6, 197, 199-202, 203-11, 212-17, 286

and sport 201-2
and violence 153-4, 198, 199, 204, 208, 214, 215-16
*see also* Andromeda; Arne; Chris; Cole; Mmabatho; Nasuib; Peter; Sarel, *Uncle*; Saunders, Mr; Sebastian; Shaun; Steamy Windows; Themba; Tshepo; West; Zebron

race *see* literature, South African, and race
rainbow nation 173-4, 175, 192, 240
rape 36-7, 153-4, 157, 161, 163, 169, 170, 172, 199, 213, 214
*Red Dust* (Gillian Slovo, 2000) 152
religion *see* literature, South African, and religion
Rheinallt Jones, Edith 52-3
*A Ride on the Whirlwind* (Sipho Sepamla, 1981) 91
Rive, Richard 95
Rivonia trial (1963-1964) 122
*The Road from Coorain* (Jill Conway, 1989) 11
Robben Island 243
rule of law 50
*Rumours of Rain* (André Brink, 1978) 91

same-sex marriage 278
Samuel, *Uncle* (character in *The Smell of Apples*) 171
Sarel, *Uncle* (character in *The Quiet Violence of Dreams*) 201
*The Satanic Verses* (Salman Rushdie, 1988) 10
Saunders, Mr (character in *The Quiet Violence of Dreams*) 214
*Save the Beloved Country* (Alan Paton, 1987) 47, 50, 81

Schreiner, Olive 96
sea *see* literature, South African, and the sea
Sebastian (character in *The Quiet Violence of Dreams*) 194, 208, 210, 211, 212
*The Second Sex* (Simone de Beauvoir, 1974) 2
Serote, Mongane Wally 96
servants *see* literature, South African, and servants
Shadrack (character in *Ways of Dying*) 186
Sharpeville massacre (1960) 92, 127
Shaun (character in *The Quiet Violence of Dreams*) 203, 204, 206, 207, 211, 212
Sindiso (character in *Men of the South*) 273-4
Siyanda (character in *Men of the South*) 277
*Skinner's Drift* (Lisa Fugard, 2005) 221-9
  farm setting 41, 221, 222, 223, 226-7
  paternal narrative in 222, 223-4, 225-6, 227, 228, 286
  silenced voices in 221, 222, 227-8
  and violence 38, 223-5, 226-7, 228, 286
  *see also* Lefu; Mpho; Van Rensburg, Eva; Van Rensburg, Lorraine; Van Rensburg, Martin
Slindile (character in *Men of the South*) 272-3, 275, 276, 280, 281
*The Smell of Apples* (Mark Behr, 1995) 155-72
  and Afrikaner identity 41, 165-6, 171, 172
  and Coloured community 163, 166, 168, 169

confessional aspects 218-19
family resemblance 160
farm setting 41
and homosexuality 163
paternal narrative in 37, 155-7, 158-63, 164-6, 167-8, 169-70, 171, 172, 253, 285
and religion 163-4, 171
and sport 158-9
and Tanzania 165, 166, 171
and violence 37, 157, 161, 163, 169, 170, 172
and war 156, 160, 162-3, 169, 170-1
*see also* Doreen; Erasmus, Ilse; Erasmus, Johan; Erasmus, Leonore; Erasmus, Marnus; Frikkie; Gloria; Karla; Samuel, Uncle; Smith, Mr
Smith, Mr (character in *The Smell of Apples*) 160
Sonke Gender Justice's Fatherhood Project 30
Soweto uprising (1976) 91, 121, 122-3, 147
Spivak, Gayatri 16-17
sport *see* literature, South African, and sport
states of emergency 92, 285
Steamy Windows (in *The Quiet Violence of Dreams*) 194, 199, 201, 203, 206-7, 208, 211
Steyn, Benjamin (character in *Kings of the Water*) 258, 262-3, 269-70
Steyn, Beth (character in *Kings of the Water*) 247, 248, 249, 254-5, 256-7, 260, 261, 269-70
Steyn, Michiel (character in *Kings of the Water*) 38, 247, 249-52, 253-4, 255, 256-61, 263-5, 266-9, 270, 271-2, 287

Steyn, Oubaas (character in *Kings of the Water*) 249-50, 251-2, 253, 255, 256, 259-60, 261, 262-4, 265, 268, 269
Steyn, Peet (character in *Kings of the Water*) 257, 262, 263, 265
Steyn, Thomas (character in *Kings of the Water*) 258
*The Stone Country* (Alex La Guma, 1967) 91
*The Story of an African Farm* (Olive Schreiner, pseud. Ralph Iron, 1883) 40-1, 100
storytelling 7, 10, 193

Tanzania 165, 166, 171
Thales (Greek philosopher) 25
Themba (character in *The Quiet Violence of Dreams*) 216
Themba, Can 95
Theo (character in *Burger's Daughter*) 137
Thulani (character in *Men of the South*) 278-9
Tinaye (character in *Men of the South*) 273, 280-1
*To Every Birth Its Blood* (Mongane Wally Serote, 1981) 91
Tokkie (character in *Playing in the Light*) 231, 232, 238, 243-4
Toloki (character in *Ways of Dying*) 172, 174, 175, 176, 177-82, 183-4, 185, 186-7, 188, 189-91, 217, 286
*Too Late the Phalarope* (Alan Paton, 1953) 47
*Towards the Mountain* (Alan Paton, 1980) 46, 47, 48
traditional culture *see* literature, South African, and traditional culture

tribe (as concept) 61 n.2
*The True Confession of an Albino Terrorist* (Breyten Breytenbach, 1985) 91
Truth and Reconciliation Commission (TRC) 151-2, 173, 191, 198, 218, 220, 225, 228, 229, 274-5, 286
Tshepo (Angelo, character in *The Quiet Violence of Dreams*) 37, 153, 161, 190, 191, 192, 193, 196, 197, 198-9, 200, 202-5, 206, 207, 208, 209-11, 212-17, 277, 286
Tutu, Desmond 152, 173

Unlawful Organisations Act (1960) 92

Valkenberg mental hospital (Cape Town) 197, 200, 202, 203, 213
Van Niekerk, Marlene 271
Van Rensburg, Eva (character in *Skinner's Drift*) 29, 38, 221, 222-3, 224-5, 226-7, 228-9, 286
Van Rensburg, Lorraine (character in *Skinner's Drift*) 225
Van Rensburg, Martin (character in *Skinner's Drift*) 221, 223-4, 225, 226-7
Van Vlaanderen, Pieter (character in *Too Late the Phalarope*) 47
Vera, Yvonne 271
Vermeulen, Brandt (character in *Burger's Daughter*) 124-5, 139, 140, 141-2
Vincent, Father (character in *Cry, the Beloved Country*) 51, 59
violence 23, 29, 36-7, *see also* literature, South African, and violence and crime
Vorster, John 165, 166
Vulindlela, Zwelinzima (character in *Burger's Daughter*) 126, 144, 146

Vutha (two characters in *Ways of Dying*) 174, 181, 184-6, 187, 188

war *see* literature, South African, and war
Washington, George 24
*Ways of Dying* (Zakes Mda, 1995) 172-91
and childhood 188, 189-90
and gender 184, 187
maternal narratives in 185-6, 188-9, 190
and mourning 172-3, 174, 175, 181, 191
paternal narrative in 36, 154, 155, 167, 172, 174, 176, 177-81, 182, 183-5, 187-8, 189, 285-6
and violence 172-3, 180, 181, 183, 187, 188
*see also* Jwara; Napu; Nefolovhodwe; Noria; Shadrack; Toloki; Vutha; Xesibe
*Welcome to Our Hillbrow* (Phaswane Mpe, 2001) 154, 192
West (character in *The Quiet Violence of Dreams*) 201-2, 203, 205, 208-9, 211
white liberals *see* literature, South African, and white liberals
Wicomb, Zoë 271
women *see* literature, South African, maternal narratives in

Xesibe (character in *Ways of Dying*) 177, 184

Zebron (character in *The Quiet Violence of Dreams*) 213, 214
Zeus (Greek god) 23

Printed and bound by CPI Group (UK) Ltd, Croydon, CR0 4YY
06/04/2026

14854926-0003